My *Heart's* in the Highlands

The building of a historic Edmonton community

Ken Tingley

Edmonton, Alberta

2012

Published by The Highlands Historical Society, Edmonton, Alberta, 2012

ISBN 978-0-9813075-2-7

Copy editor: Anita Jenkins
Graphic design and layout: some production!, Edmonton
Cover photo: Carol Snyder

My heart's in the Highlands, my heart is not here;

My heart's in the Highlands a-chasing the deer;

A-chasing the wild-deer, and following the roe,

My heart's in the Highlands wherever I go.

From "Farewell to the Highlands"

Robert Burns (1759–1796)

SEC. 16.

22

Frederick Rowland

1945

Rat Creek

HUDSON'S BAY COMPANY.

Methodist Mission
David McDougall
W.S. Robertson & Jorgunt
S. Pritchard
Donald McDonald
James Rowland
Wm Rowland
Kenneth McDonald

10 12 14 16 18 20

68a 48a 81a 114.5a 116.3a 86a 85a

4
65.6a

RIV

Coal Claim

Donald Ross

Wm Borer

170a

2
Malcolm Groat
G.A. Simpson D.L.S.
704 a

R.C. Church

Road surveyed by

West. 80.85

Church of England

NORTH   SASKATCHEWAN

17   19

Alexander McLeod   William Stiff

Joseph Herbert

346.31a

15.A

Allan Oman

1.   A. Patton   116.8a

3.   5.

271.74a   258a   Laurence Garneau   Joseph McDonald   Wm F. Bradley   20.00

7.   11.

269a   John Water   235a   Thomas J. Anderson   142a   Geo A. Anderson   66a   76.00

120.88a

Surveyed by M. DEANE, D.L.S.

442.

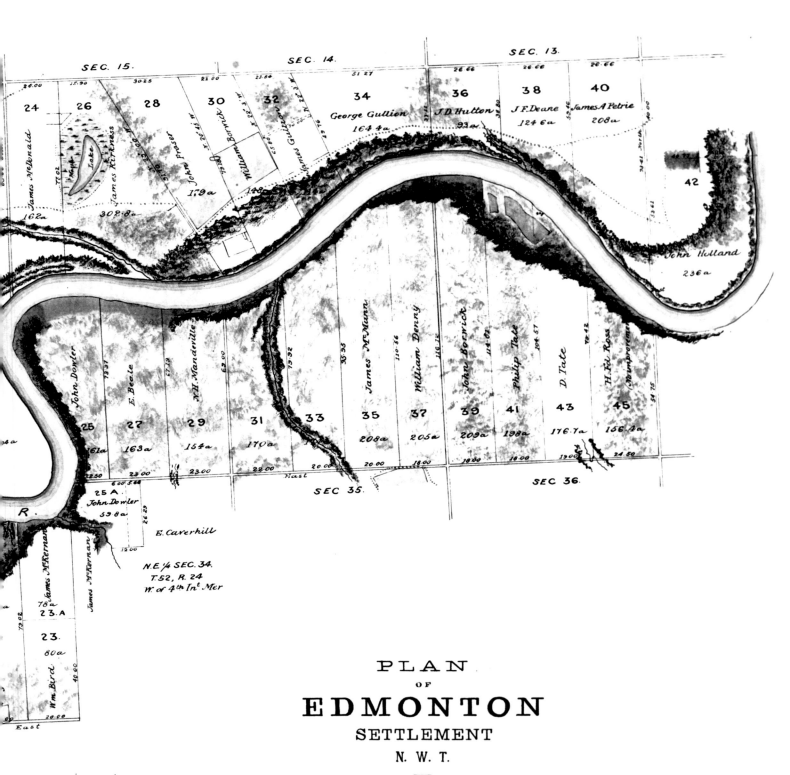

PLAN
OF
EDMONTON
SETTLEMENT
N. W. T.

Scale 20 Chains to 1 Inch

Department of the Interior
Dominion Lands Office
Ottawa, 25th May, 1883.

Approved and Confirmed

A. Russell
For the Surveyor General

EXPLANATION OF COLORS
Green. Scrub or Prairie and Woods Dotted green Water Blue
Yellow with small strokes of black Hills or Slopes. Etching or Grey Shade
(Burnt Woods) Brown Settlers Improvements Pink

Contents

Foreword ix

Project Donors xi

Acknowledgements xiii

Introduction 1

1 The Call of the River 3

2 The River Attracts the First People 5

3 Early Days in the Lower Edmonton Settlement, 1870–1899....................7

4 The Highlands: A Name to Conjure With, 1910......................................11

5 Optimistic Expansion, 1911 21

6 The Greatest Year, 1912 25

7 Magrath's Last Hurrah 39

8 The Boom Ends, 1913 47

9 Old Highlands in Decline, 1914–1919 55

10 A Decade of Faith and Perseverance, 1919–1929..................................69

11 Weathering the Great Depression, 1929–1939 89

12 Life on the Home Front, 1939–1945 103

13 The Second Boom, 1946–1959 113

Afterword: Hope and Renewal, 1960-2011 127

Notes 129

Key to Historic Edmonton Street Names 133

Thank You 135

About the Author 137

Index 138

Foreword

In September 1998, my husband and I were lucky enough to stumble upon a gem of a character home situated along a sun-soaked, tree-lined street bathed in a canopy of orange and yellow leaves. Who knew this home purchase would be the start of our own love affair with the Highlands neighbourhood? Now, we can't imagine creating a legacy of family memories in any other location.

The Highlands is one of Edmonton's best kept secrets. It's no wonder that many families have several generations living here, or that for 100 years individuals who grew up here have continued to return to to raise their own families. This intrinsic sense of community attachment is fueling a living and evolving history that the Highlands Historical Society wanted to capture in a book commemorating the neighbourhood's centennial year, 2012. We hope it will identify and preserve the Highlands' history and cultural heritage.

Author Ken Tingley, a public historian and Edmonton's Historian Laureate, has brought the history of the Highlands alive. His interpretation of historical events, people of importance, and architectural highlights inspires passion and appreciation for our neighbourhood. Within his account, the defining elements of the Highlands emerge: a sense of history and nostalgia, heritage homes and architectural diversity, tree-lined walkable streets, an abundance of gardens and green space, and neighbours connecting with neighbours.

Aligned with the Highlands Historical Society tagline, "honouring the life and times of a neighbourhood," this book re-enforces that the Highlands has an important history and a lot of soul. It is, quite simply, a great place to live. Display the book with pride!

Back in 1998 at our housewarming party, I would have loved to have displayed *My Heart's in the Highlands* on my coffee table – to highlight the proud history of the Highlands and reminding me, my family, and my neighbours that history is continually in the making, in our own living rooms.

Shelli Carder Drozd
Communications Committee Chair
Highlands Historical Society

Project Donors

The Highlands Historical Society gratefully acknowledges significant funding and support from the Alberta Historical Resources Foundation.

Thank you to the following organizations, businesses and individuals:

Corporate Sponsors
Wild Rose Antique Club,
The City of Edmonton, The Edmonton Heritage Council

Platinum
Pat and Al Barkway, Direct-Line Insurance Inc.

Gold
Sid and Nellie Braaksma, Chris and Robyn Fowler

Silver
Nancy Power, Ted and Pauline Smith

Bronze
759060 Ab Ltd., Anonymous, Morley and Susan Bleviss, Cathy Chalmers,
Margaret Chalmers (née Dalziel), Dr. Jerry and Laurie Cotter,
Stuart Drozd and Shelli Carder Drozd, Betty-Jean and John Wm Duke, Yvette Dumont,
Laurel and Al Erickson, Gisele Ferland and David Ryning, Helen Gillespie,
Glenrose Pediatric Occupational Therapy Staff, Francine Gregory and Matt McCorquodale,

Judith Hibberd, The Howell-Pick Family, Mr. and Mrs. Korpesio, Jim and Joy Leskewich
Albert and Christina, Albert Jr. and Joyce Lesnik, Jennie Monson,
Don and Ann Morrison, Don and Dolores Parkhill, Laurie Parkhill,
Stuart E. and Ethel Pearce, Harold E. Rydman remembering Helen Day (née Rydman),
Judy Shewchuk and Lonnie Johnson, Robert and Carol Snyder,
Doug and Cheryl Toshack, Judy Wagler (in memory of Walt and Ella Kern), Vicki Wheeler,
Johanne and Ted Yakula

Pewter
Carolyn Arnold, Wayne Brix, Pat Dawson, Carole Tyson Flyn, Valerie Lineham,
Rhoda McDonough, Ernie Pallister, Mary Shewchuk, Dalton and Diane Smarsh

Acknowledgements

Every book is a joint effort by many people, and this book is no exception. Johanne Yakula had the vision to initiate the centennial book project, and she oversaw the research, writing, editing and design processes. The book owes a debt to the original Highlands Historical Foundation, now very active as the Highlands Historical Society. Special thanks are due Ted Smith, an original Foundation member, who made available his material regarding the Highlands Golf Club. Carol Snyder laid a solid foundation through the oral history project, the transcriptions of which can now be accessed in the City of Edmonton Archives. All those who were interviewed and who are identified in the text have added a personal flavour. It would have been impossible to capture the earlier period of the community's development without their cooperation.

Several former residents like Margaret Husband were especially helpful and supportive, providing many wonderful photographs. I also extend special thanks to Van Tsiclas for his excellent photographs of Highlands homes, many of which have been commemorated by special plaques.

Finally, I thank the readers and reviewers who saved the author from a few of those embarrassing errors dreaded by all historians.

– Ken Tingley

Introduction

The Highlands exerts a strong attraction on those who live there. It might almost be said, "Once a Highlander, always a Highlander." Despite some who view the later development of smaller lots north of 112 Avenue as creating two Highlands, most Highlanders feel a common sense of community. Many residents have grown up in the neighbourhood and moved away, only to return. Others, descendants of the original Highlanders from before the Great War, remained for two or three generations. Many have remained all their lives.

Violet Macleod was one such resident. Her memories are typical of life in the Highlands, and a clear reminder of what that life was like for many in the early years. Born in west Edmonton in 1908, Violet moved to the Highlands in 1918 with her father, Malcolm Macleod, her mother Loretta Conley Macleod, and siblings Bruce, Marjorie, and Norman (Bill). Sister Jean was born there the following year. Violet would live in this special place for the next 75 years, watching life carry on around her. In 1996 she provided an invaluable interview to the Highlands Historical Foundation (now the Highlands Historical Society), reminding us of what has made the Highlands special over its century of existence.

Violet lived at 6116 Jasper Avenue (now 111 Avenue) from 1918 until 1939; at 11130 – 65 Street from 1939 to 1954.

Then, after a year in a downtown apartment, she lived at 11119 – 62 Street, now known as the Margaret Marshall Residence, until 1993. Her first memories are of driving down 112 Avenue in a taxi when the family moved into their new home, and thinking that there was mud everywhere. "It was terrible." Only an elevated boardwalk ran along that main commercial route in 1918; for years water would squish up through the planks, while the sidewalk moved up and down as pedestrians walked along it. Decades later Violet still appreciated the workmanship of Jack Raymond and his sons, who built many of the 12-inch concrete basement walls and sidewalks in the Highlands. Quite a few of those sidewalks, which made getting around much easier, remain in place today.

She also recalls the Spanish influenza pandemic in 1919, and having to wear a protective mask to avoid the contagion. Frances Martell also remembered her father, Clyde Smith, wearing a mask as he delivered soup door to door to those infected by the flu.

The Macleod family rented their first house from Magrath Holgate, next door to another community founder, Robert Walter Grierson. The Macleods and Griersons shared a large vegetable garden on a lot rented from the city. Only two other houses seem to have been located in this eastern part of the district in 1918, with much "bush and swamp" that required filling. "It was like a mini-ravine with a wooden sidewalk bridge over it," Violet noted. Most people did their own filling, although Roy Towns had a huge pile of dirt to help with building up yards.

On a more positive note, Violet remembered picking hazelnuts, chokecherries, and saskatoons in the river valley. Many families still observed a quiet Lord's Day and attended church on Sunday. Sometimes a walk down Ada Boulevard after church would end at a little ice cream gazebo with a screened porch. In the winter skiing and tobogganing also took place in the valley before the golf course was built in the area.

Most families had live-in maids who would also look after the children. Violet recalled Mrs. Damsell, a German woman who served as the neighbourhood wash woman. This was before the opening of the Snowflake Laundry, where two dollars would cover a week's laundry, "and everything came back neatly folded."

Residents almost always ate at home, and found their entertainment close at hand as well, with school dances, church events, and house parties. Most of the early residents were of British descent, and the community remained a Conservative outpost for many years, with Highlander A. U. G. Bury exerting his strong political influence. The commercial centre was located near 112 Avenue and 65 Street, and most shopping, with the exception of clothing, was carried out at the local meat market, grocery store, drugstore, and bakery.

What follows is an account of how the Highlands originated, how it developed, and the way in which it spread to fill the entire subdivision after the Second World War. This chronological narrative is related to broader events where appropriate, but essentially describes the built heritage of the Highlands within its own community boundaries. Primary sources such as building permits and city street directories have been used to show exactly the scale and speed of Highlands development, year by year. Within this context, the book describes the role of important organizations such as the Highlands and District Community League (one of the first in Edmonton), the United Church ladies' aid society, and other active groups central to Highlands life.

1
The Call of the River

The summer view from Capilano Bridge while driving north reveals the lush green of the North Saskatchewan River valley downstream. It reminds us of the reason most Edmontonians value the river as their city's most outstanding characteristic. This has been the case for well over a century, although at first the deep river valley posed significant obstacles to urban growth and commerce. Bridges and roads welded greater Edmonton into its present form, which is the result of several significant amalgamations preceding the First World War.

As Edmonton developed during the boom years before the war, it began to spread out into suburbs in all directions, but especially towards the west and east ends. The allure of the river valley was a constant factor in the development, and in the case of the Highlands it was paramount. The Highlands community is a quintessential expression of the importance of "location, location, location." Most of the first to live in the Highlands came because of the "view lots."

The Highlands has always been closely connected to the North Saskatchewan River and its deep valley, ravines, and flats. As the community began to develop in 1912, it was building on a relationship that the undeveloped locality had held with the river for years. The life of the lower Edmonton Settlement, downstream from the main settlement near the Fort Edmonton upstream, at first was concentrated in the river traffic and river lots.

On 4 August 1883 the *Edmonton Bulletin* reported that "Burbank's river improvements party" was set to descend the river, "to commence the work of clearing the steamboat channel of boulders, all the way down to Prince Albert." The efforts of this dozen men in their two barges with mechanical hoists signaled the importance of charting and keeping the river channels clear for the steamboats upon which the upper and lower Edmonton settlements now relied.

By 1912, the year the Highlands really began to develop, the river valley flats upstream were a series of industrial anthills swarming with hundreds of men digging up the gravel and sand, and making the brick and excavating the coal required to build the newly amalgamated Edmonton, Strathcona, and North Edmonton. Greater Edmonton relied on the river for its production, and much of the building materials in the Highlands would come from Gallagher's Flat, Ross Flat, Walter's Flat, and Riverdale. "The river is more like a street," declared an article in the *Edmonton Bulletin* in March 1912, "and it is at the present time one of the busiest thoroughfares of the city."

During the winter hundreds of teams used the frozen river trail, the teamsters steering from point to point and occasionally crossing snowy sand or gravel bars, like that at Gold Bar across the river from the Highlands. Gravel for construction, and for gold mining, was gathered along the shores and thawed out by bonfires as the spring approached, to be shoveled onto sleighs and wagons. At several points in the high river escarpment the river had created large deposits of sand that were prized by contractors for plaster, pavements, and sidewalks. The ice was sometimes cleared, marked off, and sawn into cakes for storage, to be used in ice chests and coolers when the hot summer arrived. Brickyards relied on the deep clay banks to provide materials for the rapid house construction taking place during the pre-war boom.

2

The River Attracts the First People

Early aboriginal peoples came to what we call the North Saskatchewan River valley for millennia before the coming of Europeans. They were attracted by the shelter, fuel, and game in the winter; sustaining herbs and other plants in the spring through fall; and plentiful water and fish during most of the year. The flat, sheltered areas protected within the river bends deep in the valley reliably sustained these people in most of their needs. The highlands above on the river escarpments provided lookouts from which they could spot game or other people.

Anthony Henday was the first European to visit the area that would become Edmonton. He passed through in 1754, and again in 1755 on his return to York Factory from a mission to seek out new sources of fur for the Hudson's Bay Company. The land still seems to have been recognized as Blackfoot territory, although Cree and Assiniboine were moving west along the river, encouraged and strengthened by their better access to European trade

goods. During the spring of 1755 Henday observed the Cree band with which he was travelling stop just downstream from the future Edmonton, at a site where they gathered birch bark, built canoes, and met many Cree visitors. It seems that by this time the greater Edmonton area was already a significant gathering place for aboriginal groups.

Fort Augustus was built by the Northwest Company near the present location of Fort Saskatchewan in 1795, soon followed by the first Edmonton House across the river. The area was on the western edge of expanding Cree territory, a transitional zone between Cree and Blackfoot that would shape its history during the fur trade period. This area also stood at the junction of woodland cultures to the north, and plains cultures to the south. The posts were moved upstream to the present site of Edmonton in about 1802, where they remained until 1810 – on what much later became known as the Ross Flat. A series of posts followed until the fifth and final Fort

Edmonton was built high on the north river valley terraces above Ross Flat in 1830, five years after a serious flood damaged the fourth post.

During its heyday the Hudson's Bay Company hired men from the Orkney Islands to build York boats, so called because they were used to carry seasonal fur harvests downstream to York Factory on Hudson Bay. Some of these Orcadian company men were among the first occupants of what came to be called the Highlands. Fort Edmonton dominated the administration and growth of a vast western commercial empire between 1795 and 1870. Some of the first influences of this history would be felt in the Lower Edmonton Settlement that grew up downstream from the fort after the sale of the North-Western Territory to the Dominion of Canada in 1869.

3

Early Days in the Lower Edmonton Settlement, 1870–1899

"Towards the close of the nineteenth century," Tony Cashman writes, "the most exciting sound of the Edmonton summer was the great steamer *Northwest* whistling as she passed the Highlands on the approach to Edmonton." Of course, the name *Highlands* would not be applied to the neighbourhood until 1910, but the lofty escarpment that defined the north side of the North Saskatchewan River was clearly a "highlands," officially or not (*The Best Edmonton Stories*, p.197). Cashman notes that the *Northwest* whistle alerted people in the Upper Edmonton Settlement that the steamer was on the way, giving them plenty of time to hustle down to Ross Flats to greet it.

The first steamboat to pass the future location of the Highlands was the *Northcote*, which arrived in 1874, the same year that the North-West Mounted Police crossed the river and ascended Rat Creek to establish Fort Saskatchewan just to the north. It had only been four years since the Hudson's Bay Company had relinquished its northwestern domain to

the newly confederated Dominion of Canada. Before that time the vast western wilderness dedicated to the fur trade had been better known to the world as "the Great Lone Land." Five versions of Fort Edmonton had presided over the fur trade on this stretch of the mighty North Saskatchewan River since 1795, but few buildings existed outside the forts' palisades until 1870.

After the land transfer that year, things began to percolate across old Rupert's Land and the newly formed Northwest Territories. For decades the Hudson's Bay Company had discouraged settlement and agriculture fairly consistently, but after 1870 settlers began to take up residence outside Fort Edmonton on narrow river lots similar to those first laid out in New France. The Highlands would be located far to the east of any such early nodes of settlement for almost another 40 years.

Secondary officers of the Hudson's Bay Company, as well as former employees, began to leave the company and take up river lots. They were among the first permanent settlers

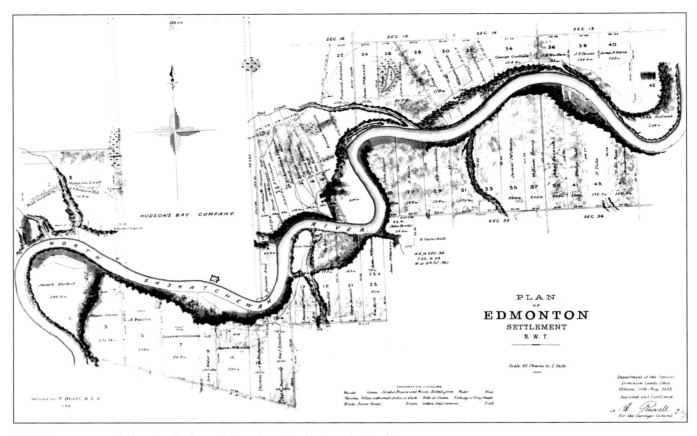

This 1883 survey map of Edmonton Settlement shows the original rectangular river lots.
City of Edmonton Archives EAM-85.

outside Fort Edmonton. Most established themselves as farmers on both sides of the river, along the riverbanks downstream from the fort. Frank Oliver recalled in 1921 that "[the] settlement of Edmonton was comprised almost entirely of this class of people." Others established homes around the first Methodist church and manse near the present site of the Chateau Lacombe.

Colin Fraser, John Sinclair, Donald McLeod, James Rowland, William Rowland, Kenneth Macdonald, James Kirkness, John Fraser, James Gullion, and George Gullion

took up the first river lots downstream from Fort Edmonton. Donald Ross, John Walter, "Edmonton's first millionaire," and Malcolm Groat took up other properties. The Gullion brothers would sell River Lots 32 and 34 to John A. McDougall in 1898. These river lots were the core of what would become the Highlands twelve years later.

In 1918 McDougall recalled the first River Lot settlers. "They did a little farming, freighting, and buffalo-hunting," he remembered. "After getting this little crop in, in the spring, they would generally go down to Winnipeg with a string of ponies and carts after freight for the Company, and in the fall, after their return, and when their small crops were gathered in, they would all start for the plains for a buffalo hunt, and to lay in a winter's supply of meat."

Among this list of Edmonton pioneers, the Gullions are of the most interest in the history of the Highlands. James Ingram Gullion first settled River Lot 32, in the heart of what became the Highlands. The obituary in the *Edmonton Bulletin* on 19 September 1902 marked his passing by noting that he "was one of the land marks (sic) of the district and was among the first to begin farming operations here which he did in the early '70's." James Gullion, born at Eday in the Orkney Islands in 1837, lived on the same farm on River Lot 32 until his death.

James Gullion came to Fort Edmonton in 1857, while his brother George came to the Northwest in 1851, taking up a river lot next to his brother in about 1870. George Gullion had moved to Athabasca Landing by 1902. James Gullion's wife, who was a sister of Henry and Colin Fraser, died in 1899.

James Gullion was adventurous in his youth, crossing the Atlantic several times before finally beginning to work for the Hudson's Bay Company. "He was a boat builder by trade, and also acted as a guide on the Saskatchewan in the days when the Hudson's Bay Company carried their freight in inland boats," the *Edmonton Bulletin* reported. "He was also a river guide and took part in the military expedition from Edmonton to Fort Pitt under General Strange in the rebellion of 1885." His funeral, on 18 September 1902, was attended by many of his fellow Edmonton pioneers.

Talk of a transcontinental railway linking the Edmonton Settlement with the outside world was rife during the 1870s, and the growing community hoped to benefit from a northern route through Yellowhead Pass. While Edmonton would be discouraged in this hope, a telegraph line connected it to the outside world by 1879, and it had a newspaper three years later. Edmonton was on the cusp of an amazing boom that would see its population mushroom.

In August 1899 a devastating flood hit the North Saskatchewan River, destroying everything in its path. The *Northwest* steamboat had stopped operating in 1897, and had been

Floods were a continuing menace in the river valley. The year 1915 marked another very destructive flood, when a loaded train had to be parked on the Low Level Bridge to prevent it from washing out. CEA EA-160-1399.

pulled onto Ross Flats to serve as a warehouse. The 1899 flood washed her away, and as her wreckage floated down the river past the Highlands, where it had so proudly plied its way, Edmonton found itself on the edge of the greatest period of growth in its history.

During the coming decade Edmonton would grow from town to city, and be transformed, seemingly overnight. The boom would attract builders, speculators, developers, and real estate men by the hundreds. Among them would be two who envisioned something special for the highland properties to the east of the growing city.

4

The Highlands: A Name to Conjure With, 1910

By 1910 Edmonton, Strathcona, and their satellite communities like Beverly, Jasper Place, and North Edmonton were in the middle of a phenomenal burst of growth and development. In 1901 the population of the combined cities of Edmonton and Strathcona totaled 4,176 residents, where as recently as 1899 Edmonton had held only 2,212, with a few hundred in the newly named Town of Strathcona. By 1903 Edmonton had grown to 6,995; in 1906 14,088; the Dominion census showed a population of 27,000 in Edmonton alone in 1909.

Agriculture was the basis of prosperity in the Canadian North-West, which became known in the first decade of the 20th Century as "The Last Best West." The American frontier had been pushed beyond its historical limits and officially closed in 1891, the year the first rail connection reached the south bank of the North Saskatchewan River across from the Edmonton Settlements. A rival city sprang up at the end-of-steel located in South Edmonton (renamed Strathcona in 1899), but both Edmonton and Strathcona, known as "the Twin Cities" between 1907 and 1912, benefited from the rail link. The railroad brought a flood of immigrant townspeople and home-steaders to the district.

The policies established by Clifford Sifton, Minister of the Interior in the new Liberal government of Sir Wilfrid Laurier after 1896, promoted waves of British and European immigration based on the lure of virtually free farm lands in the west. First initiated by the completion of the Canadian Pacific Railway in 1885, the westward tide of humanity surged in along the proliferating rail lines. Dominion Land Offices were established in the many new towns across the North-West. In 1910 Duncan Marshall, provincial Minister of Agriculture, appointed Charles S. Hotchkiss as the Alberta Immigration Commissioner for the year. Hotchkiss was charged with overseeing this vast land rush. Edmonton continued to grow rapidly: 31,064 in 1911; 53,611 in 1912; 67,243 in 1913, following amalgamation of the Twin Cities. City population would peak in 1914, the first year of the Great War of 1914–1918, at 72,516. After this, the population would decline due to the war and post-war economic lethargy. It would not reach this level again until 1929, on the eve of the Great Depression.

The birth and early development of the Highlands was an integral part of the sweeping events that were transforming Alberta's capital city. Between 1910 and the early years of the First World War, Old Highlands, the original area constructed before the First World War, would see most of its core surveyed, planned, and built. The character of Old Highlands' distinctive community culture and lifestyle would also be determined during these pivotal years.

These were also the years during which the City Beautiful movement envisioned a civilized city living graciously in accord with nature. The *Edmonton Capital* (26 January 1910) reported that a "beautiful driveway along both the north and south banks of the Saskatchewan river is something that the imagination has drawn for nearly every Edmonton and Strathcona citizen." The Edmonton municipal parks committee was reported to be in negotiations with the provincial government to construct such a scenic driveway during 1910. "The intention is to have the scenic route extend east on both sides of the river as far as the Clover Bar bridge and four miles or so up the river." The first efforts were made around Capitol Hill and the new Lieutenant-Governor's residence in Glenora. The war would halt the downstream construction, although Ada Boulevard became a later legacy of this early planning.

In the same year the east end witnessed the movement of the Edmonton Exhibition into the vicinity of the future Highlands development. The two formed a dynamic relationship thereafter. However, City Commissioner A. G. Harrison complained when the exhibition grounds were moved to the East End Park in 1910: "At present visitors to the grounds have to pick their way along a winding trail, which has refuse scattered along the edges." (*Edmonton Capital* 3 February 1910) Harrison asked that Pine Avenue and other approaches be brushed out to facilitate access to the exhibition grounds. This situation was soon to change, not least since a "high class" neighbourhood was about to rise on the southeastern flank of the exhibition precincts. And such a neighbourhood would demand more than a path through the bush.

Subsequently, the question of access to East End Park and the exhibition grounds centred on radial railway construction. Extension of the Edmonton Radial Railway (ERR) to the park along Jasper Avenue, Kinnaird Street, and Pine Avenue was on the agenda of a special meeting called by city council for February 28 to consider a report by ERR Superintendent C. E. Taylor. The *Edmonton Capital* reported that "quite a discussion arose as to whether the north or south routes should be taken for the east end extension. A delegation for Norwood Boulevard advanced the northern route, which was supported by Superintendent Taylor, but the southern route was supported by the councilors. Alderman Joseph Clarke, who lived in the district, argued for the Norwood Boulevard group, noting that there was no adequate supporting population for the Jasper Avenue route east of Government Street, and that during the winter the south route would have to be discontinued or run at a loss. Clarke also argued that the south route would serve only about 500 people, while the north route would serve some 2,000.

Mayor Robert Lee toured the east end with Superintendent Taylor and the public works committee on March 10 to consider the merits of a street railway "belt line" to service the exhibition grounds. These were to be single-track lines having turnouts to avoid any level crossings. "I think also that two stub lines like these would be far more serviceable in handling crowds at the exhibition," Lee stated, "than would a belt line." (*Edmonton Capital* 11 March 1910)

As the debate continued, construction was delayed. A special meeting of city council on May 26 was held to discuss the issues again. City Commissioner A. V. Bouillon reported that it would be virtually impossible to complete the rail connection in time to serve the 1910 exhibition. To push it through in time would add greatly to the costs. "If it was intended that the line should be in use by the time the exhibition opened, work should have been started on it at least two months ago," Bouillon stated. "As it is, nothing has been done. All the materials have to be bought yet, the plans have to be drawn, and in fact nothing whatever has been done so far toward the construction of the line." (*City Capital* 26 May 1910)

What would become the Highlands on the east side of Edmonton and Glenora on the west were notable examples of residential developments courting streetcar expansion. The Highlands was an exclusive district on the outskirts of the city developed by Magrath, Holgate & Company beginning in 1910. Magrath Holgate marketed the development as a natural paradise of refined, graceful homes situated above the scenic North Saskatchewan River valley.

Car No. 11 at the end of its run, at City Park (Borden Park), in the summer of 1913.
Glenbow Archives photo NA-1328-64585

While isolation may have appealed to those who valued exclusivity, the Highlands nevertheless expressed a desire for streetcar service, and the developer went about achieving his goal in a way that foreshadowed contemporary public-private partnerships. On 29 August 1911, Magrath Holgate proposed to pay for construction and cover any losses for the first eighteen months of streetcar operation if the city supervised and administered bringing service to the isolated district. The cash-strapped city fathers accepted the offer a week later. In just ten months, the line was running from the boundary of East End Park (renamed Borden Park after Prime Minister Robert Borden visited Edmonton in 1914) along Pine Avenue to Irwin Street. The line was soon extended two blocks further east.

During 1910 Magrath, Hartt & Company was becoming one of the most successful among a legion of real estate developers taking advantage of the spectacular growth in Edmonton and Strathcona. On Friday, 25 March 1910, Magrath's development business, reorganized as Magrath, Holgate & Company, purchased 278 acres adjoining the newly developing exhibition park in the east end of the city. This land was located just east of the Bellevue subdivision, and was purchased from Hon. John A. McDougall MPP for $150,000. The *Edmonton Bulletin* reported that this was the largest sale of real estate in Edmonton to that date. Magrath Holgate announced that the purpose of the purchase was the creation of a residential neighbourhood, to be subdivided into 66-foot lots "laid out on crescent streets to be graded shortly." This district was briefly known as McDougall Heights.

In September 1910 the city announced the creation of Beverly School District #2922, sometimes called the "Edmonton Highland School District," and plans to build two wood-frame school buildings at the present location of the Highlands Junior High School. Then somewhat after the fact, the Highlands was annexed during 1911. It was at this time that Magrath Holgate offered to pay for the streetcar extension to the Highlands, and to protect the city from financial responsibilities associated with this service for eighteen months. These negotiations committed the Edmonton Radial Railway to hourly service to the Highlands, with a line running east along 112 Avenue to 63 Street, and soon extended to 61 Street. Magrath Holgate and the city also agreed to build an elementary school in the Highlands, with the bid of $144,440 accepted on 1 August 1913. A news story stated:

The property commands a fine view of the city and Mr. Magrath will build there

himself. Trees will be planted and a sewerage system installed. The part of the property lying on the flats will be reserved for park purposes. The street car service now extends to the corner of the grounds and also the water, electric light and telephone systems.

Magrath, who had just returned from a tour of the west coast to look over real estate developments in Victoria and Vancouver, reported to the *Bulletin* that as a result of his investigations he had "greater faith than ever in Edmonton realty."

One large advertisement announced in April 1910: "We have marked so many of our listing cards SOLD during the last few weeks that we find it necessary to completely revise our lists. Property Owners are invited to list their property here. Few have the buyers and can sell if the price is right. Call, phone or write: Magrath Hartt & Co., Opposite Merchants Bank." (*Edmonton Capital* 20 April 1910)

Magrath, Hartt & Company regularly posted "Real Estate Bulletins" in the local newspapers, listing properties across the city: a lot in Groat Estate "near brow of high bank"; three lots near Norwood School, "high and dry"; a new house and two lots on Ross' Flats, "the low price will soon sell this property." (*Edmonton Capital* 22 April 1910) Other successful speculative ventures included "one of the best Jasper Avenue double corners... directly opposite the C.P.R. Station site." The advertisement also noted that Jasper Avenue and 109 Street were the two widest business streets in Edmonton. "The main entrance to the Station will likely be on 9th Street, opposite this property." The asking price was $50,000. Such large transactions (for the day) were not uncommon for Magrath, Hartt & Company. (*Edmonton Capital* 2 May 1910)

On 10 September 1910 the newspapers in Edmonton and Strathcona offered readers "cash for a thought." What was that thought? The new Magrath Holgate company was offering $50 in gold in a contest to suggest a name for their new subdivision in Edmonton's east end. Their firm's recently purchased land needed a good name before being placed on the market. The *Edmonton Capital* noted further: "[From] almost any portion of it an absolutely ideal view of 15 miles is obtainable, embracing Clover Bar and the range of hills in the distance, while nearer the river the scenic beauty is beyond adequate description." Moreover, the newspaper stated, "A charming feature of the subdivision is the elevation, rising several feet above the city level, as it affords a surprising view that cannot be equaled in and around the province."

Magrath and Holgate needed a name "that will suitably designate this property and be consistent with the high class of residence that will be erected as it has been decided to place a building restriction of $2,500 upon the sites." No lots were to be sold until the name had been selected. It was reported that already this large property, bounded on the south by the North Saskatchewan River and on the north by Alberta Avenue, was "rapidly being cleared by the new owners...."

Such contests were fairly common in the years before the First World War. The month before, on February 4, the *Edmonton Daily Capital* and *Saturday News & Alberta Homesteader*, offered a grand prize of a $600 Nordheimer piano for the "candidate" who obtained the most new subscribers for the *Capital*. There was another piano as second prize, and an array of "district prizes." This contest, in the newspaper favoured by Magrath, Holgate & Company, was probably the inspiration for the contest.

Daily advertisements appeared in the local newspapers, warning that only five days, four days, three days remained to enter the contest. The contest closed at midnight the following Saturday, September 17. On September 19 the five judges were to meet "in a private room, and after being locked in securely will open up the huge lists of names sent in and then each coupon will be thoroughly examined." These five prestigious judges were Judge H. C. Taylor; D. S. MacKenzie, Deputy Minister of Education; T. M. Turnbull, Manager of the Bank of Commerce; E. C. Bowker, Manager of the Dominion Bank; and H. Bewlay Stevens, the Advertising Manager of the *Edmonton Bulletin*.

Advertisements reported on 20 September 1910 that, "owing to the extraordinary number of Coupons sent in for our name contest, it is impossible to announce the winner until *tomorrow afternoon*." Two contest entrants suggested the name "Highlands," S. Loughlin and Mary MacKenzie, but after consideration Miss Loughlin won the prize since the other entry was dated September 9, and the winning entry on September 4. Miss Loughlin then called at the Magrath and Holgate office, was identified, and awarded the gold. "The prize is now on view in our window," it was announced. "The Highlands" became the official name for the new subdivision on the autumnal equinox, 21 September 1910.

Several times during September, bucolic views of the Highlands taken by photographers Byron-May appeared in the local press. Another advertising campaign kicked off during the remainder of September. The following

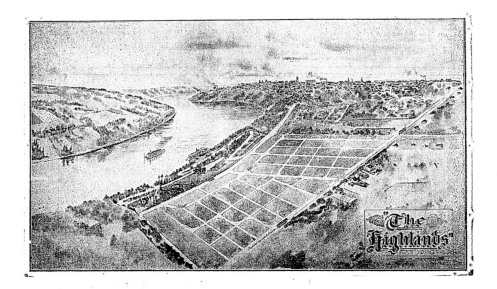

"The Highlands"

"The Land You Hear So Much About"

aptly describes the property we are shortly placing on the market called **"The Highlands."** Everybody is interested in the sub-division because it is so delightfully situate—the scenery is one of the finest to be obtained in this City—the land rises high above the river thus affording a magnificent view of the pretty bends that abound—the lack of City noises that worry those living in and around the busy centres—the building restriction of $2500 demands a residence of fine structure being built upon its lots and thus ensuring the owners of property a certain high class social set.

As an investment **"The Highlands"** offers inducements hitherto unheard of in Edmonton and we can safely guarantee anyone a good increase over their deposit within a short time. Speculators will find in **"The Highlands"** a good turnover in a comparatively short time on account of the improvements to be entered upon at once in every way possible to make this sub-division one of the most select and desirable in and around the district. Anyone wishing further information can have all their enquiries answered upon application at the office where any member of the staff will be glad to meet you.

Should you desire to see the property we will be delighted to run you out in the auto in a few minutes from leaving the City.

Not Yet—But Soon!

Magrath, Holgate & Co.

(Successors to Magrath, Hart & Co.)

Jasper Avenue, E.   Edmonton,   Alberta.

Ad from the
Edmonton Capital,
September 24, 1910,
page 5.

full-page advertisement, with the newly-named "The Highlands" still printed in quotation marks, provided information on "The Land You Hear So Much About" in the *Edmonton Capital* on 23 September 1910.

> *Everybody is interested in the sub-division because it is so delightfully situated – the scenery is one of the finest to be obtained in this City – the land rises high above the river thus affording a magnificent view of the pretty bends that abound – the lack of City noises that worry those living in and around the busy centres – the building restriction of $2500 demands a residence of fine structure being built upon its lots and thus ensuring the owners of property a certain high class social set.*
>
> *As an investment "The Highlands" offers inducements hitherto unheard of in Edmonton and we can safely guarantee anyone a good increase over their deposit within a short time. Speculators will find in "The Highlands" a good turnover in a comparatively short time on account of the improvements to be entered upon at once in every way possible to make this sub-division one of the most select and desirable in and around the district.... Should you desire to see the property we will be delighted to run you out in the auto in a few minutes from leaving the City.*

The next day another advertisement featured a bird's-eye view of the Highlands, as envisioned "not yet, but soon."

The Highlands lots went on sale on 1 October 1910, heralded by yet another festive and heavily advertised event. Magrath, Holgate & Company kicked off the preceding week in the Monday newspapers by advertising a special opening-day offer, which allowed for one-quarter cash down payments and the balance in equal payments spread over three years. After this the terms were to include a one-third cash down payment, and the remainder spread over four years. The Highlands, "brimfull (sic) of beauty spots – literally bristling with inducements for speculators and investors – is ready for immediate building operations and can offer any homemaker advantages," the advertisement continued, "such as modern and up-to-date improvements, street grading and sidewalks, whilst the street car runs up to the corner of the property." On Tuesday a photograph of the Highlands showed a view of the river. "This Sub-division is intended for a home site for all those who are seeking a reserved, quiet and select site, and the illustration aptly displays the charm of this property," Magrath, Holgate & Company proclaimed. "We intend making this the sweetest and most desirable sub-division for select and critical householders in Edmonton."

On Wednesday Magrath Holgate challenged a prevalent theory of the day, in which classy neighbourhoods were supposedly built in the west ends of cities. It listed the following cities that had build prestige neighbourhoods to the east: Seattle, Portland, Los Angeles, San Francisco, Oakland, Vancouver, St. Paul, Minneapolis, and Spokane. A special streetcar, with autos taking interested people into the area from the end of track, were advertised for the Friday preceding opening day, as were the $9 per front foot lot rates. "If you compare these terms and the price with other offers in the market we believe you will be convinced of this fact, that "THE HIGHLANDS" IS THE CHEAPEST, SAFEST, MOST DESIRABLE AND MOST REMUNERATIVE ON THE MARKET."

On Thursday a special pitch was made to "the ladies."

LADIES

We will be looking for a chance to take you to "THE HIGHLANDS" by special car on Friday. Come along as many as you like. We extend a special invitation to you.

On Friday and Saturday (opening day) other groups, from the wealthy professional to the upwardly mobile, were targeted with reasons they should be interested in the Highlands – under an oversize headline asking WHY?

Doctors

You are keen of discernment and discretion – able to diagnose disease and suggest remedies – always ready to handle something that will add laurels to your reputation, take advantage of the opportunities in "THE HIGHLANDS". People are already located on the adjoining property and will soon be on this sub-division. Sometimes they may need your advice – be there to give it. See the point?

Lawyers

Some of your superfluous cash needs good investment. Why not consider "THE HIGH-LANDS"? Locate your country seat in the midst of natural beauty. Let the scenery that nature has planted there call you to a quiet and peaceful home site. It is really worth it.

Merchants & Bankers

Holding responsible positions in the city, you should most certainly avail yourself of this money maker. A small investment in "THE HIGHLANDS" now will enable you to raise a valuable sum next year should you require extra money for your financial undertakings. It is good security, too!

Gentlemen at Leisure

When reading this announcement and wondering what to do with your income and bank balance, may we suggest you make a resolve to handle some of "THE HIGHLANDS." This property appeals to the wealthy class. It is high and dry and has a building restriction of $2500 upon it, which bars all shacks and assures you of high class residences.

Speculators and Investors

Who are looking for a "good thing" need not go any further. As a speculation this sub-division is the best – it is full of all kinds of improvements that impel an increase of price rapidly. As an investment it guarantees practically a sure income on account of the street grading – sidewalks and boulevards to be laid down – besides its natural scenic wonders.

High Class Mechanics

Who are waiting for a fine home site can now have it. You will be able to build a residence here that will be worthy of your efforts – it will enable you to be away from the rush of city traffic and will be the means of assisting you to have a respite from toil and worry. All we ask is that you will enable us to take you out as an opportunity.

Magrath, Holgate & Company advertised two days after the opening sale that it had realized $37,920 in sales, which it claimed as a record sale for one day in the history of Edmonton. The first purchaser of a lot was the Hon. J. A. McDougall MPP. A further sale, extending the original purchase conditions, was put on for Tuesday, October 4. This included sixteen lots, as well as three view lots, "in order to give those who could not get down on Saturday an opportunity to purchase this desirable property...."

While the Highlands was the flagship project for Magrath, Holgate & Company, the firm continued to sell real estate across the city. In mid-October 1910 it had a lot for sale on Griesbach Street, four lots on Kirkness Street, three lots on Carey Street (in Norwood), an eight-room house on a view lot on Stewart Street, all of Lot 18 Block 18 in River Lot 10, two lots with sewer, electrical, and streetcar connections, and "a good list for business and warehouse sites."

Other developments were selling natural beauty in October 1910. Starke & Franklin were selling Dovercourt as "Nature's Beauty Spot" in "The Beautiful West End." The company reminded its investors, "When this Subdivision is sold there can be not more."

However, not everyone was in favour of urban sprawl, not even in 1910. On October 25 the Municipal Improvement League held its first meeting in William Griesbach's office, and expressed the view that the future development and progress of Edmonton depended on compact growth, including the centralization of the commercial and industrial districts. The league opposed "unwarranted extensions to the city east and west," and felt that if this pattern persisted beyond the boundary of the utility systems "huge expenditures for trunk sewers, and electric light, telephone, waterworks, and street car additions, would be incurred for which insignificant revenue in comparison with the outlay per capita, would be realized...." The league also expressed the view "that it was a bad policy to incur such an expenditure when the population of those outlying districts could easily be accommodated within a small and compact area between Kinistino and Twenty-first streets, which it was said could accommodate at least 150,000."

This early expression of "densification," as embraced nearly a century later, was part of the league platform in the 1910 election. Nonetheless, most people, then as now, looked favourably on a nice quiet home in the suburbs, and the more pastoral the setting the better.

The Edmonton Exhibition as Friendly Neighbour

The Edmonton Agricultural Society organized the first local exhibition at Fort Edmonton on 15 October 1879. This was the first event of its kind ever held in what was then known as the North-West Territories. Edmonton's first fair showcased locally produced livestock, grain, vegetables, and handiwork and attracted 500 people.

In 1893 the organization held the city's first spring exhibition, and in 1899 the exhibition grounds were relocated to Rossdale Flats. The first parade to promote the fair was held in 1903, although the fair did not organize community parades during the 1930s and 1940s.

By 1904 the exhibition attracted over 20,000 attendees, with 5,200 on opening day alone. As attendance grew during the first decade of the 20th century, the exhibition relocated to its present, more expansive site in 1910. In 1912 the fair was extended to six days. It continued to be held through the First World War, even though the facilities were at the disposal of the Canadian Army. A similar arrangement was made during the Second World War, though this time with the Royal Canadian Air Force.

The exhibition was rebranded Klondike Days in 1962, with the theme revolving around the Klondike gold rush. The public embraced the theme with relish, dressing up in period costumes for the Klondike Days opening parade.

In 2004 Northlands Park celebrated the 125th anniversary of the fair and exhibition. The Klondike Days Parade was also themed to commemorate the city of Edmonton's 100th anniversary in the same year. Fair attendance continued to climb upward, having broken the 800,000 attendance mark in 2005. However, in 2006 attendance fell to 688,369, coinciding with the year the name of the exhibition was changed to Capital EX.

The Edmonton Exhibition Grounds as seen from the Grandstand in 1931. CEA EA-160-682.

5

Optimistic Expansion, 1911

The reorganized Magrath, Holgate & Company Ltd. was incorporated, with capital of $200,000, at the beginning of February 1911. W. J. Magrath was elected president and managing director at the first meeting of the board. Bidwell A. Holgate was elected the first vice-president and Rev. A. W. Coone the secretary-treasurer. During that spring Rev. Arthur Coone met with R. J. Robinson and Thomas Young at his house to discuss the need for a Sunday School in the new Highlands subdivision. All three had come to take up residence in the Highlands, and Rev. Coone used his influence with Magrath to advocate for the church. At this time there were very few houses in the Highlands, although more development had taken place north of Alberta Avenue and to the west in Bellevue. Still, everyone was optimistic that things were about to change rapidly.

R. J. Robinson, the former superintendent of Grace Sunday School, became superintendent of the new Union Sunday School that held its first meetings in the Highlands School.

This in turn would lead to the first Highlands Methodist Church, forerunner of Highlands United Church, built on land donated by Magrath Holgate.

The new Magrath Holgate charter indicated that the company now sought wide powers, and that it would focus its energies more on the loan and mortgage business. In a mere five years Magrath had become one of the major players in the real estate development of his adopted city. Magrath Holgate Ltd. would now try to concentrate much of its attention on the development and improvement of its flagship neighbourhood in the Highlands.

A week after the reorganization Magrath Holgate announced that it was going to begin immediate construction of a brick addition to its real estate office on Jasper Avenue. F. A. Saunders began construction under a thousand-dollar contract. The company was growing, and looking to the future as Edmonton continued to boom. Edmonton showed a surge in property assessments between 1901 and 1910. Evaluations increased from

Highlands
Methodist Church.
Glenbow Museum
Photo NC-6-890.

$2,580,986 in 1901, to $15,980,212 in 1906, to $20,903,910 in 1908, to $30,105,110 in 1910. Only Calgary and Lethbridge showed similar increases in value among western Canadian cities. In the same period Edmonton had increased in population by over 146 percent. In 1911 the city seemed to be riding a wave of real estate wealth with no peak or decline in sight. Magrath Holgate was positioning itself to ride that wave.

A long session was held in city council chambers on 16 February 1911, at which W. J. Magrath met with the city commissioners and the public works committee. After Magrath petitioned for a water line to the Highlands, his petition was referred to the commissioners, the city engineer, the superintendent of water works, and the city solicitor, with instructions to come to an agreement between the city and Magrath Holgate. The basis for the agreement was that the city would undertake the

construction, while Magrath Holgate would assume all liability. The company would meet all interest and capital charges on debentures issued for the construction of the proposed twelve-inch water main. As a result of this agreement, the first major hurdle in providing services to the Highlands was met.

Competition in the real estate market was fierce, with the *Edmonton Capital* reporting on February 17 that there were up to 36 subdivisions in Edmonton. "All of them are being taken up and no doubt there will be many more during the summer," it added.

Magrath Holgate continued to develop other parts of the city as well. During March 1911 it advertised a lot with a railway spur on Fourth Street, just three blocks north of Jasper Avenue, for $13,000. During April the company advertised a wide range of real estate, including a prime lot just north of Norwood Boulevard on First Street; a wholesale site with a double corner and railway spurs on Upper Fraser Avenue ("Nothing as cheap in the Wholesale District"); another double-corner commercial lot on Fraser ("There is $1,500 profit in this corner in the next month"); a store for rent on New Market between Queen's and Fraser ("This is the only store now ready, directly on the new market"); "snaps" like a lot with house and barn on Namayo Avenue between Griesbach and Sutherland; a "beautiful home site" in Oliver across from the new school ("This is positively the cheapest corner on 16th, 17th or 18th Streets"); the only corner lot for sale on First Street in Norwood; and the "Most Desirable Home Site in West End" on 16th Street between Jasper Avenue and the Canadian Northern Railway tracks; property in Groat Estate. Magrath Holgate also continued to pursue ventures outside of the city, including "A Going Business" for exchange or sale in a west coast city during June 1911.

At this time the Highlands remained largely open land, and the company continued to promote the sale of lots. During the 1911 Easter holiday it suggested in an advertisement that during Good Friday it would be a good idea to "take a rest and spend a few hours walking over 'The Highlands'. Its locality will be a tonic."

On June 30 it was reported that the Magrath Holgate business had had total profits of over $110,000 during the preceding week. During July the company remained busy in the city of Strathcona, as well as Norwood, Parkdale, and Belvedere. The east end continued to grow, with much activity in Norwood and Delton.

Property adjacent to the packing plants that were appearing in this part of the city continued to sell, and increased in value by about 25 percent during August. Many residents of the Highlands would work for the packing plants in the next several years as the neighbourhood grew, and former residents Enid Hart and Jean Robbie recall that these employees were numerous by the 1920s.

Things were flourishing for Magrath Holgate by August, when the company advertised itself as owners and selling agents for the Highlands, Bellevue, Bellevue Addition, City Park Annex Addition, and Tuxedo Park. It also was advertising itself as specialists in acreage for subdivision purposes for "out-of-town clients." Finally, the company as reorganized was branching significantly into fire insurance and work as financial brokers.

During July 1911 the new Industrial Pavilion for the exhibition grounds was announced. Of course it was to be second to none in the west. An impressive drawing in the newspapers further spurred interest in the east end development.

As the fall of 1911 approached, Magrath's efforts on behalf of the Highlands met further success, although at some expense to his company. For some time he had offered to construct at his expense a street railway line from East End Park (now Borden Park), where the line ended, to Irwin Street in the Highlands. City council agreed to permit this construction on September 5, and on the same day Magrath Holgate exercised its option to purchase an additional 839 acres of land lying just to the west of the Highlands (River Lots 36 and 38, Edmonton Enlargement) from William Short for $300,000. This appears to have been the largest acreage purchased for subdivision purposes in Edmonton to that date, but had been contingent upon securing city council's permission to construct the street railway connection. On September 6 Magrath Holgate placed $25,000 in the Dominion Bank to be used by the city to construct the line from the east side of East End Park to Irwin Street. The city agreed to build the line from the west side of East End Park to the grove of trees which marked the east side of the park. It was hoped the line would be completed during the fall, and opened for public use as soon as it was finished.

By September 1911 Magrath Holgate held an enormous tract of 1,117 acres of land for subdivision. The *Edmonton Capital* reported on September 6 that this land "would be placed on the market as soon as is practical." This land included the recent purchase from William Short, extending from Alberta Avenue to the river, "and which is about the finest view property in the city." This property adjoined the Highlands on the east, and the northwest quarter section of Section 13, the south half of Section 13 adjoining Alberta Avenue on the south, and the northern quarter of Section 14 through which the Grand Trunk Pacific Railway ran "and which presents a fine trackage proposition." The city quickly took an option on adjoining properties at this point.

The building season was drawing to a close in November when a shortage of bricks was announced, due to an unusually wet season. Pete Anderson reported that his plant in Gallagher's Flat was short two million bricks that season. The 1912 building season was already felt to be in jeopardy as the building boom continued.

6
The Greatest Year, 1912

An editorial in the January 22 issue of the *Edmonton Capital* declared 1912 to be Edmonton's year. "Every indication which could possibly be relied upon points to the greatest year's growth for Edmonton that a western city has ever known," trumpeted the editorial, "and the indications quite as conclusively point to a continued expansion without cessation for at least five years ahead." Pointing to the unprecedented growth of the city, as well as its agricultural and resource hinterland, the piece concluded: "Nineteen hundred and twelve is to be Edmonton's year, and the time when the rush of construction and development will commence is now only a very few weeks away. And this is the question to you, brother: Are you ready?"

Other real estate companies were developing the east end. The Sage-Appleton Company opened the Beverly Heights subdivision in mid-January, advertising its easy access to streetcar lines, water and sewer lines, and electric lights ensured within a few months. "According to the terms of all agreements," as with the Highlands and other aspiring prestige districts, "a certain class of residences must be erected thus guaranteeing that there will be no unsuitable or unsightly dwellings on any part of this property." Also like the Highlands and other east end properties, it offered "Choice Elegant Beautiful Riverview Lots...." Such view lots were becoming *sine qua non* in the east end.

The Wellman-Gibbs Company put Mount Royal lots up for sale immediately east of the Highlands on 8 February 1912. This new subdivision was located south of Alberta Avenue and north of the river, and abutted Beverly Heights to the east. This tier of developments was seen as a prestigious area for the immediate future. Magrath Holgate cooperated with Gowan and Company, and York and McNamara, to begin development of the New Hagmann area on 15 March 1912. "This is strictly inside property," an advertisement declared in the heated terms typical of the day, "the most desirable in every respect on the market in any city in Western Canada today."

McCutcheon Bros. summed up the atmosphere in its advertisement for Boulevard Heights that March.

The Eleventh Hour Man
We all know him.

The man who is always a little behind his opportunity. Consequently – He never can see the real chance when it presents itself. Do YOU belong in his class or are you of those who are willing and eager to take advantage of such an opportunity for quick profits as is offered in Boulevard Heights?

By the spring of 1912 shortages of construction materials and labourers, along with the rapid influx of people to the city, had led to a severe housing shortage. This was most noticeable among recent immigrants and working people, many of whom lived in a tent city on the Hudson's Bay Reserve until evicted in March. But many recent newcomers among the business and professional classes also felt a pressing need for a home. The time seemed ripe to develop the Highlands.

On Monday morning, 13 May 1912, the Hudson's Bay Company opened the greatest land sale in Canadian history. Magrath Holgate had already acquired tracts of land for sale in the Hudson's Bay Reserve on the first morning of the sale, hiring men to stand in a line that stretched around several city blocks.

The development of the Highlands really began to percolate during the spring of 1912. On 19 April 1912 William F. Brown, of 624 – 15 Street, obtained a building permit for a frame house on Lot 23 Block 23, Highlands Survey, on West Houston Street*, valued at $4,000. He was the first occupant listed in 1913 at this house at 1804 Houston Street (11150 – 64 Street), the first house for which a permit was issued in the Highlands. Many more soon would follow.

On 25 April 1912 two more building permits were issued. A "Mr. Truman" of Edmonton obtained Building Permit 893 for a frame house valued at $4,500 on Lot 16 Block 1, Highlands Survey, East Houston Street (6306 – 111 Avenue). The house was to be built by F. H. Webb.

Harold H. Parlee of 451 – 5 Street obtained Building Permit 894 for a frame house on Lot 15 Block 1, Highlands Survey, on East Houston Street, also to be built by F. H. Webb, and valued at $5,200. Parlee was already a prominent lawyer, and would become very influential in Edmonton. Boyle Parlee & Co. included partners John R. Boyle, H. H. Parlee, Churchill L. Freeman, Percy W. Abbott, and William J. A. Mustard, Barristers (155 Jasper Avenue East). In 1913 Parlee was still living at 3246 Jasper East, and was with Parlee Freeman and Abbott, but would move into the Highlands soon after. The original Parlee residence would later burn down, but another would be built on an adjoining lot.

Violet Macleod, who lived at different Highlands homes between 1918 and 1993, recollects how the Parlee house remained at the centre of Highlands social life for decades. The Parlees and their sons Steven, Bill, and Jim hosted many fabulous parties. "In the winter they had sleigh rides and tobogganing parties where two toboggans were attached to the back of each car and they would drive to Fort Saskatchewan with the teenagers on the toboggans," Violet Macleod remembered in later years. "When they returned, Mrs. Parlee had a huge turkey dinner."

On 21 May 1912 Robert G. Dunsmore obtained Building Permit 1207 to build a frame garage on Lot 9 Block 3, Highlands Survey, on West Irwin Street, to be built by the owner,

🔨 BUILDING PERMITS

William F. Brown
11150 – 64 Street

"Mr. Truman"
6306 – 111 Avenue

Harold H. Parlee
Lot 15, Block 1

Robert G. Dunsmore
11344 – 63 Street

*See "Key to Historic Edmonton Street Names" at the back of this book.

and valued at $100. Robert Dunsmore was the first occupant of 1778 Irwin Street (11344 – 63 Street) in 1913. This would be the first of many early garages built. Longtime Highlands resident Violet Macleod recalled that there were cars in the neighbourhood from the beginning, reflecting the professional background of many residents. It was common to have a car after about 1920," she stated.

Magrath Holgate Limited, working as brokers for J. A. McDougall, obtained its first building permit for a dwelling in the Highlands on 26 May 1912, on Lot 8 Block 8 of the Highlands Survey, located on West Johnston Street. This frame house was to be constructed by F. H. Webb, and was valued at $3,300.

At this time Magrath Holgate Limited consisted of William J. Magrath, president; Bertram A. Taylor, first vice-president; Bidwell A. Holgate, secretary-treasurer; Fred J. Whitcroft, second vice-president. It had already branched out as "Real Estate and Financial Brokers, Insurance, Loans and Investments." Its office was at 44 Jasper Avenue East. Other houses were soon being constructed by Magrath Holgate or by the owners of the Highlands lots.

On 4 April a permit was issued to George C. Clarke for a frame house at 1650 West Houston Street (11142 – 64 Street). Clarke was a salesman for Western Canada Properties Ltd. His home was listed as one of three "new houses" in the 1913 *Henderson's* Edmonton directory. George C. Clarke was the first occupant, and he lived there for a number of years.

On 27 May 1912 Norman B. Wellman of 649 - 6 Street obtained Building Permit 1266 to build a frame house on Lot 7 Block 7, Highlands Survey, located on East Irwin Street, to be built by the owner, and valued at $3,000. Norman Wellman, a carpenter, was the first occupant of 1765 Irwin Street (11239 – 63

Street) in 1913, making the house built sometime during 1912-1913. Clarence Smith, an engineer with the Swift Canadian Company, moved in next during 1915. He was the first of many packing plant managers and employees who would live in the neighbourhood.

On 27 May 1912 George E. Gibson obtained Building Permit 1267 to build a frame house on Lot 6 Block 7, Highlands Survey, located on East Irwin Street, to be built by the owner, and valued at $3,000. George Gibson, a carpenter with Nesbitt and Miller, was the first occupant at 1755 Irwin Street (11233 - 63 Street) in 1913. Gibson was also a teamster with Magrath Holgate. Edward J. Bond then moved into the house in 1915. Today this foursquare dwelling is known as the Bell Residence, acknowledging the long-term residing of the Bell family, 1921-2000..

On 7 June 1912 C. Durham obtained Building Permit 1372 for a frame house on Lot 5 Block 1, Highlands Survey, on East Houston Street (11149 - 64 Street), designed and built by architect E. Kean and valued at $3,000. This residence was still listed as a "new house" in 1913, with Ambrose C. Faulkner the first occupant between 1914 and 1915. He then rented the house to a series of tenants, returning to his home after retirement in 1945. Ernest Brown, the influential and famous Edmonton historian and photographer, lived at this house between 1919 and 1921. A two-storey addition was built on the back in 1971.

On 11 June 1912 Garnett M. Meiklejohn obtained Building Permit 1408 for a frame house on Lot 5 Block 7, Highlands Survey, on East Irwin Street. The house, valued at $2,500, was to be "built by owner." Garnett Meiklejohn, a carpenter, was the first occupant of 1745 Irwin Street (11227 – 63 Street).

⚒ BUILDING PERMITS

J. A. McDougall
Lot 8, Block 8
George C. Clarke
11142 - 64 Street
Norman B. Wellman
11239 – 63 Street
George E. Gibson
11233 - 63 Street
C. Durham
11149 – 64 Street
Garnett M. Meiklejohn
11227 – 63 Street

Holgate residence, 1912
6210 Ada Boulevard.
Photo courtesy of
Van Tsiclas.

One of the most prestigious Highlands residences then was commenced. B. A. Holgate obtained Building Permit 1541 on 19 June 1912, for a "B. V. Hse" (brick veneer house) on Lots 12–13 Block 9, Highlands Survey, located on North Ada Boulevard. The house was designed by the successful local firm Nesbitt and Morehouse. The Holgate Residence was valued at $19,000, a considerable sum even at the height of the pre-war boom. Eventually Holgate would spend $49,000 on this property, including $10,000 for the carriage house.

Nesbitt and Morehouse at this time were involved in "Building Superintendence, Plans, Specifications, etc." Arthur Nesbitt and Ernest W. Morehouse, Architects, had their offices at 27 Jackson Block, Jasper Avenue East.

Morehouse, who had set up his own firm, essentially became the in-house architect for Magrath Holgate projects. He designed many Highlands residences, including the homes of Magrath and Holgate. Morehouse left his mark on thirteen buildings constructed in the Highlands between 1912 and 1915, while he is credited with others beyond those for which building permits make the connection. He was born in Chatsworth, Ontario, in 1871, and trained as an architect in Toronto, where he began his career as a contractor. He pursued his studies in Chicago and Detroit. He arrived in Edmonton in 1910, where he went into partnership with Arthur Nesbitt before launching out on his own. After leaving a permanent impression on the built heritage of Edmonton, Morehouse left for Detroit in 1929, and died there in 1937.

Other permits issued on 19 June 1912 included one to Magrath Holgate Limited (Building Permit 1542) for a frame house on Lot 3 Block 17, Highlands Survey, on East Campbell Street, also designed by Nesbitt and Morehouse, built by owner, and valued at $3,600. J. D. Blaynay was the first listed occupant at 1725 Campbell Street (11215 – 61 Street) in 1914. Roland G. Vanderburg, a wireman with Edmonton Telephones, then moved in during 1915.

The *Edmonton Saturday News* reported on 22 June 1912 that the recently completed Edmonton Radial Railway streetcar line to the Highlands already was being "well patronized."

> Many have taken advantage of the opportunity to see that part of the city and have not only enjoyed the pleasant ride which is given, along the river bank and then through the city park, but have been surprised at the number and character of the houses that have been built in the Highlands. The Activity has been spreading to the subdivision beyond. Both Beverley Heights and Beacon Heights are within a few minutes of the end of the car line and many buildings are projected there, the attraction of such admirably situated property at the present reasonable prices being one that is not easily resisted. The development that is going on in that direction is well worth taking half an hour off some day to see for yourself.

Following the establishment of the Union Sunday School, many Highlanders felt the need for their own church. A committee met in the Magrath Holgate offices on Jasper Avenue East on 3 July 1912 to discuss organizing a Methodist congregation in the Highlands. Rev. Thomas Powell, chairman of the East Edmonton District, chaired this meeting, and a board was appointed for the new church, including Rev. Arthur Coone, Herbert Baker, R. J. Robinson, and B. R. Orser. Baker was the first treasurer and Robinson the first secretary.

Two weeks later E. W. Morehouse was asked to prepare plans and specifications for a temporary church to be built on Lot 3 Block 3. This frame church – only 28' x 34', and two and one-half stories high on a concrete foundation and with a full basement – was to serve as

the church until a later church could be raised. Later, this building was used as a manse.

The first service was held on 1 December 1912 under Rev. Stephen Bond. At the same time the ladies aid society was set up at the home of Mrs. J. D. Blayney, who was elected its first president. Mrs. Coone then was elected president of the new Women's Missionary Society on November 25, soon replaced by Mrs. Herbert Baker. During construction of the church, services were held in the curling rink.

Rev. J. W. Smith wrote in 1933:

> The building of the little white frame church that for many years stood on the corner of 64th street and 113th avenue is an example of what real community effort can do! For, aside from the cost of building materials and equipment, very little was spent. Men who were busy all day came and worked on the church in the evenings as long as it was daylight.

The dedication services were held on 21 September 1913, with Rev. Kirby, later principal of Mount Royal College in Calgary, presenting the sermon, and Rev. Thomas Powell performing the dedication ceremony. Rev. L. S. Wight served as the first minister from 1913 until

⚒ BUILDING PERMITS

Highlands Methodist
Church
64 Street and 113 Avenue

Gladys Griffith and Marjorie Humphreys playing tennis at the Magrath Mansion. Photograph courtesy of Margaret Husband.

Ward Residence, 1912,
11125 – 60 Street.
Photo courtesy of
Van Tsiclas.

1917. In 1914 two classrooms were added to the church. Rev. G. H. Cobbledick then served the church from 1917 until 1921. Next, Rev. W. A. Smith oversaw plans to build the new brick church; Rev. W. J. Haggith assumed the duties of minister in 1925; and Rev. J. W. Smith took over the congregation in 1932.

Between 19 June and 5 December 1912, 47 more building permits were issued for the

Highlands Survey. Of this number, 29 were issued to Magrath Holgate on November 22 alone.

On July 2 Edward J. Bond obtained a permit to build his house on West Houston Street (11424 – 64 Street), Cephas Sisson to build a house and barn on the same street (11312 – 64 Street), and Henry J. Hoff, the contractor, to build a house on East Houston Street (11341 – 64 Street). That August another house designed by E. W. Morehouse and built by F. H. Webb was permitted on Lot 1 Block 16, Highlands Survey.

In August as well, Ernest W. Morehouse took out a permit for his own home on East Houston Street (11153 – 64 Street).

The Grierson Residence, 6124 Jasper (111) Avenue was one of the many houses for which building permits were issued in November 1912. Robert Walter Grierson and his wife Allie purchased the house in 1916. Robert Grierson was the younger brother of Edmund Grierson, and an early city pioneer and hotelier. Robert Grierson began as a real estate agent in 1910, but his R. W. Grierson and Co. suffered the ups and downs of the building cycles in Edmonton. Allie Grierson remained in the house until 1972. This attractive residence, suggesting a strong Queen Anne influence, was designated a Provincial Historical Resource in 1983.

The Hooson Residence (11119 – 60 Street), is another surviving reminder of the Magrath Holgate initiative to gain substantial building permits in the Highlands during November 1912. Kenneth Mackenzie was a tenant of the Hooson Residence during 1922 and 1923. Mabel Holgate purchased the house in 1924, keeping it until 1940. The Hooson family moved into the house in 1932, purchased

🔨 BUILDING PERMITS

Edward J. Bond
11424 - 64 Street

Cephas Sisson
11312 – 64 Street

Henry J. Hoff
11341 -– 64 Street

Ernest W. Morehouse
11153 – 64 Street

Robert Walter Grierson
6124 - 111 Avenue

Hooson Residence
11119 - 60 Street

Three generations of Highlands women. Gladys Griffith with her mother and grandmother pose near their rented home at 11312 – 63 Street in 1915.
Photograph courtesy of Margaret Husband.

it in 1943, and remained as residents for many years. William Knight Hooson moved to Edmonton in 1911, and in 1916 became co-founder of the Hooson-Racey insurance company, which became the Hooson Company in 1919.

W. J. Magrath obtained building permit 2142 on 24 August 1912 to build a brick veneer house on North Ada Boulevard, to be designed by E. W. Morehouse and valued at $30,000. This was the Magrath Mansion, the principal landmark of the Highlands to this day, and a social centre for the community for decades.

On 20 September 1912 Magrath Holgate obtained a building permit for a dwelling on Irwin Street (11127 – 63 Street), designed by Nesbitt and Morehouse, and built by O. J. Haugen. The following day a building permit was issued for a dwelling on Lot 4 Block 23, designed by Morehouse, built by F. H. Webb, and valued at $4,900. On the same day a permit for the Methodist parsonage located on Houston Street (11305/17 – 64 Street) was issued. The parsonage was designed by Morehouse, built by Webb, and valued at $4,500.

By the fall of 1912 other developers were taking a hand in building up the core of Old Highlands. The carpenter E. J. Bond took out a permit to build a house at 11312 – 63 Street. Frederick and Helen (Ella) Griffith later would rent this house with their daughters May and Gladys.

Ella G. Griffith was born in Thamesville, Ontario, in 1868, and married Frederick Lawyer Griffith in 1892. They moved to Edmonton from Melbourne, Ontario, in 1910, and first purchased a home in the west end on Thirteenth Street (113 Street). The family traveled to California in 1913 for Frederick's health, with their close friends, Will Brown

and his wife. Frederick died in 1914 at an early age, and on 17 July 1923 Mrs. Griffith and her two daughters moved to the McLuhan house, 11342 – 64 Street, which Gladys Griffith had purchased. (After the McLuhan family left in 1918, the house had been rented out until 1923.)

Hooson Residence, 1912
11119 – 60 Street.
Photo courtesy of
Van Tsiclas.

Mrs. Griffith and daughters
at new house in 1923.
Photograph courtesy of
Margaret Husband.

🔨 BUILDING PERMITS

W. J. Magrath
North Ada Boulevard

Magrath Holgate
11127 – 63 Street

Methodist Parsonage
11305/17 – 64 Street

Frederick Griffith
11312 – 63 Street

This view shows Margaret Husband's grandparents (on the left) with Mr. and Mrs. Will Brown (third from the right), sightseeing in Long Beach, California in 1913. Brown and his partner Sisson built nine houses on 64 Street.
Photograph courtesy of Margaret Husband.

⚒ BUILDING PERMITS

W. Brown / Cephas Sisson
11127 – 64 Street
11133 - 64 Street
11141 – 64 Street

William Gibson
11223 – 63 Street

Thomas Gibbard
11141 – 63 Street

Gibbard Block
6427 – 112 Avenue

Gladys, born in Melbourne, Ontario, on 11 October 1894, began teaching on the permanent staff of Highlands School in 1914 at the age of eighteen and remained until 1924, serving as assistant principal during that period. Gladys married on 14 August 1924, moving with her engineer husband William S. McDonald to Calgary. Gladys rented out the McLuhan house until 1928.

Walter Husband was born in Bridlington, Yorkshire, and had moved to Pincher Creek with his family in 1910. He arrived in Edmonton in 1919, and would spend almost a half century as a representative for the Alberta National Drug Company. May Griffith married Walter on 3 August 1926, at the McDonald (her sister's) residence in Calgary. Their daughter, Dorothy May Husband, was born in June 1927. After living briefly in the Gibbard Block, the Husbands moved for several months into 11217 - 64 Street, one of two adjacent houses built by Will Brown for May Griffith in 1924.

Walter and May Husband moved into 11342 – 64 Street (the McLuhan house) in June 1928. Twins Margaret Jean and Frederick Mowbray were born at this house on 31 August 1930.

The Griffiths and Husbands were long-term Highlanders who contributed a great deal to the early life of the neighbourhood.

Will Brown and Cephas Sisson also took out permits in 1912 to build three houses at 11127 - 64 Street, 11133 - 64 Street, and 11141 - 64 Street. On 9 October 1912 William Gibson received his permit to build on a double lot on Irwin Street (11223 - 63 Street), while on October 29 Thomas Gibbard got a permit for his house at 11141 - 63 Street.

As demands for housing escalated during the pre-war boom years, apartments became an important part of the Edmonton housing scene. The Arlington, completed in the fall of 1909, was the first apartment building in Edmonton. Like other apartments at that time, such as LeMarchand Mansion (begun 1909, occupied 1911), the Algonquin (1915), and Westminster Apartments (1912), the Gibbard Block offered its tenants modern conveniences, an appealing atmosphere, and a central location near the streetcar line and commercial centre of the Highlands. For a while the Gibbard Block was notable as the tallest building outside downtown Edmonton.

The Gibbard Block (6427 – 112 Avenue), built during 1912–1913 and named for William T. Gibbard, president of the Gibbard Furniture Company of Napanee, Ontario, remains a Highlands landmark within its main commercial district. Ernest W. Morehouse, the favoured architect for Magrath Holgate projects, designed the Gibbard Block.

Magrath and Holgate wanted a luxurious apartment block in the Highlands. Distracted by the enticing rewards of the real estate boom, they leveraged their assets to acquire more and more prime real estate and other diversified industrial investments. Another investor was required to build the desired apartment block, as most of their resources were tied up in speculative ventures. In this way William Gibbard, an Ontarian, became an investor in Edmonton real estate and added his name to the apartment. Also, until 1914, 57 Street between 112 Avenue and 118 Avenue was named Gibbard Street.

The land was purchased in 1912, and an apartment able to compete with LeMarchand Mansion and the Arlington Apartment opened the following year. The timing was bad for the investors however; the 1913 real estate crash, coupled with the subsequent outbreak of a European war, saw the collapse of the dreams of wealth fostered in Edmonton's speculative hothouse. The cold wind of reality withered such dreams, and following Magrath's death in 1920, his family even lost their magnificent home. William Gibbard also died in 1920.

Over the years the Gibbard Block was the location of several businesses important to the Highlands. The First World War hit the community hard, and the space at 6423 – 112 Avenue remained vacant from 1916 to 1921. The Highland Drugstore operated from this location between 1922 and 1943; the Corner Drugstore then continued at the location until 1959; and Agnew Drugs continued the service until 1964. Next door (6427 – 112 Avenue), also in the Gibbard Block, grocery stores offered their services to Highlanders in 1914, and again from 1917 to 1948. This location became a variety store between 1949 and 1960, a ladies' fashion shop from 1961 to 1963, and was vacant after this date until its revival years later.

Magrath Holgate also received a permit to build a curling rink on Lots 1–3 Block 3

(11305/17 – 64 Street) on 22 November 1912. The rink was actually built closer to 62 Street. This was the first curling rink in the Highlands, built at a cost of $9,000. Curling and lawn bowling were particular interests of W. J. Magrath, and this fact is reflected in later years by the many Highlanders who participated in the sports, and the convenient proximity of facilities in which to play. The establishment of the Thistle Curling Club in 1920 developed from this early commitment to the game. The

Gibbard Block, 1913
6423 – 112 Avenue.
Photo courtesy of
Van Tsiclas.

Lawn bowling at the
Magrath Mansion.
Glenbow Archives Photo
NC-6-3695.

curling rink and its property were returned to the city in June 1922 due to tax arrears, as were many other lots in the Highlands.

Because of Magrath's interest in lawn bowling, many believe that he organized the first club in the Highlands as early as 1912. The Highlands claims the oldest lawn bowling club in Alberta. At first the spacious Magrath mansion lawns were used as bowling greens, and a cup was presented as early as 1918 for a competition held there. The Highlands and District Community League, established in 1921, laid out and prepared its bowling green, as well as a baseball diamond. The Highlands Lawn Bowling Club restored the greens in 2004.

The Magrath Holgate company also was permitted to build "stores" on Knox Avenue (112 Avenue) valued at $25,000, beginning to add to the commercial services available along Knox. This also was another seed from which an important part of the Highlands would grow.

On December 7 the *Edmonton Saturday Mirror* complained of the lack of provision for new east-west Edmonton Radial Railway lines along the river on the north side. "Is it not natural that a very considerable population should grow up in that direction within ten, fifteen or twenty minutes of the terminus of the Highlands?" it asked. "Indeed, it is growing up already, and before long there is little doubt that it will pay to build out to it, plan or no plan."

The Highlands, although developing fairly briskly, retained its semi-rural aspect, as it would for years to come. This was further reinforced by the condition of some of the roads to the east end. In many people's minds the Highlands remained a fairly vague area in the east end. In 1912 Henderson's city directory described the Highlands simply as being located south of Alberta Avenue (118 Avenue) and east of Wilton Street (65 Street).

The Davidson Residence (5650 Ada Boulevard), an expansive two and one-half storey foursquare dwelling occupying two lots, is another reminder of the early relationship between the Highlands and its rural "hinterland." Built in 1913, to a design attributed to E. W. Morehouse, this home was rented by Adam J. Davidson in 1921, and purchased from Ada Magrath three years later for $10,000. He would live in this house until his death in 1945. His daughter Cora sold the house in 1981.

Adam James Davidson was born in Galt, Ontario, in 1864, and inherited the hard work ethic of his Scottish parents, working on the farm during the summers and attending school in the winters. He started as a teamster about 1884, and was appointed superintendent of the public works department in Galt between 1905 and 1910. He arrived in Edmonton in 1912 and moved into the Highlands in 1913. His first business venture was with his brother-in-law George Robertson, with whom

Davidson residence, 1912
5650 Ada Boulevard.
Photo courtesy of
Van Tsiclas.

The Magrath-Holgate Limited office, next to the Robertson-Davidson office, busily competing by marketing East End properties in Beverly Annex.
City of Edmonton Archives
EA-160-489

he established the Robertson-Davidson Real Estate Company. In 1920 he and Robertson also became involved with W. J. Magrath's Western Foundry and Machine Company Ltd. Robertson-Davidson began as real estate developers, purchasing a tract of land with its mineral rights in Beverly Heights, between 50 Street and 34 Street, and south of 118 Avenue to the river. Davidson then opened a coal mine, which he operated in Beverly Heights between 1918 and 1928, after which he leased it to the Bush Mine and took up dairying.

Davidson would later be elected president of the Holstein Friesian Breeders' Association of Alberta. When he died at his home at 5650 Ada Boulevard in 1945, Davidson owned a herd of 69 purebred cattle that grazed on the river road just east of the Highlands. The Beverly Mine finally went into receivership in September 1959, and was purchased by C. I. Clark. This mine had produced some 50,000 tons of coal annually at its height. Mrs. Del Davidson died in the house in April 1949. A section of 112 Avenue was named Davidson Avenue, while Davidson Street was the name of 131 Street until 1914.

In August the *Edmonton Capital* complained of the condition of the Jasper East road out to the exhibition grounds, which it described as being "in a disgraceful and deplorable condition." The report called on the city to improve the road for the great crowds of fairgoers that would arrive in the east end in the coming week. The swampy Kirkness Lake area near the grounds had just been filled in during 1911. In fact, the area around the Highlands would remain somewhat un-serviced by its roads for years – an issue to be debated and agitated over by community leagues and business groups for some time.

By August 1912 Magrath Holgate was advertising the Highlands as "the highest class

The new Highlands
School, 1914.
Glenbow Archives
Photo NC-6-760.

We will build you a home per our own plans – you pay monthly, half-yearly or otherwise.

You can own your home in this beautiful section and pay no more than rent.

The building restrictions guarantee you a future high class residential district.

Several of the foremost businessmen of Edmonton are now building here. It will pay you to investigate.

residential section of the City." Many of the river view lots had been sold and built on, but the company advertised on August 27 that it still had "some beautiful homesites left in the Highlands. Let us show you their advantageous points, scenic beauty – as well as convenience to the Heart of the City." In addition the following points were made:

In September Magrath Holgate announced plans to build an office and apartment block in Bellevue Addition, designed by Ernest Morehouse and located near the Magrath and Holgate residences in the Highlands. This three-storey brick building (the Gibbard Block) was to provide a focus for future growth in the neighbourhood during the coming years, and to symbolize the prosperity and success of the company.

On 17 October 1912 the Edmonton Public School Board building committee recommended the construction of a permanent school on the Highlands school property, with the number of rooms to be decided later, based upon the growth of the Highlands. On 5 December 1912, in the final building permit let out for the Highlands that year, the school board was allowed to build a "temporary school" on its property on Johnston Street (11425 – 63 Street). This school was designed by school architect G. E. Turner, built by George Watson, and valued at $3,800.

On 3 October 1912 it was announced that Magrath Holgate had sold its interests to B. H. Taylor and Fred Whitecroft, former employees

🔨 **BUILDING PERMITS**

"Temporary School"
11425 – 63 Street

of the company. Taylor was appointed the new president, while Whitecroft was appointed vice-president and secretary-treasurer. Between 1905 and 1912 Magrath Holgate developed over 20 subdivisions, the *Edmonton Capital* reported, "some of which owing to the rapid growth of the city, are now very close in." The Highlands was numbered with the new

Gladys and May Griffith are seen in the foreground in this Husband family photograph. The two original wood frame schools as well as the new brick Highlands School completed in 1920 are in the background.
Photograph courtesy of Margaret Husband.

Magrath residence, 1912 6240 Ada Boulevard. Photo courtesy of Van Tsiclas.

Chown Residence, 1912, 11141 – 62 Street.
Photo courtesy of Van Tsiclas.

Bury Residence, 1912, 111422– 62 Street.
Photo courtesy of Van Tsiclas.

subdivisions of Kennedale, Mount Lawn, Bellevue, City Park Annex and Addition, Beacon Heights, Industrial Place, and Victoria Place.

> *W. J. Magrath ... is one of the city's old and best known realty dealers, having put upon the market some of Edmonton's most promising subdivisions. Seen today [October 3], Mr. Magrath stated that he had decided to leave the arduous real estate game and devote his time to other things. Mr. Magrath takes a deep interest in civic affairs and has announced that he will be a candidate in the next mayoralty campaign.*

During 1912 the Highlands began to fulfill Magrath's dream of a "high class" neighbourhood located on the river escarpment in the east end of the city. It was well established as a desirable location for the managerial and professional classes of the booming capital city, newly amalgamated into a Greater Edmonton. Magrath himself was looking to build on his reputation as an influential community builder to launch a political career. All seemed bright for the future of the community, and the city.

7
Magrath's Last Hurrah

The fortunes of the Highlands, W. J. Magrath, and Edmonton seem to have been closely entwined by late 1912, and would suffer similar outcomes with the hard times that descended on the community beginning in 1913.

William Magrath was born near Deseronto, near Peterborough, Ontario, in 1869. He began his career working in the cheese exporting business in Belleville, for many years known as the home of the world's largest cheese, building up a considerable enterprise there. He married Ada Thirsee Lake in Shannonville, Ontario. Ada had been born in Tamworth, Ontario, on 24 October 1894. They had one son, named Adrian, who would live in the Highlands for years.

The Magraths moved to Edmonton from Belleville, where he had been an alderman for two terms. They moved west in 1904 or 1905, one account having them arrive on the first Canadian Northern train west from Battleford, Saskatchewan. Ada would serve on the first board of directors of the YWCA in Edmonton. William, as John Blue has it in his Alberta history, "ever recognized the value of clean sport, knowing that an even balance is maintained only by the man who can play well and work well."

He was the first president of the Alberta Curling Association, and a principal organizer of the Highland Curling and Bowling Club. In 1914 he became president of the Edmonton Baseball Club, operating the franchise within the Western Canada League. He was active in the Highlands Methodist/United Church where he organized the Sunday School department.

In December 1907 Magrath, Hartt & Company made what the *Edmonton Bulletin* called "the biggest deal in farm lands ever executed by any firm in the city of Edmonton [over 51,000 acres]."

Magrath formed his partnership with Bidwell Holgate in 1909, when Holgate bought out Hartt. During 1910 Magrath Holgate convinced city council that development in the Highlands district would benefit the city and obtained 278 acres in the far east end. They invested $10,000 to provide streetcar service, electric light and power, water, sewer, and telephones to attract residents. Schools were needed in the new neighbourhood as well. Beverly School District #2922, sometimes referred to as the Highlands School District, was announced in September 1910, just as lots in the newly named Highlands subdivision began to be sold. The first two temporary wood frame "cottage" schools were constructed in the Highlands in the fall.

The year 1912 would be a very important year for both Edmonton and Magrath, who had made his fortune and was ready for a change. Early in the new year William and Ada left for a five-month tour of Europe and Asia, leaving behind the cold Edmonton winter. They visited the island of Madeira. "Peculiar customs prevail in the city of Funcha where the natives travel by means of oxen attached to a sledge," the *Edmonton Bulletin* reporter noted in his account of an interview with Magrath that June. Their world tour would include Spain, Gibraltar, North Africa, the Mediterranean, the Dardanelles, and Constantinople. They also saw the Holy Land with its many sites "of biblical mention," and the great cities of Germany, Italy, Austria, Scotland, and Ireland. The Magraths returned from their tour on June 8.

That fall it was announced that Magrath and Holgate were retiring as president and vice-president of Magrath-Holgate Ltd., ending their seven-year partnership. The company name did not change, and it continued to carry on business as one of Edmonton's foremost realty concerns. Bertrum Taylor, who had joined the firm in 1910, would succeed Magrath as president, and F. J. Whitcroft, who had joined

in the summer of 1911, would replace Holgate as vice-president.

Magrath now devoted his energies to public life, and would build a mansion in the Highlands worthy of the city's chief administrator.

On 24 August 1912 Magrath took out a building permit for a $30,000 residence in the Highlands, on Lot 17, Block 19. E. W. Morehouse was the architect. The building permit was adjusted upward as the work progressed, to a $40,000 value on 11 September 1913. This landmark residence, designated a Classified Historic Site in 1977, is even today the flagship property in the Highlands.

Magrath was now ready for the next phase of his plan to redefine his civic role.

It was announced in the Edmonton newspapers in mid-November 1912 that "a public meeting in the interests of W. J. Magrath, *the people's candidate* for Mayor" would be held at Shirtcliff and Harvey's Theatre on Alberta Avenue on November 19, and in the Royal Hall on Kinistino Avenue (96 Street) on 21 November.

Meanwhile, William Short had held his first organizational meeting on the evening of November 13 in his committee rooms at 544 First Street. This meeting was chaired by Claude Gallinger, another very prominent real estate man. This address would become Short's campaign headquarters after this time.

Magrath's campaign got off to a rocky start. Edward McQueen, one of his supporters, turned in a faulty voter's form, which quickly was splashed across the November 16 issue of the *Bulletin*. A certain E. J. Lee, living in Victoria Place, just north of the Highlands and east of Santa Rosa, was judged invalid, but what appears to have been a small error was quickly turned into a suggestion that fraud was involved. Since both Magrath and the High-lands were involved, suspicions were aroused that would dog Magrath's campaign.

Magrath issued his mayoralty platform to the press on November 19. The Magrath manifesto began: "Everything in connection with the city's administration should be done in the open. There can be no occasion for star chamber proceedings in the handling of the people's business or in the spending of the people's money. There will be no balancing of one problem against the other, nor lining up prejudice against duty." Having suggested se-cretive, underhanded dealings, Magrath prom-ised instead "honest, economical, efficient and business-like administration...." He also pledged "to protect the interests of the people by giving them a hundred cents' worth of work for every dollar expended." His vision called for "a systematic plan of civic improvements, designed to meet the exigencies of this com-munity for years to come."

Street railways were at the very heart of civ-ic politics in Edmonton at this time. Magrath argued that "a permanent and complete street railway plan should be a skeleton or framework made by looping up the present lines and new adopted loops added as the population war-rants [like] our water, sewer and light lines...."

He also wanted to "bring the scattered workers into touch with each other through frequent conferences ... a fair wage clause which will work and which will be binding upon every contractor who does work for the city and every department of the city's affairs... [and] the eight hour day...." Such arguments were probably aimed at Joe Clarke's labour supporters.

Sensitive to the argument that support of street railways and other services could be seen as self-serving for realtors, Magrath expressed

his support for public utilities, but added that "I am in favor of their improvement and betterment and extension to where they are required and where they will be needed to in-crease the permanent pay roll of Edmonton." However, while he rejected city ownership of gas utilities, he endorsed civic support for a private gas supplier and supported industrial development generally. In a nutshell, Magrath favoured "improvements and betterments and extensions [that] are imperative, if Edmonton is to grow."

Magrath also was in favour of the City Beautiful movement. A. U. Morell, the influ-ential landscape architect and urban design innovator representing the Minneapolis firm Morell and Nicholas, would appear before the city commissioners, park commission, and heads of civic departments on November 20 to promote a comprehensive plan for Edmonton that included residential, industrial, business, and wholesale zoning, "municipal housing and workmen's colonies," playgrounds, parks, and boulevards. Magrath defined City Beautiful as promoting "a clean, wholesome, healthy city; a city that is worth while to the resident as well as to the visitor; a city of which the province of Alberta and the Dominion of Canada may be reasonably proud because of its enterprise and progress and its achievements."

Magrath truly launched his campaign at Shirtcliff and Harvey's cinema that November 19. Calling Edmonton a high-spirited steed, Magrath proclaimed that, if elected, he would "let her go!"

> We are in a race here, and there is no rea-son under the heavens, as far as I can see, why Edmonton should take second place in this beautiful province. Edmonton has been made the capital city of Alberta, and the University has been placed here

because this was conceded to be the best location for it, but if we are going to go to sleep on the job the capital and the University will be moved somewhere else. This city has the natural advantages; it has the railroads, it has the coal, it is the distributing centre, and is the hub of a great agricultural country.

Magrath's role as a developer was an important part of the campaign. "A great deal has been made of the fact that I am a real estate man," he admitted. "A heinous offence, isn't it? I claim that my business has given me an insight into the needs of the city of Edmonton, and I defy any man to come forward and say that W. J. Magrath has wrongfully treated him or not carried out what he promised."

He then attacked Mayor Armstrong's administration for inadequacies in the radial railway, water supply, lighting, and paving programs. Furthermore, a recent typhoid outbreak was attributed to a sewage leak above the main water intake. "I believe we could get a gravity system by which it would be possible to draw water out of the river several miles up, and store it in a large reservoir, which would also be a settling basin." Chronic power shortages led him to conclude that, "Surely a business administration would not be constantly running short of power," such as in the route connecting Jasper Avenue and Alberta Avenue. All of this was laid at the feet of Mayor Armstrong. "By the way things have been going in the city affairs during the last two years," he trumpeted, "you would think that the mayor had been used to some little town back east where they did not go in for progress." Finally, J. J. Thompson, the owner of Victoria Place, was called forth to refute the charges of registration fraud, and he indicated

that the city had told him his subdivision was located within municipal limits.

George Clark, a magistrate from Orillia, recalled for the audience a time when Magrath was driving his car down a hill, and landed in a mud hole at the bottom. He said the way Magrath backed up hill made him hold his breath, and added, "That is the way that Mr. Magrath will run the city." After a silence, someone shouted, "Backwards?" Someone from Victoria Place then shouted, "We came to the city as strangers and he took us in," to much further laughter.

Next Magrath addressed a crowd of over 200 at Ross Hall in Strathcona, where he admonished Armstrong for the poor lighting on the south side, the crowded cross-river streetcar service, and an inadequate plan for the proposed Strathcona Hospital, while praising the pre-amalgamation Strathcona council for its ambitious paving project. Again he felt he had to defend himself for being a real estate man. "I wonder how many of you are not interested in real estate?" he queried. "Hands up." None were raised.

At this point Alderman Joseph A. Clarke entered the fray, holding a nomination meeting in Moose Hall on 20 November 1912, at which "both of the candidates already in the field were declared unsuitable, and it was unanimously decided to tender a nomination for the mayoralty contest...for 1913...."

The *Edmonton Bulletin* was clearly the voice of the Short campaign, with a banner headline above a steely-eyed portrait of Short on the front page on November 21: "No Empty Promises But Ripe Experience; Efficiency Big Plank in Short's Platform." Short then launched his campaign in the Bijou on Whyte Avenue, stressing his *experience and efficiency,* the catchwords of the campaign to come. Candidate Short had to answer suggestions that he was an agent for the railways, as his firm represented several of them. The disagreement over the Grand Trunk Pacific crossing of Kinistino Avenue and the need for a subway underpass of the railway right-of-way had received a great deal of public attention. But Short declared that charges of conflict of interest were made "only by those to whom the word 'honor' is an unknown quantity."

The fight really heated up when a three-candidate meeting was held at the North Side Orange Hall on November 25. Joe Clarke called the campaign "the most prolific booze contest ever carried on in Edmonton." Clarke continued by stating, "I can take you down town to half a dozen places where you can get all the drinks you want free from now until the ninth of December." When challenged by Magrath and Short to name names, Clarke declined.

At a meeting held at Westmount School, Magrath reminded people that the electric light department superintendent had been requesting customers to close down between 5:00 and 7:00 pm on work days and from 5:00 to 10:00 pm on Saturdays. "This shows a state of affairs at the power house that should be remedied," he declared.

Of course, Fightin' Joe continued to get off memorable, albeit irrelevant, lines like, "I love a man that has his coat half off all the time in his fight against the enemies of the people." Or, "The only way by which I can be beaten for mayor in this campaign now is for one of the other candidates to drop out."

More substantively, A. F. Ewing spoke for Short, who had returned to Salem, Ontario, because of the sudden death of his father on November 23, declaring that as mayor of Edmonton for three years Short had introduced the concepts of municipal ownership and a land tax, as well as the administration by city commissioners. As for Magrath, Ewing said, "Do you want to see [Edmonton] boomed to the skies? Whom would that profit? Not those citizens who have a stake in the city; only those who have recently come here and have real estate to sell at a big profit."

"Edmonton has never had a big boom," Ewing said, glossing over the truth slightly, "and never a serious set-back. And have you considered this, that the man who comes here and buys land at, say $50,000, and then goes away to live in some other land, is levying tribute from us for all time on the interest on that money."

Meanwhile, Clarke was having his own voting fraud imbroglio. Robert Hamilton, his campaign committee representative, had been called before the city council "court of appeal" on the voters' list on November 18. Hamilton was asked to explain how he had compiled Clarke's list, especially those of Japanese waiters at the Alberta Hotel and many Chinese names. Fraud was becoming a big election issue, and a *Bulletin* editorial noted that while Short, its favoured candidate, had been the father of the tenants' franchise in Edmonton, he was "opposed to allowing the voters' lists to be stuffed with the names of persons who are not tenants under the pretense that they are such."

Magrath, by now described as "the only candidate whose chief argument so far has been to knock Edmonton," had made the mistake of negative comparisons with pavement laid in Victoria and Calgary during 1912. Alderman J. M. MacDonald questioned this in the *Bulletin*, stating that while Calgary had contracted 55 miles of paving, only about half of this had actually been laid. Edmonton had broader streets than Victoria and Calgary – why not compare square yards of pavement laid, thundered Macdonald. The *Bulletin* headline: "What Mr. Magrath Says – And Actual Facts on Some Paving."

Clarke accused Magrath of holding out a public park in the Highlands as an inducement to live there, then demanding $8,000 from the city to provide such a park. Magrath denied this. Clarke contended that this could easily be proven, but as usual declined to do so.

Things got even more heated as December dawned. Clarke and Magrath went *mano a mano* at Riverdale School, after Fightin' Joe accused Magrath of wanting to extend utilities to property rather than people. Magrath said he held no properties except the Highlands, which already had utilities. At Westmount School that night, Alderman Livingstone was arguing that, in fact, the Highlands streetcar line was losing the city $54 daily, based on 900 passengers using the line each day.

Clarke rose to stake out his position as a man of the people, saying that his two opponents were merely two representatives of the same class. "One gentleman represented large property interests. The latter bought sub-divisions and, of course, believed that water, light and sewer should be taken to the sub-divisions. Instead of putting the utilities where the people were, the sub-division men would put them where the property was, and then take the people out there. That was the difference between people's men and property men." John Blue gave one of the key speeches at the Riverdale meeting, praising Magrath's energy but pointing out his lack of political experience, and calling for the voters to go back to "the man

who started to pilot the ship on its present era of progress." Remaining a stalwart supporter of public ownership, Blue cited Short's opposition to plans by Cyrus Eaton for a gas franchise, and George Tretheway's plan for Glenora.

On December 4 the *Bulletin* convincingly reminded its readers of the role played by Short during 1902–1904, pointing out that the four public utilities in Edmonton were owed to his vision.

The city held at that time a charter for a street railway system, but by common consent the place was not as yet large enough to support such an enterprise. A proposal arose to grant a franchise to a private company for the construction and operation of this utility. Mr. Short put forth the proposal in council and on the public platform, and when a referendum resulted in favor of giving away the franchise he refused to be a party to the transaction, left the mayor's chair, and an acting mayor had to be elected to sign the agreement....

Thus preserving the chance for the Edmonton Radial Railway four years later.

When Short returned on the evening of December 4, it was like the Second Coming according to the front page of the *Bulletin*, which reported 800 supporters at the downtown Bijou for the ratepayers meeting. Although other candidates addressed the meeting, it seemed to be largely in support of Short.

Chief Justice Horace Harvey brought in his decision in the Alberta Supreme Court case stemming from another of Clarke's wild claims that several aldermen had benefited from the widening of Elizabeth Street. All were exonerated.

The *Bulletin* continued its attack, calling Magrath's platform a program "as long as a transcontinental railway, and calling for a huge expenditure of public money" while criticizing past administrations as inefficient. A front-page cartoon by "Stan" showed a beleaguered citizen holding his hands over his ears as Clarke and Magrath loudly assailed him from a platform. Magrath is shouting: "Let me save Edmonton!! Once I was a Councilman back in Belleville!" Stan had earlier portrayed Magrath trying to pry up the tracks of Short's "progressive street railway development program" as it steamed toward him, as Short cried out: "Hi there, clear the track."

By the time a third large meeting was held in the Empress Theatre, Short was focusing his attack on Clarke, having apparently written off Magrath. "I came before you ten years ago. Edmonton was small then. I left the mayor's chair three years later and Edmonton was a city," he declared. "Today it is called the Chicago of western Canada." On the same night, in Norwood, Magrath was sticking to his guns, although the steam seems to have gone out of the paving issue. "Edmonton should have as many miles of paving as Calgary, and yet Calgary has three times as much paving as Edmonton, while Victoria has twice as much. What I stand for today is doing what is necessary and getting our paving done in a systematic way... Let us have the electric light we want, and not have our street cars tied up for an hour or so and prevent people getting home from their work. Let us have the surplus of power." George O'Connor responded by branding the Magrath plan as costing $30 million and therefore being unaffordable.

On election day the wisdom of William Short adorned the masthead of page one in the *Bulletin* under the heading "Eternal Vigilance is the Price of Good Government." Short

was quoted: "Edmonton's name for good and progressive government is not local nor provincial. It is known wherever the English language is spoken. Our people have always stood for substance, not shadow. To the extent to which the right to vote is exercised today by *the men and women who comprise our real citizenship*, will the present high name and prestige of the city be maintained." Below this was a cartoon showing a giant voter's hand marking an x by Short's name, while at the same time smashing a black cat labeled "wild cat propaganda." A Short advertisement compared the candidates one last time. There was Clarke, "The Stormy Petrel" "erratic, unsafe, free of tongue with other peoples' good names" who started in the Yukon as a candidate for labour men against the government, and ended as a government supporter. Magrath, who only had served as an alderman in Belleville, Ontario, in 1896 and 1904, had never served on the Edmonton council, was inexperienced and "reckless in statement." Short himself, of course, fared much better, including his "absolute honesty."

The outcome was predictable by this time. Short took the mayoralty in what we might call a landslide, and the *Bulletin* headline proclaimed the "biggest majority in civic history," voters favouring him over his two opponents combined by over 1,400 votes. The next morning Short was reported to have 3,732 votes, Magrath 1,220 and Clarke 1,111.

When a victory meeting was called at the Empress Theatre, Magrath was invited and showed up to congratulate Short. "To tell the truth," he stated, "it is something that I have been expecting for several days past. In fact, I called up Mr. Short just at seven o'clock this evening and congratulated him, but he suggested that it was too early yet, so I will repeat my good wishes now. A man cannot be a good sport unless he is able to take defeat as well as victory. And I hope that I can do that. I do not mind at all when a man like Mr. Short beats me." Magrath promised to be of any assistance that he could in the coming year. Short responded by saying that Magrath was more than an also-ran, calling him a good sport, and leading the theatre in three hearty cheers. Clarke did not accept the invitation to attend.

Holgate-Magrath remained active, and the day after the election took out permits for 26 houses in the Highlands, costing $2,600 to $4,500 each, as well as a curling rink on Magrath Avenue, to cost $9,000. The company also took out building permits for stores on Knox Avenue, in the Bellevue Addition, at a value of $25,000.

During the following year Magrath disposed of his half section and "devoted his energies to encouraging payroll industries for the city." For example, Western Canadian Foundry and Machine Company located in Edmonton, as did the Twin City Manufacturing Company. Magrath was vice-president of both of these companies. He also became president of Apartments, Ltd., with plans to build apartment blocks in Edmonton. The company retained heavy investment in the old Bush Coal mine as well.

The fabulous growth of Edmonton during 1912 went into decline in 1913, and in August 1914 the Great War broke out in Europe. By this time Magrath was president of the Edmonton Industrial Association. In November he was approached to run for the mayoralty again, but declined. Assuring newspaper readers of his confidence that he would certainly win should he run, he declined on the basis that the city now needed harmonious administration. "Therefore, as a loyal citizen of Edmonton, looking toward its best interests, I feel that I should not be a candidate for the mayor's chair at this time, as it would only keep up the agitation which has been going on in our city so long and of which all loyal citizens of Edmonton have had enough." He then threw his support to William T. Henry, his old supporter, who would become the successful candidate.

Magrath died at his Highlands residence on Sunday afternoon, 7 November 1920. He was only 51 years old, but he had been confined to the house for the previous two months and had been "in failing health" for the past year following a paralytic stroke in late 1919. His body was taken from his residence to Mount Pleasant Cemetery for interment the following Wednesday afternoon.

The family fell upon hard times, but kept its connection with the Highlands mansion for the next two decades. Adrian attended the University of Alberta, and lived in the family house for a while. Ada Magrath died on 6 June 1941, following a long illness. She had remained in the mansion until 1931 through the acquiescence of the city even though the taxes had not been paid for several years. At the time of her death she was living with her sister and brother-in-law W. J. Hamilton.

8
The Boom Ends, 1913

The year 1913 opened with high expectations. The east end, among other Edmonton districts, was expanding rapidly. The Clover Bar Heights Land Co. Ltd. opened the real estate competition on January 10 with an advertisement that declared: "The 1913 Boom will be in the East End and particularly in Clover Bar Heights, Edmonton's Fastest Selling Subdivision." On 20 February 1913 Robertson-Davidson Limited, now calling itself the largest owners of subdivision property in the city, and the owners of Beacon Heights, Beacon Heights Annex, and Beverly Heights, announced the "opening date" for its new Beverly Heights Annex, immediately east of the Highlands along the east end of Alberta Avenue. This east end district already had a plank walk extending from the end of the "Packing Plant" streetcar line to the east end of the new annex. Robertson-Davidson announced plans to grade its roads as well. "An 80-foot boulevard runs through Beverly Heights Annex from Alberta avenue to Ada Boulevard, and this thoroughfare will be nicely

graded and a walk laid for its entire length," the *Edmonton Capital* reported. "From the end of the Highlands [street]car line Knox avenue will also be graded and provided with a plank walk to connect with the road and walk on the boulevard." The Alberta Avenue to Ada Boulevard walk was commenced on February 22.

G. D. Robertson also proposed to city council at this time that Robertson-Davidson construct a mile of streetcar line to "connect with the Highlands line which was donated to the city by the Magrath Holgate company last year." This Highlands line proved very successful in its first year, and now Robertson wished to extend a similar line from the end of the Highlands route eastward through Beverly Heights to the new addition. At the same time, Magrath Holgate was advocating for the paving of the line along Knox Avenue, that is, for track laid on a concrete base with paving between the rails. This plan would meet with much opposition. On April 14 Robertson-Davidson indicated their readiness to finance the streetcar line.

Beverly Heights Annex is just east of the Highlands where many fine homes have been built, and which was quickly snapped up last year in spite of the building restrictions. It is also just east of Beacon Heights, but on the opposite side of Alberta avenue. Last year [Robertson-Davidson] sold 2,900 lots in Beacon Heights, principally to local people, and today there are over three hundred families living there, a fact which illustrates the rapid developments that are taking place on the east side.

By 1913 several east end districts were becoming popular for working class and managerial buyers, located as they were near to two packing plants, a large tannery, a "casket and wooden ware factory," the Western Foundry, and other industrial development just to the north. Robertson-Davidson were eager "to make their new offering especially attractive to Edmonton workingmen" who would seek employment in these factories. With these new neighbourhoods becoming more "blue collar" in their character and the economy taking a downturn, the Highlands soon would find itself also attracting more workers as purchasers of homes in the area. Many managers of these adjacent businesses would come to call the Highlands home with the passing years. Thomas L. Dando began construction in Beverly Heights Annex on about 1 March 1913. As east-end neighbourhoods began to grow up around the Highlands, with their attendant services, the community soon began to lose its splendid isolation at the eastern extremities of the city.

In February 1913 the future of the east end looked promising to the real estate community. The *Edmonton Capital* summed things up on 26 February 1913:

The Highlands have shown wonderful building growth since the street car line was laid down, while in the subdivisions held by the Robertson-Davidson company there are already 300 residences occupied and a large number contracted for this year. When these are completed there will be at least 1000 residences in this territory which would be tapped by the car line proposed [by G. D. Robertson].

However, there were setbacks to the developers' grand plans. The Magrath Holgate proposal to the city commissioners on January 21 for the paving of Pine and Knox avenues with their streetcar lines met with resistance. The commissioners recommended that this plan not be accepted:

In connection with the paving of Pine avenue for which we understand the residents in the vicinity of the Highlands are willing to meet the cost, if this avenue is paved it will necessitate the construction of double tracks along the same on a permanent basis, the cost of which is estimated [at $80,850].... In this connection your commissioners feel that the cost of this permanent work, not at present required by traffic in that section..., the interest and sinking fund of this permanent work should be borne by the property desiring this improvement, until such time as the capital expenditure on this line is declaring a revenue.

At this time Magrath Holgate had peaked in their real estate ventures. A special supplement to the *Illustrated London News* on 1 March 1913 praised the Highlands as a good bet for the international investor. Noting that streetcars were servicing the area, and that the streets had been graded, the article reported that some $700,000 had been spent on residences. "As a result of the substantial improvements which are being made in the district, there is a constant appreciation in value," the article concluded.

But as Magrath Holgate itself began less direct management of their Highlands development, independent real estate developers began to build on and sell many properties. For example, The Imperial Agencies Ltd., with offices in the Imperial Bank Building downtown, were selling large properties in the core of Old Highlands by April 1913.

Despite early enthusiasm in the building market at the beginning of 1913, as early as April the local press was noticing a slowing of construction. The *Capital* noted on April 4 that "this spring it seems more quiet than within the past, due, undoubtedly to the stringency of the money market, for the program that had been mapped out for the coming season would have made it the busiest in the history of the city." Although architects were reporting the cancellation of large projects, apparently residential construction still was holding its own in districts like the east end, "and if all reports are correct, the number this year will double that of those erected last year. At that it will hardly be sufficient to accommodate the ever-increasing population of Edmonton," the report continued. "At the present time houses are at a premium in the city." Although the decline in the pre-war Edmonton boom had already commenced by the spring of 1913, significant construction would continue in the Highlands during that summer.

The first building permit for the Highlands during 1913 was issued on February 10 to Dr. R. G. Montgomery for a store and "lodgeroom" located on Alberta Avenue and 63 Street.

Bidwell Holgate obtained a building permit for a "stable, garage and living room" on Lots 10–11 Block 9, Highlands Survey. At the time this property still retained its Jasper Avenue East street address (now 111 Avenue). E. W. Morehouse was the architect for this $6,000 project. About a week later W. J. Magrath was issued a permit for a "garage and Living Rooms" at his property on Lots 7–8 Block 9, also designed by Morehouse. Magrath also was issued a permit for additions to his residence on Lots 17–19 (6240/6250 Ada Boulevard), now valued at $40,000. He continued to build up his property on Ada Boulevard, and on September 11 he again added value to his permits for Lot 19 on Ada Boulevard. On the same day Holgate added to the value of his property on Lots 12–14 on Ada Boulevard, bringing it to $20,000.

Other dwellings followed intermittently during the spring despite the slow economy. On April 21 Thomas Young received his permit to build a house at 11330 – 63 Street. On May 7 E. M. Kreig arranged for construction of a house at 11128 – 62 Street. F. C. Newland then took out a permit for a house at 11129 – 61 Street on May 29.

Gladys and May Griffith at the new Highlands School as it neared completion. Photograph courtesy of Margaret Husband.

⚒ BUILDING PERMITS

Dr. R. G. Montgomery store and "lodgeroom"
Alberta Avenue and 63 Street

"Stable, garage and living room"
Lots 10–11, Block 9

"Garage and living rooms"
Lots 7–8, Block 9

Magrath Residence additions
6240/6250 Ada Blvd.

Holgate Residence addition
Lots 12–14, Ada Blvd.

BUILDING PERMITS

Thomas Young
11330 – 63 Street

E. M. Kreig
11128 - 62 Street

F. C. Newland
11129 – 61 Street

W. J. Sageon
11224 – 63 Street

Magrath Holgate
11158 – 64 Street

William F. Brown
11330 – 64 Street

G. F. Jeffrey
Lot 13, Block 6

Edmonton Pubic School Board
11507 – 62 Street

Highlands School,
1913–1920
11509 – 62 Street.
Photo courtesy of
Van Tsiclas.

W. J. Sageon received his building permit for a house located at 11224 – 63 Street on June 3, built by L. F. Toby, while the Magrath Holgate Company took out a permit for another house at 11158 – 64 Street on June 9. Local real estate developer and builder William F. Brown received a permit for his house at 11330 – 64 Street on June 18.

G. F. Jeffery arranged to build a temporary house for $200 on Lot 13 Block 6 on 24 June 1913. He presumably lived in this building during construction of a larger dwelling on this lot, for which a permit valued at $4,000 was granted on July 7.

By the end of July the need for a larger school was becoming clear, and the Edmonton Public School Board was given a permit to build the Highlands School on its property located on 62 Street and 113 Avenue. This new school, valued at $3,500, was designed by school board architect G. E. Turner, and built by Pepper and Sons. On 23 September 1913 another permit was granted to the school board, allowing for the construction of a $10,000 foundation for the school. The final permit for the Highlands School was let out on 26 June 1914, with a value of $35,000. Turner designed the school as a twin of the Collegiate Gothic King Edward Park in Strathcona.

It took several years to complete the school, coming as it did during a period of financial stringency and war. Although the first floor appears to have been finished and in use by 1915, the second floor was not finished until later, when it became the first Normal School in northern Alberta. Highlands School was not completed until 1920.

The Highlands was beginning to fill up with new houses by the end of 1913, despite the slowing of the general economy. Along the north side of Ada Avenue, according to the 1913 Henderson's city directory, several impressive residences were located. The residence of W. T. Ash, of Ash Brothers, W. J. Magrath's "new house," and B. A. Holgate's "new house" formed an imposing phalanx on the south boundary of the neighbourhood. These three elegant homes overlooked the North Saskatchewan River valley from its high escarpment. Beyond the intersection with Grace Street was another "new house" towards the intersection with Johnston Street. William C. Cunningham and George L. Siddell already had built their homes on the south side of Ada.

Houston Street was becoming quite developed by 1913. Along its east side were three "new houses," including the M. Francis Webb home, and another "new house" (#1865) before the intersection with Knox Avenue. W. J. Magrath (#1735) still had a home located south of Magrath Avenue, across which, to the north, was the Highlands Methodist Church. R. G. Montgomery (#1871) occupied the only other residence before Adrian Avenue, and north of that Mrs. Bertha White was the sole resident until reaching Alberta Avenue.

On the west side of Houston Street, south of Knox Avenue was the residence of George C. Clarke (#1650). No further houses had been constructed then, except for north of Magrath Avenue, where William F. Brown (#1804), Cephas Sisson (#1814), E. Clifford McPhee (#1836), and Herbert McLuhan (#1864) lived. Herbert McLuhan would live at this house until 1918. Herbert's son, Marshall McLuhan, who later became a famous philosopher of the impact of mass media on global society, was born in Edmonton in 1911. Marshall lived in this house with his parents between 1912 and 1918. The house appears to have been rented out until Gladys Griffith purchased it in 1923. North of Adrian Avenue were the homes of Dr. R. G. Montgomery and Robert J. Houston, a butcher, who lived at #1964. Alberta Avenue intersected Houston north of these homes.

The south end of Irwin Street was anchored by the Magrath mansion. Progressing north on the east side of Irwin Street, Frank Pugh (#1645), Manley R. Cryderman (#1655), and a vacant house (#1665) were located, before Knox Avenue intersected 64 Street. William Gibson (#1725), L. A. Palmer (#1735), Garnett M. Meikeljohn (#1745), George Gibson (#1755), and Norman B. Wellman (#1765) had their homes further north toward the Magrath Avenue intersection. Thomas M. Scott (#1825) occupied the single residence before Adrian Avenue. No other houses were built to the north boundary of the Highlands at Alberta Avenue.

In 1913 no houses were built yet on the west side of Irwin Street south of Knox, except for the William Mitchell Residence. Between Knox Avenue and Magrath Avenue were a "new house," and the homes of Harry A. MacLean (#1726), Dr. W. A. Atkinson (#1765),

and Robert G. Dunsmore, (#1778). Another "new house"(#1816) and Robert J. Robinson's home (#1856) were located between Magrath Avenue and Adrian Avenue.

Fewer houses were located along the east side of Johnston Street. A "new house" and the William J. Beecroft residence were already built south of Magrath Avenue. J. D. Blayney (#1725) resided between Magrath Avenue and Knox Avenue.

The Morrison Residence (11350 – 67 Street), another noteworthy house, was built in 1913. Wesley R. Morrison moved into his new residence that year. Morrison was a clerk for Alex C. Dempsey, confectioner, who operated a store at 10071 Jasper Avenue. Morrison later worked as a warehouseman for Woodwards.

Dorothy Aird, whose family moved into the Highlands during the 1913 financial crunch, describes how the contractor building their house went broke during the decline, leaving this house still under construction. Her father, George Green, purchased the house from the contractor and finished the

A schooner built for Inuit clients at The Highlands boat yard, 1927. Glenbow Archives Photo ND-3-3540.

Highlands Community
League Hall
113 Avenue at 62 Street.
Photo courtesy of
Van Tsiclas.

work himself. Located on the corner of 66 Street and 113 Avenue, it was in fairly undeveloped territory. The family obtained water from a well at first, and boasted a double outhouse for a while. The Green residence (11305 – 66 Street) remains to this day, a very nice example of early Craftsman influence in the Highlands. Green lived there from 1913 until 1962.

Other familiar sights for years in the Highlands were the home and boat yard of Captain John Matheson, master of the SS *Northland Light.* He lived at 785 – 5 Street in 1913, but moved into 11346 – 67 Street (originally 1892 Wadleigh Street) in 1914, and lived there until 1942, when the boat yard was closed.

Matheson was the manager of the Northern Boat Building Company, and was listed as proprietor after 1923. He is said to have worked alone with his sons to find contracts, procure materials, design the boats, and oversee construction. Clients included the Hudson's Bay Company, the RCMP, and northern fishermen. His boats worked throughout the north.

Stuart Pearce, who grew up in the Highlands, recalled the Matheson boat works located at 11321 – 68 Street, operated by the captain and his four sons Don, Bruce, Gordon, and Rod. "It took one year to build a large boat for Eskimos from up north," he remembers. "The Eskimos came with their families and lived that whole time on the grounds of the boat works, returning north when the boat was finished." Dorothy Aird recalled the tents in which they lived, and that Highlands kids played with the children. Enid Hart and Jean Robbie, growing up in the area during the 1920s, later recalled the impression left by the boat yard:

> The boathouse was stuck way back in the bush and it was a scary place. They all thought maybe it was haunted. The boathouse was closed in the summer and they built the boats in the winter. They employed some people in the summer making skis and snowshoes.... They all knew spring was here when the boat was taken by horse

Margaret Marshall
Residence, 1914
11119 – 62 Street.
Photo courtesy of
Van Tsiclas.

and wagon [to] the NAR (Northern Alber-
ta Railway) yards. Then it went on a flat
car to Waterways, now Fort McMurray.
Captain Matheson would ride in the boat
and there would be a parade atmosphere.
Everyone would line up on 112 Avenue to
wave as the boat went past.

Occupants remained the same at both houses
from 1915 until 1939, when 11350 – 67
Street was listed as "vacant." In 1940 Stanley
G. Deane, a teacher at Riverdale School, was
first listed as living at 11350 – 67 Street. The
occupants remained the same at both houses
again until 1946, when Mrs. Annie Matheson
was listed as the sole occupant at the Matheson
residence. By this time Deane was teaching at
McKay School. In 1947 W. Harland McDonald lived at the rear of 11346 – 67 Street, with
Mrs. Matheson still at this address as well. Mc-
Donald was an employee at the U.S. Airport
in Namao. This was typical of the entire city
during the war and the immediate postwar
housing shortages.

In 1950 McDonald became the sole occupant of the Matheson residence. Occupants
remained the same at both houses then until
1956. In 1957 Harold "Harry" B. C. Madison,
a well-known barrister, and his wife Jean,
moved into 11350 – 67 Street. W. Harland Mc-
Donald, now a traveler with Burrows Motors,
remained at 11346 – 67 Street. The next year
Howard G. Poff, a salesman with C. W. Carry
Ltd., and his wife Fern were the occupants
of 11350 – 67 Street. C. W. Carry Ltd. was
a member of Canada Iron Foundries Group
of Companies, "fabricators of structural steel,
joists, reinforcing, etc. Steel merchants, bolts,
capscrews, etc.," located at 10530 – 103 Street.
Such middle class managerial occupants and
owners were becoming even more common in
the Highlands.

Another family lived near the Matheson
boat yard. Dorothy Reynolds recalls the Raymond family, English immigrants who built a
house from furniture crates, and who provided
Eccles cakes for the neighbourhood kids, as

well as sharing a large cheese on the kitchen table. Dorothy enjoyed that custom as a kid playing with the Raymond children.

In October 1913 construction in the Highlands was slowing. Highlanders began organizing to promote their community interests as the wave of prosperity since the last financial crunch in 1907 subsided. Money was tighter, and community services began to require more concerted efforts to obtain them. On 21 October 1913 at a meeting of prominent residents in the Highlands Curling Club rink, the East Edmonton Municipal Association was established. The association would cooperate with similar organizations already set up in Norwood and North Edmonton to select candidates for the civic election. Herbert Parker was elected president; J. A. Bullman, vice-president; and R. C. Chown, secretary-treasurer. The executive committee consisted of William F. Brown, A. W. Coone, Bidwell A. Holgate, H. H. Parlee, George C. Clark, and E. W. Morehouse. In addition to drafting a platform in cooperation with the other east end groups, R. C. Chown was directed to write to the city commissioners asking for improved streetcar service on the Highlands line. From this beginning emerged a long tradition of community advocacy that would lead to the establishment of one of the first community leagues in the city, and similar campaigns to the present day.

9

Old Highlands in Decline, 1914–1919

Following the amalgamation of Edmonton and Strathcona in 1912, Greater Edmonton demanded more efficient streetcar service, with each new district making its own voluble case to city council. The Edmonton Radial Railway announced that the Low Level Bridge and Highlands lines would be merged on 31 January 1914, operating from Main Street (104 Street) and Whyte Avenue directly to the Highlands. The new service ran every fifteen minutes, with half-hour service after 10:30 in the evening. However, by February 10 the city made it clear that no new services would be offered during the 1914–1915 fiscal year due to the financial stringency of the times. Commissioner of Operation J. Chalmers and ERR Superintendent W. T. Woodroofe declared on that day that "the biggest invasion of delegations cannot force the city council to authorize the further extensions of the street railway this year."

The boom had encouraged a rising demand for services in the new subdivisions, and the Highlands had just made it through the last window of opportunity before the crash, thanks to Magrath, Holgate, and many energetic, organized Highlanders pleading the cause of their special neighbourhood. The Highlands was among the districts approved for the laying of sewers at the city council committee of the whole on 5 February 1914. Such services would be harder to obtain after September, when the Great War of 1914–1918 turned everyone's attention to defence and home-front austerity. Many dreams had to be deferred. The East End Park (to be renamed Borden Park during the war) had been offered the likelihood of a wading pool, a streetcar shelter, a bandstand, and an auditorium. This plan would not be fully realized until 1957.

The numerical system of street identification began to be implemented during the spring of 1914. The so-called "Edmonscona System" recommended implementation of the street numbering put into place in Strathcona following amalgamation in 1912, while the "All-numerical System" would be centred on the axis of Jasper Avenue and 101 Street, with

Atkinson Residence, 1912
11234 – 63 Street.
Photo courtesy of
Van Tsiclas.

⚒ BUILDING PERMITS

J. E. Wright
11242 – 64 Street

A. Montgomery addition
6401 Alberta Avenue

Sisson and Brown
11122 – 64 Street

A. C. Meyer
11123 – 61 Street

W. McKay Smith
11224 – 64 Street

Mr. Williams
Grace Street

G. Patrick
Store, 11155 - 70 Street

the city divided into quadrants like Calgary. However, after a vote by Edmontonians an alternative system, as it exists today, was implemented instead. Street names like Houston and Irwin, which had been in place throughout the Highlands for a little over two years, now were changed to a numbering system to conform with the rest of the city. House numbers also were changed to accommodate the new system.

This change took some time, and met with considerable resistance. Commissioner Chalmers, for example, refused to adopt the new system for the ERR streetcars, although it was changed after his term ended in the fall of 1914. The rest of the board of city commissioners then took a firm hand to implement the change in October.

Sporadic construction continued here and there in the Highlands during the first half of 1914. J. E. Wright took out a building permit on March 17 for a house on Lot 17 Block 24 (11242 - 64 Street). A. Montgomery received permission to make an addition to the property at 6401 Alberta Avenue on April 8. Sisson

and Brown then received a permit to build a house on Lot 28 Block 23 on April 15, while on June 10 they took another permit to build a house on Lot 27 Block 23 (11122 - 64 Street). On April 15 A. C. Meyer received his permit for a house designed and built by Joseph W. Oakes, on Lot 2 Block 18 (11123 - 61 Street).

By late July 1914 newspapers were declaring in screaming headlines that the panic of 1907 had been less damaging to Edmonton than the existing money crunch. Meanwhile many foreign workers already were returning to their home countries as the war loomed. Many Serbians were heading back home, while members of the 3,000 Austrian families living in Edmonton were flocking to the *Nowyny* offices on Kinistino Avenue to arrange passage home. Much of the manpower of Edmonton began to disappear as thousands of young men from different immigrant populations on both sides of the impending conflict left for military service.

Every aspect of local life was affected by the growing excitement. The *Edmonton Capital* reported that Miss Gimby, "the popular soprano of the Highlands Methodist Church," had entered the Royal Alexandra Hospital to take a nursing course. Many such young women would serve as Nursing Sisters in the coming four years, or with the Voluntary Aid Detachment (VAD) overseas.

Two more houses were built during July, but these would be the last until the end of the war. On July 2 W. McKay Smith received a permit to build a house on Lot 20, Block 24 (11224 - 64 Street). On July 21 a Mr. Williams obtained his permit for a house located on Grace Street, to be built by the College Construction Company. Dr. W. A. Atkinson and C. W. Monaghan received permits to construct garages on their properties. The final permit of the year was issued to G. Patrick, for his owner-built store on Lot 16 Block 12 (11155 – 70 Street), valued at the very low figure of $200.

The Dr. Atkinson Residence (11234 – 63 Street) was one of the many houses built by Magrath Holgate after taking out numerous permits in November 1912 in an effort to jump start development of the subdivision. The house, finished in 1913, would become one of the outstanding landmarks of the Highlands while the doctor lived there between first occupancy and 1945.

While operating his medical practice in downtown Edmonton, Dr. Atkinson also served the nearby packing plants and coal mines. He became a beloved figure in the community. He made regular house calls as required, especially during the great Spanish influenza outbreak in 1918 and 1919, and for children quarantined with diphtheria, whooping cough, measles, and other maladies. His home office, located just to the right of the front entrance, was often opened for night emergencies as well. Dr. Atkinson was elected Conservative MLA from 1930 to 1935, and his early advocacy of state medical coverage is still remembered. Allan H. Wachowich, a notable member of the Alberta judiciary, owned the home from 1969 to 1991.

The Ward Residence (11125 – 60 Street) was another house for which a permit was issued in November 1912. Edward (Harry) Ward and his wife Muriel, came to the Highlands from Hamilton, Ontario, in 1913, and took up residence at this house in 1914. Harry Ward had already established a hardware store in Morinville, but worked in Edmonton for the Alberta Marble and Granite Company from 1913 to 1923, and later with James Ramsay

Highlands United Church celebrates it fourth anniversary. Photograph courtesy of Margaret Husband.

Company and the Independent Memorial Company. Harry died in 1949, and Muriel stayed in the house until 1974.

By 1914 the east end had grown considerably since the opening of the Highlands in 1912. Beverly had grown from a new village of 300 on 21 May 1913, to over a thousand residents by 10 July 1914. It was noted in the press on that day, as the village sought town status: "The roadway along the river bank will in time become a beautiful driveway in conjunction with the driveway through the Highlands." Magrath Hartt & Company were part of this development, operating its small mine there, working a single seam of 7 feet 6 inches at a depth of 54 feet, but without the benefits of a rail connection. David Jones was the engineer in 1914, while Carmie H. May was the "overman," or foreman. Some Highland residents worked in the Beverly mine at this time. Adam J. Davidson, through his influence in developing Beverly Heights and his mining interests, was another prominent founder of Beverly.

Work in Edmonton virtually ground to a halt on Saturday, 1 September 1914, as newspaper headlines screamed "War Now Declared!"

BUILDING PERMITS

Dr. Atkinson Residence
11234 – 63 Street

Edward (Harry) Ward
11125 - 60 Street

Men swarmed to enlist, and the war took precedence over everything else. The fervour was stoked by the rhetoric and poetry of the day. Rudyard Kipling's "For All We Have and Are," published in Edmonton newspapers on 3 September, warned:

For all we have and are,
      For all our children's fate
Stand up and meet the war
      The Hun is at the gate.

Many Highlanders rushed to sign up, and Rev J. W. Smith, Highlands United Church, wrote in 1933: "The years of the Great War were hard on the little Church as they were on all churches throughout the country. We are proud of our Honor Roll with ninety names upon it – ninety men that answered the call to do their duty to Home and Country." Others not associated with this church added to the contribution from the Highlands.

Also on September 1, the board of city commissioners met and proclaimed that because of the "threatened stringency in the money market, due to the great probability of war of long duration among the powers of Europe, in which event it will be impossible to float the authorized treasury note issue of $4,600,000, measures for the curtailment of public construction work are now being considered by the board of city commissioners." This spelled the virtual end of construction in the city for some time.

While St. Mary's Anglican Church congregation dates its existence in the Highlands from 1914, it would not be able to construct a large church to house its parishioners. The little St. Mary's church became a landmark of sorts as the location of a streetcar siding where two cars could pass each other, one car

stopping there while the other passed by in the other direction.

Futile efforts were made to encourage residential development. On October 16 the Alberta Lumber Co. Ltd. advertised: "Lumber at War Prices." This ad reflected the dire predicament in 1914. "Build now while the war is on," it implored. "You'll save enough on the lumber to pay your labor." Farmers were enticed by this message: "Bring in your wagons. We'll load them up and feed your teams."

Conditions were worsening for Magrath and Holgate as well. In November attempts were made to draft Magrath as a mayoral candidate, but on November 12 he announced he would not run. He had been a big promoter of the Viking natural gas field during 1914, as president of the Edmonton Ad Club and a member of the Edmonton Industrial Association; he subscribed $5,000 to promote development of the gas field and offered gas to the city at cost if the well was successful. On March 11 members of Magrath's gas committee took the Grand Trunk Pacific Railway to Viking to turn the first sod for the first drilling operation. The spade with which he turned the sod later was put on display at the Industrial Association office in the Tegler Building.

No building permits were issued for the Highlands Survey from 30 July 1914 until 7 May 1917, when A. G. Baker received a permit for a $1,000 alteration to his house on Lot 1 Block 18 on 61 Street. No other construction occurred until 6 June 1918, when a garage was built at 11142 - 64 Street. Over a year then passed before another permit was let on 17 October 1919, for a garage at 6403 Ada Boulevard.

Carleton G. Sheldon was granted one of the last building permits issued in the Highlands before the wartime construction hiatus.

⚒ BUILDING PERMITS

A. G. Baker addition
Lot 1 Block 18, 61 Street
Carleton G. Sheldon
6018 - 111 Avenue

In June 1914 he received a permit for a Crafts-man bungalow at 6018 Jasper (111) Avenue. Sheldon was an American teacher who had moved to Toronto in 1906. Sheldon moved to Edmonton in 1913, where he became general manager of the Western Foundry and Machine Company, in which W. J. Magrath was vice-president. During the war Western Foundry manufactured shell casings for the Canadian military. In 1916 Sheldon became the business manager for the Humberstone Coal Company. In 1922 he worked for Coal Setters Ltd., and in 1932 he established the Sheldon Coal Com-pany, with which he was involved until his death in 1943.

Clyde Smith, an auctioneer, his wife Min-nie, and their four children moved into the house at 11243 – 58 Street (the "Buttercup Farm" house) in 1918. Although this house was built in 1912, it does not seem to have been occupied until the end of the First World War. Smith's daughter Frances recalls that when the family moved there it was the only dwelling located between 57 Street and 61 Street, from 112 Avenue to 118 Avenue. Frances wondered how the Faulkenbergs, who built the house, got the materials onto the site since her father had to cut a road into the house after moving in. A large slough extended from 58 Street to 60 Street, which was good for skating in the winter and navigating on makeshift boats in the summer. The sewer was not extended to the house until 1946; it had a compression tank and well. The land north to 113 Avenue served as wheat fields until 1946, when the subdivision began to be developed once again.

The Martells and Griersons were early neighbours who built in the vicinity, and the children of these families formed strong friend-ships, playing in the open country around

their homes. Still, Frances recalls that it was quite terrifying to be walking home through the bush to her Buttercup Farm house at night. Some mothers prohibited their daughters from visiting because of the isolation. Miners from the east end workings and "hobos" from the North Edmonton rail lines were common in the district, and they frightened some.

Frances also recalls that although Dr. At-kinson was available to the community, many medical situations at first were handled out on the farm. She had her tonsils removed on the dining room table by a cousin who was a doc-tor, and Grandma Smith handled other emer-gencies, keeping a sterile needle and thread handy on the back of the stove to deal with gashes and cuts.

Land values declined dramatically after the outbreak of the First World War, and A. J. Davidson, who would become a long-standing Highlander after the war, lost most of his remaining Beverly land due to munici-pal property tax arrears. He managed to keep the mineral rights, however, and substantial properties along the riverbank. Davidson bought out Robertson's share of the company

W.J. Magrath, President of the Edmonton Industrial Association, uses a ceremonial spade to turn the first sod at Viking Number One natural gas well, Viking, Alberta, 11 March 1914. Glenbow Archives Photo NA-1072-15.

at this time. In 1917, using his mineral rights in Beverly and along the river bank just east and south of 38 Street and 104 Avenue, Davidson started a coal mining operation registered as the Beverly Coal and Gravel Co, Ltd. #707. This company later became known as the Bush Mine.

The first drift mine was cut into the banks just above the riverbed, where the company built a horse barn that included an engine room. Coal chutes allowed loading onto sleighs on the ice in winter or on top in the spring and fall. Horse-drawn coal sleighs made deliveries into the Highlands and other districts in the winter.

Davidson also became a shareholder and director in a munitions foundry (Western Foundry and Machine Co.) located at 53 Street and 124 Avenue next to the CNR tracks. His granddaughters recalled that a lamp made from one of the shells sat on a small desk by Davidson's easy chair in the Davidson Residence all the years they were growing up. There was also a large empty shell standing by the fireplace where the fireplace pokers were kept. One year into the First World War, the Highlands had reached its initial plateau of development. It had rapidly been surveyed, subdivided, and built up within its southwestern quarter between 1912, the peak year of the pre-war boom, and the gradual onslaught of the economic decline during 1913 and 1914. The Highlands also had established its identity and character as a distinctive and prestigious suburb of Edmonton within this remarkably short period of time.

Ada Boulevard remained the defining street for the Highlands in 1915. Harry W. Ritchie lived at #5650 (the Davidson House), and no other houses were found between 60

Street and 62 Street. Beyond this stood the Holgate Residence (#6210), the Magrath Mansion (#6240), the William T. Ash Residence (#6256), and the George L. Siddell residence (#6403).

The Holgate Residence (6210 Ada Boulevard) was one of the first grand signature homes in the Highlands. Holgate, like most original Highlanders, was born in Ontario, in this instance in 1877. Following the deterioration of the Magrath and Holgate holdings after 1913, the Holgates had to leave their magnificent mansion. In 1920 after selling out, they moved to 6010 – 111 Avenue. Bidwell Holgate retired in 1923 and died in 1928. Architect Richard Vanderwell restored the house after purchasing it in 1983. The Holgate Residence was designated a Provincial Historical Resource in 1987.

In 1913 William Thomas Ash and his family rented the Ash Residence (6256 Ada Boulevard), another signature Ada Boulevard mansion attributed to E. W. Morehouse. William and his brother Sidney established Ash Brothers Diamond Hall in 1907, specializing in wholesale diamonds, watch making, and jewelery manufacturing. Ash finally purchased the house in 1921, but sold it in 1924. Ash Brothers closed in 1928, and the family moved to Ontario. Matilda Singer, wife of Philip Singer, bought the house in 1927, and owned it until 1962.

Knox Avenue, renumbered 112 Avenue in 1914, continued to develop a small commercial core. Magrath, Hartt and Company had offices at 6228 – 112 Avenue, although nothing yet had been constructed between 63 Street and 64 Street. A vacant store stood at 6423 – 112 Avenue. The Gibbard Block (6425 – 112 Avenue) stood as a significant reminder of the aspirations of the Highlands. Bill Smith, its janitor, lived at 11308 – 67 Street (formerly #1814) before the war. Tenants or the Gibbard Block in 1915 included John Martaugh (#3), H. M. B. Adams (#4), C. S. Fyfe (#5), Andrew Myles (#6), J. E. Rymer (#7), Sydney M. Miller (#8), and James Allardice (#9). James Allardice owned the Allardice Grocery next door at 6427 – 112 Avenue. A possible rental unit with a rear entrance at this store was listed as vacant in 1915. Beyond this, *Henderson's* 1915 directory notes "no houses to 70th St."

The only buildings on old Magrath Street (113 Avenue) were the Highlands Curling Club, east of 62 Street, and the Highlands Methodist Church, between 63 Street and 64 Street. Nothing was yet built along Willow Street.

Alberta Avenue was beginning to show some commercial development north of the Highlands by the outbreak of war, mostly near its intersections with 57, 58, and 64 Streets. A few houses were scattered up and down the avenue near the commercial buildings. Among those in business by 1915 were the Highlands Grocery Store (6401 – 118 Avenue), William A. Ferguson's Highlands Hardware Store and residence (6327 – 118 Avenue), and Sidney Gray's Highlands Meat Market and residence (6403 – 118 Avenue). William Hudson lived at 5202 – 118 Avenue, Jesse Oliver at 5606 – 118 Avenue, a vacant house stood at 6212 – 118 Avenue, and Charles McKinney lived at 6512 – 118 Avenue. Other than this, several businesses had been established to serve the emerging residential area: City Park Grocery, at 5702 – 118 Avenue; City Park Meat Market, at 5704 – 118 Avenue; and a vacant building at 5706 – 118 Avenue. A vacant store remained at 5802 – 118 Avenue, while James Good lived at 5806 – 118 Avenue. Two vacant buildings

stood to the west at 5808 – 118 Avenue and 5812 – 118 Avenue. Nothing at all was built west of this except one vacant house, until the Victoria Pool Room and Barber Shop was built at 6406 – 118 Avenue, adjacent to another vacant site at 6416 – 118 Avenue, and the residence of the Rev. Arthur W. Coone at 6424 – 118 Avenue (formerly #3006).

The Field Residence (5610 – 111 Avenue) is a reminder of the entrepreneurial group that developed the commercial strip along 112 Avenue. One of the earliest houses in the Highlands, it was occupied by James Williamson Field and his wife Ethel in 1915. They stayed there until James (who had moved to Edmonton in 1914) died in 1933.

In 1915 Field was the founding proprietor of the Highlands Cash Grocery in the Gibbard Block, later known as Field's Cash Store. This business was central to filling the needs of the community for many years. Although he established a pharmacy in another neighbourhood, Field maintained his home in the Highlands. His daughter Ethel, an artist and art teacher, then lived there until her death in 1975.

By 1915 the eastern boundary of the Highlands had developed sporadically along Campbell Street. Six houses were spread along the east side of the street by the end of that year. (Many of these dwellings were renumbered, and the street redesignated as 61 Street in 1914, as were all the houses, streets, and avenues in the Highlands.) No houses were yet constructed along the west side of the street. For years, the Edmonton Radial Railway lines would end at 61 Street.

Howard G. Baker's home (11119 – 61 Street; originally #1663 Campbell Street) was the southernmost residence on its street, with that of A. E. Meyer, a financier, located

61

Field residence, 1912
5610 – 111 Avenue.
Photo courtesy of
Van Tsiclas.

immediately to its north at 11123 – 61 Street. Frank G. Newland's house (11129 – 61 Street; originally #1675) was the last of this grouping of three located on the east side of that block. Only Roland G. Vanderburg's house (11215 – 61 Street; originally #1725) stood between 112 (Knox) Avenue and 113 (Magrath) Avenue. Roland Vanderburg was a "wireman" for the municipal telephone system at the time. North across 113 Avenue stood two houses: William J. and Mamie Beecroft's home (11305 – 61 Street; originally #1805), and a vacant house at 11317 – 61 Street. Nothing else was built to the north of this before the houses of Alfred Snew at 11825 – 61 Street, and George Brown, a painter, at 11831 – 61 Street.

Further west on 61 Street, eleven dwellings had been completed by 1915. South of 112 Avenue, Albert M. Vail, a representative for the Mooney Biscuit and Candy Company, occupied the southernmost one at 11122 – 62 Street (formerly #1636, and the Bury Residence from 1919 to 1946). Next came William H. Edwards' house (11128 – 62 Street); Edwards was then a teacher at Oliver School. A vacant house stood at 11136 – 62 Street (formerly #1676).

Harry L. Wells, a traveler for Revillon Bros. Wholesale, had the northernmost house on this block, at 11142 – 62 Street (formerly #1696). This house is one of the oldest in the Highlands, in that the building permit was issued in March 1912. Herbert Baker purchased the property that August, having received a mortgage in July. L. H. Webb appears to have been the contractor who constructed this attractive foursquare residence. Baker lived here until 1914, and then rented it to Leonard Humphreys, a schoolteacher, who lived there from 1916 until 1936 when he died. Humphreys purchased the house in 1922.

Eldon Tanner, Minister of Lands and Mines under the Social Credit government, rented the house from 1937 until 1939. The caragana originally planted there at this time survives to this day, as do a number of very old caragana hedges in the Highlands.

In the mid-1940s Humphreys' daughter Erica married Adrian Magrath, son of W. J. Magrath, and the couple lived next door at 11136 – 62 Street. Adrian had lived there with his mother, Ada, and his uncle William Hamilton after the death of W. J. Magrath in 1920.

Only J. Lyle Anderson, a real estate agent, occupied a house in the next block, north of 112 Avenue, at 11212 – 62 Street (formerly #1717).

Frederick Cresswell, co-owner of the Cresswell and Atherton Grocery (12005 – 66 Street), occupied the house at 11322 – 62 Street, next to a vacant house. His partner John Atherton also lived in the neighbourhood, near 62 Street and 112 Avenue. The Highlands School Annex (temporary school) was the only other building that stood further north on 62 Street, also on the west side of the street. The Highlands School itself was located on the east side of the street, across from the Annex. Only two other houses stood on the east side of 62 Street: those of William Pring Williams at 11119 – 62 Street, and Russell C. Chown, superintendent of the City Stores and Works Department, at 11141 – 62 Street (formerly #1667).

The first of these houses, 11119 – 62 Street, is now known as the Margaret Marshall Residence, for the famous owner and occupant from 1928 until 1952. Katherine Tardrew, a "spinster," received the lot on which the house was built in 1914, as a gift from Mary Tardrew. Katherine soon married William Pring Williams, and in July Williams received a building permit to build a house on what appears to be the smallest lot in the Highlands. The family moved out in 1916, and the contractors, the Cottage Construction Company, resumed ownership of the property in 1920. After this it remained a rental property until Margaret Marshall purchased it in 1931, having rented it since 1928.

The Chown Residence (11141 – 62 Street), valued at $4,800, was the most ambitious of the Magrath Holgate homes built along Grace Street, with a design often attributed to the architect E. W. Morehouse. Its story encapsulates one of the distressing aspects of life during the economic troubles after 1913. In 1912 Chown moved to Edmonton from Belleville, Ontario, taking up residence in his fellow townsman Magrath's new development in the Highlands soon after. His family already had opened Chown Hardware in the city in 1906, and apparently he moved west to join them. He was soon secretary-treasurer of the Chown company, and managed one of its two Edmonton stores. He purchased his house from Magrath Holgate on 31 December 1913, taking

Owen residence, 1912
11227 – 63 Street.
Photo courtesy of
Van Tsiclas.

up residence near his brother Leroy who lived at 11145 – 63 Street.

Chown Hardware was a victim of the financial downturn in 1913 and the advent of the First World War, and was liquidated in May 1916. In 1914 Chown was hired by the city as its superintendent of Stores and Works Department. When the department was cut back in 1917 due to wartime restrictions he became a traveling salesman and then a labourer, and was sometimes unemployed. Chown returned to Ontario during the 1920s. Magrath Holgate foreclosed on the mortgage in 1922, and two years later the house was divided into two suites. Under new ownership it has been restored to its former impressive character and was designated a provincial Registered Historical Resource in 1993.

Irwin (63) Street, one of the earliest streets to be developed, boasted more residences, with more closely grouped blocks of houses giving it a less tentative look than some of the more recently developed streets in the Highlands. To the south of 112 Avenue on the east side of 63 Street were: Arthur W. G. Scriver, a broker, at 11107 – 63 Street; John L. Bond, a traveler for Canadian Consolidated Rubber Company, at

11127 – 63 Street (formerly #1615); Manley R. Cryderman, a postal clerk, at 11135 – 63 Street (formerly #1655); and William F. McSweyn, a clerk for the provincial department of education, at 11141 – 63 Street (formerly #1555).

North of 112 Avenue on the east side were: William Gibson, a farmer, at 11215 – 63 Street (formerly 1725); a vacant house at 11223 – 63 Street (formerly #1735); Herbert W. Owen (the "Meteorological Service Office") at 11227 – 63 Street (formerly #1745); Edward J. Bond, the contractor, at 11233 – 63 Street (formerly #1755); and Clarence Smith, an engineer with Swift Canadian Company, at 11239 – 63 Street (formerly #1765). C. B. Bennett, a barrister, had the only home on the east side of 63 Street between 113 Avenue and 115 Avenue, at 11317 – 63 Street (formerly #1825). No other residences were built south of 118 Avenue on the east side of this street.

Along the west side of 63 Street the farmer

Alfred S. Taylor's house anchored the south end of the street at 11146 (formerly 1674 – 63 Street. North of 112 Avenue were Dr. Percy H. Van Der Voort, a dentist with his office located downtown at #726 Tegler Building, at 11210 – 63 Street; Harry A. McLean, an accountant with his office located at #410 Agency Building, at 11218 – 63 Street (formerly #1726); Henry J. and Gladys V. Saigeon, a stenographer for the Alberta Moral Reform League, at 11224 – 63 Street; Dr. W. A. Atkinson, prominent physician and early Highlands resident, at 11234 – 63 Street (formerly #1756); and the broker Robert G. Dunsmore at 11248 – 63 Street (formerly #1778). Across 113 Avenue were a vacant house (11312 – 63 Street; formerly #1816), the contractor and carpenter Charles T. Coote's home at 11330 – 63 Street (formerly #1824), the residence of Thomas Young, 11330 – 63 Street (formerly #1846), proprietor of the Highlands Grocery Store located at 6401 Alberta Avenue; and Robert J. Robinson's house at 11334 – 63 Street (formerly #1856). Robert Robinson was an agent for the Imperial Life Assurance Company (with its office at #202 Hartt Block). No other houses were located north of this on the west side of 63 Street and south of Alberta Avenue. (Charles Coote also was listed at an alternative address in *Henderson's* 1915 directory, at 11209 – 127 Street.)

Houston Street, renamed 64 Street, was one of the first developed in the Highlands and as such by 1915 was a well established residential strip in the heart of the new development. South of 112 Avenue on its east side were five houses, although three of these were vacant in 1915: 11127 – 64 Street; 11133 (formerly #1655) – 64 Street, and 11141 – 64 Street. Ambrose C. Faulkner resided north of these at 11149 – 64 Street, while Ernest Morehouse lived

Gimby Residence
11248 – 65 Street.

at 11153 (formerly #1685) – 64 Street. North of 112 Avenue Wilbur G. Grant, a salesman for Heintzman and Company, lived at 11223 – 64 Street (formerly #1735), the only house on the east side of that block. North of 113 Avenue lived Rev. Louis S. Wight, the pastor of Highlands Methodist Church, at 11317 – 64 Street (formerly #1825), and John J. Montgomery, of J. J. Montgomery and Company, a real estate business (located at 8943 Alberta Avenue), who lived at 11341 – 64 Street (formerly #1865). The only houses on the east side of the street between these houses and Alberta Avenue were James E. Carswell's home at 11429 – 64 Street and a vacant house at 11451 – 64 Street.

Four houses were located south of 112 Avenue on the west side of old Houston Street. Henry Dunkraker owned the most southerly at 11116 – 64 Street, adjacent to a vacant house at 11122 – 64 Street. George C. Clarke occupied the next house at 11142 – 64 Street (formerly #1664), while Ethel Wells, widow of Cyrus Wells, lived at 11156 – 64 Street. William S. Gourlay, a watchmaker with Jackson Brothers jewelers, lived north of 112 Avenue at 11224 – 64 Street, while the only other resident of the west side of this block was James F. Wright, a carpenter, at 11242 – 64 Street.

Four of the oldest houses in the Highlands stood north of 113 Avenue: William F. Brown, the early Highlands builder, at 11304 – 64 Street (formerly #1804); Cephas Sisson, another early Highlands builder, and partner of Brown, at 11312 – 64 Street (formerly #1814); a vacant house at 11324 – 64 Street (formerly #1836); Creighton A. Scott, proprietor of the Rex Fruit Store (10135 Jasper Avenue), at 11330 – 64 Street (formerly #1844); and Herbert E. McLuhan, president of McLuhan Sullivan and McDonald Ltd., a real estate enterprise

(#3, 10110 First Street), who lived at 11342 – 64 Street (formerly #1864). Only two houses stood between these and Alberta Avenue: Rev. Frank D. Roxburgh, pastor of Grierson Presbyterian Church, who lived at 11424 – 64 Street (formerly #1926), and Robert J. Huston, foreman at Swift Canadian Company, at 11466 – 64 Street (formerly #1964).

The lots along Wilton Street also had come some way toward filling up by 1915. Nine houses stood along its east side south of 112 Avenue. S. Royle Hurson, an electrician with the Hudson's Bay Company, lived at 11115 – 65 Street (formerly #1615); James H. Fulton, an accountant for LaFleche Brothers, occupied 11119 – 65 Street (formerly #1619); Robert Cockburn, a clerk with the municipal Assessor and Collection Department, lived at 11123 – 65 Street (formerly #1623); Dr. Powell Karrer, a dentist (with an office at #303, 9815 Jasper Avenue), lived at 11125 – 65 Street (formerly #1627); Wilmer J. Kelly at 11131 – 65 Street (formerly #1635); Thomas W. Edwards, a foreman with Canadian Northern Railway, at 11137 – 65 Street (formerly #1639); Alex S. P. Esson, a cashier with Imperial Canadian Trust Company, at 11141 – 65 Street; a vacant house at 11145 – 65 Street; and George Bishop, a clerk with Esdale Press, at 11149 – 65 Street.

North of 112 Avenue on the east side of 65 Street were found Marshall W. Hopkins, a surveyor, at 11213 – 65 Street (formerly #1721); Bruce R. Orser, a real estate agent, at 11215 – 65 Street (formerly #1727); and William Thomson, a contractor, at 11239 – 65 Street (formerly #1769). North of 113 Avenue were Edward B. Williams, at 11319 – 65 Street (formerly #1833); Herbert C. Matthews, at 11331 – 65 Street (formerly #1857); Donald A. Morrison, at 11425 – 65 Street (formerly #1913); Jonathan H. Jones,

Dorothy Husband dressed as a gypsy for her dance recital. Dorothy and Margaret both took tap-dance lessons from Dell Davidson.
Photograph courtesy of Margaret Husband.

at 11429 – 65 Street; James B. Simpson, at 11431 – 65 Street; and the former #1925 Wilton, now vacant.

The south end of 65 Street was anchored on its west side by the Alex Ross residence at 11120 – 65 Street. North of this were Fred Pearson, at 11130 – 65 Street (formerly #1634); John S. Dixon, at 11142 – 65 Street (formerly #1658); and Albert Holden, at 11146 – 65 Street.

North of 112 Avenue lived Frank G. Brown, at 11216 – 65 Street; Milton S. Somers, at 11218 – 65 Street (formerly #1732); John S. Dixon, at 11222 – 65 Street (formerly #1738); and Charles Wellington Gimby, at 11248 – 65 Street (formerly #1792). North of 113 Avenue were Morton Shook, at 11440 – 65 Street (formerly #1924), and John Crow, at 11442 – 65 Street. No other buildings were found north of this on the west side until Alberta Avenue.

The Gimby Residence at 11248 – 65 Street, completed in 1913, remains a fine example of buildings in the original Old Highlands. Charles Wellington Gimby ranched for several

years before opening Gimby and Coburn in 1921. This was a service and repair shop specializing in Ford cars until it closed in 1944, although Gimby had retired in 1933, and left Edmonton the following year. His daughter Marian Gimby, who grew up in the Highlands, had a long teaching career, and was elected the first female president of the Alberta Teachers' Association in 1951. His grandson Bobby Gimby composed and performed the famous Canadian Centennial anthem "CA-NA-DA" in 1967. After Gimby and Coburn closed, the house was sold to Andrew Miller, the Provincial Chief Inspector of Mines, in 1929. Miller lived there until 1943. The Gimbys built another house on a third lot, next door at 11242 – 65 Street after selling to Miller.

By 1917 lots in Beverly were selling for only twenty dollars each, although lots on Ada Boulevard and Alberta Avenue sold for more. However, the bust had truly come to the real estate market in the east end. In order to maintain an acceptable level of service, the Highlands streetcar line, with its yellow cars, began operating its line to Bonnie Doon, with only one motorman to allow cheaper operation.

Many of the young left the Highlands during the war, either to serve in the armed forces or service organizations, or to seek work in home-front industries such as munitions manufacturing. W. J. Magrath, as president of the Ad Club, promoted a fair for 1915, to replace the lost exhibition, after the grounds became a training depot for members of the Canadian Expeditionary Force as it prepared to serve in Europe. But it was the churches that provided the focus for most social activities.

By October 1918 it was clear that the war would soon be over, and more local entertainments were being held. Group No. 3 of the

Highlands Women's Missionary Society held a musicale at the Holgate Residence on 30 September presided over by Rev. Cobbledick. At this musicale the Highlands Orchestra performed under Mrs. Westgate, with vocal solos by Master John MacGregor, Miss Margaret McSweyn, Mrs. Willing, and Miss Pearl Hayman. There was also a violin solo by Mrs. Westgate, a reading by Master Jack Anderson, a piano duet by Miss Alice Topping and Miss Muriel Wells, as well as other musical events and refreshments. A week later Mrs. H. J. Beecroft hosted the Highlands Presbyterian Ladies Aid Society at 11306 – 61 Street.

The Highlands Orchestra was an important part of community life after the First World War. Violet Macleod, daughter of Malcolm and Loretta Macleod, would later remember the years when the orchestra was directed by Bill Cryderman. She played piano in the orchestra, while her brother Bruce performed on the trombone and drum, and sister Jean performed on the piano. The Cryderman children, Ruth, Lil, and Helen, also were members of the orchestra.

Music was an important part of life in the Highlands. Marge Roxford, the minister's daughter at Highlands United Church, taught piano, and later became a violinist with the Vancouver Symphony. Violet Macleod played the piano at weddings, and sometimes the violin, as well as "the little old pump organ" in the church. She and her friend Wilma Crispy from time to time would have singing engagements, or perform on local radio programs. Almost everyone in the Highlands seemed to own a piano, and at least one family member would play it. Violet recalled how families would gather around to sing Christmas carols and hymns in the evenings. Enid Hart and

Jean Robbie later recalled that most kids took music lessons during the 1920s, and practice time was generally agreed upon as between 4:00 and 6:00 each afternoon.

As life began to return to some semblance of normality despite the great sacrifice and loss of the war, another shock was about to hit the city. By early October news accounts of a serious outbreak of Spanish influenza in United States Army camps had reached Edmonton. Accounts of its spread into civilian populations soon followed. The epidemic in next to no time was raging up the Atlantic seaboard, and by October 8 it was reported to be spreading to the west.

The first suspected case was reported in Edmonton the following day. Plans were rapidly put in place to ban public meetings throughout Alberta. The Alberta Board of Health initiated a modified quarantine in the province on October 12, under which "inmates" in infected houses were required to affix identifying placards on their homes. For the time being, theatres, churches, and other such meeting places remained open. Advertisements for patent medicines began to appear, taking advantage of the spreading concern. Cinnform Pastilles promised "to protect the nose and throat against the germs' attack." Dr. Chase's Menthol Bag offered further relief, as did Bromo Quinine.

Eight more cases were reported throughout Alberta by October 14, with another eight reported in Edmonton the following day. Alberta nurses were volunteering to go into isolated villages to help as the flu spread. As a preventative measure, by October 21 passengers on the streetcars were required to wear gauze masks, sold for ten cents at local drug stores. The Edmonton Board of Health almost immediately extended this measure to include all places of business. Dr. W. A. Atkinson addressed the Beverly Board of Health, recommending that it take action to forestall the spread of the disease in the east end. Seven deaths had occurred by October 24, with 1,381 cases reported across the province.

Helen Carswell Newnham still remembered the impact of the flu on the Highlands 75 years later: "The whole community was devastated." Three members of the Topping family died, including Mrs. Topping's daughter Eileen and son Frank.

Life went on despite the flu, and the Presbyterian Ladies Aid Society held a silver tea and sale at the Roxburgh house (11212 – 62 Street) on Friday afternoon, October 18. The women of the Highlands Methodist Church also were gathering gifts to send to "the boys" overseas by October, under the direction of Mrs. O. W. Cunningham (11324 – 64 Street). These gifts were collected at the Magrath Mansion, and shipped out on October 28.

On Saturday morning, October 26, city clergy met at the Civic Block to help set up a "district nursing scheme" to supplement the activities of the Board of Health among those not in the overcrowded hospitals, but confined to home. The Highlands zone was under the direction of the Rev. Arthur W. Coone. Where entire households were incapacitated, support could be provided from central kitchens and visiting nurses. By November 11 the provincial board of health announced that the flu had reached its peak, with only 27 cases reported in Edmonton.

That Monday thousands of Edmontonians turned out to parade and celebrate Armistice Day despite the rampant Spanish flu. By November 18 A. G. MacKay, Minister of Public Health, reported that Edmonton had

suffered three times the incidence of the disease that Calgary had. There had been 4,997 cases, with over 330 deaths. Three days later, MacKay announced that flu masks were no longer required on the streets. On December 16 the Highlands Women's Missionary Society met, hosted by Mrs. Herbert Baker at 6318 Jasper (111) Avenue. Things were beginning to return to normal.

With Christmas past, the war over, and the Spanish flu subsiding, ten inches of snow fell on the city during December 28–29. As the neighbourhood began to dig out of the snowdrifts, and streetcar service was restored, Highlanders gathered in their homes to celebrate the conclusion of the hard times they had endured.

On 2 January 1919 the high schools reopened, while excluding students who came from homes afflicted by the flu, or who had been infected within the past two weeks, as well as those with "la grippe." Students in these categories would be admitted, however, if they had a certificate of health issued by the city medical health officer. The schools had been closed for ten weeks because of the Spanish influenza pandemic, and most of the students were by the beginning of January eager to return to their friends and classes. H. E. Dobson, formerly principal of the Highlands School, served overseas during the war, and in November 1919 was appointed principal of Norwood School. F. G. Sutherland then took over in that position at Highlands.

As 1919 commenced, it was hoped that the city might return to its former energy, but the demands upon it had been too extreme. For the remainder of the year, the Highlands seemed to turn in upon itself and pursue its own neighbourly and family interests.

10

A Decade of Faith and Perseverance, 1919–1929

The "Roaring Twenties" did not live up to the name in Edmonton as fully as it did in many other places. The 1920s could be more accurately described as a decade during which Edmonton tentatively sought a new direction for the city, as it very slowly but surely seemed to recover from the devastation of the Great War and the Spanish influenza pandemic. Discovery of oil at Fort Norman in 1920 resulted in a brief outburst of oil speculation in Alberta, but that interest soon sputtered out. Only one building permit was let in the Highlands that year, on 21 April 1920, for a dwelling designed by E. W. Morehouse, and constructed by Greenough and Blair. Situated on Lot 30 Block 23 on 110 Avenue, it was valued at $4,600.

Several people would rent in the Highlands, however. In 1920, for example, A. J. Davidson rented what the family would call "the Big House" on Ada Boulevard from William Magrath, to be closer to his mining operations. This house would become one of the most interesting and locally important

locations in the district in the coming years. This lack of residential construction characterized almost the entire city. Despite the sluggish economy, Edmonton retained its role as a supply centre for the growing agricultural industry in central and northern Alberta. This sector retained some steady commerce to support the municipality.

The Mackenzie residence at 6010 Jasper (111) Avenue exemplifies the hard times in the Highlands during the post-war years. Magrath Holgate built this house in 1912, its gambrel roof making it unique in the neighbourhood. Kenneth W. Mackenzie rented it from 1916 until 1922. Mackenzie remains best known as the first mayor of the city of Edmonton, elected to the position by acclamation of city council on 5 December 1904, until a civic election could be held. When the Holgate family were forced by financial reversals to vacate their house on Ada Boulevard in 1922, they moved into this house. Bidwell Holgate died in 1928, and his widow stayed in the house until 1931, but retained the property until 1938. Dr. T. H. Field,

Highlands School served as the Edmonton Normal School from 1919 until 1923.
Glenbow Archives
Photo NC-6-9009.

modest Edmonton strike, but the sense of bitterness among veterans ran deep. The militant One Big Union, established in Calgary that same year, soon had adherents across the West.

By 1920 the dislocations of the war had led to the closure of 557 (mostly one-room) schools across the province because of a lack of teachers. Of these, 377 had been closed just since the beginning of the year. "A large number of teachers are taking their vacation in January and February in lieu of the summer vacation," the *Red Deer News* reported on 17 March 1920, "because the severe cold and heavy snowfall this winter make it difficult to operate many of the rural schools."

The Highlands Normal School, which had presented its first short course in the winter of 1919–1920, now had 108 teachers in training, according to the Hon. George P. Smith, Minister of Education. Alberta had three normal schools by 1920, in Edmonton (Highlands School), Camrose, and Calgary. The first long session of teacher training was held in the Highlands School between 24 August 1920 and 15 April 1921. This normal school operated until 1923, and a number of its students roomed in Highlands homes during these years.

the son of James W. Field, then purchased the house.

In this atmosphere people longed for the opportunity to help each other and try to find strength for the future. On 24 January 1921, the Edmonton Federation of Community Leagues was established as one response to the deep need for community. It rapidly grew to the largest organization of its kind in Canada with both social and political power. The Highlands and District Community League was one of the first members, holding its organizational meeting on 15 February 1921.

Early hopes for post-war reconstruction and civil re-establishment were slow to be realized, with a persistently high unemployment rate among returning military personnel. The Great War Veterans' Association championed the cause of local veterans, but many of the disillusioned and embittered returned men found little opportunity for work. Such challenges led many to join the brief and partial Edmonton general strike that hit the city between 26 and 31 May 1919. The Winnipeg General Strike significantly overshadowed the

Another local educational opportunity became available in 1925 when the Lutheran Church's Missouri Synod established Concordia College at Ada Boulevard and 71 Street, to the east of the Highlands. The college, founded in 1921, had held its first classes at Caledonia Temperance Hall. Until the Schwermann Hall student residence was completed, many Concordia students also boarded in the Highlands. Between 1929 and 1931 Grace English Lutheran Sunday School operated out of a store (7543 – 112 Avenue) that had been largely vacant since its construction in 1921. For a while Concordia's "Faculty Row," consisting of four residences, was located on Ada Boulevard. These houses were demolished during construction of the Capilano Freeway.

Though life in Edmonton during the 1920s did not rival the excitement of the prewar era, it was not without its entertainments. The Edmonton Commercial Grads women's basketball team rose to world prominence after the war, and Edmontonians took special pride in their achievements. When the team disbanded in 1940, they had won an amazing 96 percent of their 522 games, a record never rivaled by any North American basketball team since.

New technologies also helped ease the bleak winters. CJCA, the first radio station, went on the air on 1 May 1922, and in 1927 the University of Alberta launched radio station CKUA.

Kids from the Highlands had the nearby Borden Park to amuse them. Enid Hart and Jean Robbie, friends growing up together in the neighbourhood during the 1920s, later recalled the zoo located there, especially the polar bears, coyotes, peacocks and other exotic birds, and elk and bison. Often the zoo porcupine would wander out of the park into Enid's family garden. They would place a barrel over it until the city sent someone to return the vagrant beast to its home. The bison were easily seen from the passing streetcar. Another favourite was the carousel that operated on weekends, and the huge all-wood roller coaster north of the bison pen.

Enid also remembers that much of the land north of 116 Avenue was still open, and that she could walk along a trail bordered by wildflowers in that part of the Highlands.

Large cracks resulting from operations at the Premier Mine appeared in Highlands Drive (Ada Boulevard) during 1928. City of Edmonton Archives Photo EA-75-341.

Other summer pastimes included impromptu gatherings of ten or twenty kids playing kick the can or run-sheep-run, and "there were lots of trees to climb, huts to make, caves to play in, and no one ever lacked for things to keep busy with." Saturday afternoons saw many taking in a matinee for a nickel at the Dreamland or Gem downtown, or at the new Avenue Theatre on 118 Avenue.

Young and old gathered to skate at open-air rinks, and met at each other's homes for card parties and entertainment that they provided themselves. In the Highlands the churches and community league remained the centres of community activity. The atmosphere of wartime severity was beginning to moderate somewhat. Prohibition was repealed in 1923, but "beer parlours" were required to have separate entrances for men and another for "ladies and escorts."

Until the 1920s the city had many coal mines within its limits, such as the Premier Mine, Standard Mine, and Bush Mine, all of which would have a major impact on the Highlands. But this situation also was changing rapidly. On 9 November 1923, Mayor D. M. Duggan lit a flare from the first natural gas to arrive via the pipeline from the Viking gas field located east of the city. Although W. J. Magrath had been instrumental in promoting this field, he had died in 1920 and so did not live to see that dream fulfilled. As natural gas began to replace coal for heating homes over the next three decades, the familiar coal delivery wagons disappeared.

The Premier Mine, located in what would later be the middle of the golf course (immediately below Concordia College), continued to play a role through its very presence and its destabilizing effect on the river-top roadways. The wooden superstructure of the tipple was a local landmark for some time, acting as a magnet for local kids who loved to climb on the giant steel wheel that remained, a reminder of the old hoisting mechanism. A house that belonged to the mine manager also remained for some time below the river bank. Another mine once operated near the intersection of 112 Avenue and 75 Street.

The real estate market languished for almost three decades after 1912. The Edmonton Real Estate Exchange, established in 1909, represents the first real effort to regulate the rapid growth in real estate dealings. In that year over 60 agencies and companies were listed in Edmonton and Strathcona, a number that would peak at 333 in 1914. Between 1903 and 1914, 274 new subdivisions were laid out in the city, many not to be developed for years. Although the Real Estate Exchange lasted only a short time, it introduced the first local multiple listing service and laid the foundation for subsequent organization following the disruption of the First World War.

Edmonton struggled to recover after the First World War, and in 1919 only about a

hundred real estate agents remained in the city. It was not until 1927 that the Edmonton Real Estate Association was established, leading finally to the first legislation requiring the licensing of real estate sales agents.

The Highlands and District Community League held its organizational meeting in the Highlands Public School on Tuesday evening, 15 February 1921. "Despite the severe weather conditions of the evening," its Minute Book reported, "some 50 residents were in attendance." A. U. G. Bury was voted to chair the meeting, and reported that the meeting had grown out of an earlier informal gathering of neighbourhood residents, and consultation with the Highlands Parent-Teachers' Association, established in 1912. The PTA expressed its wish to merge with a local community league as the enthusiasm for such local groups began to sweep Edmonton.

A committee of Highlands residents under G. McManus was set up to draft a constitution and by-laws. It was decided that the community league would represent residents living within the Highlands Public School District. Article 3 stated: "The objects of this organization shall be the development of intelligent public spirit among its citizens by the holding of meetings for the presentation and free discussion of public questions and such other activities – civic, social and recreational as shall promote the general welfare of the said district. Its policy shall be non-partisan and non-sectarian." Annual membership fees were set at one dollar. Provision was made for Associate Members between the ages of 16 and 21.

The community league elected five vice-presidents, the first to be a person who had a child currently attending school and was prepared to chair the parent-teachers' committee; the second to chair the program committee;

the third to chair the local improvement committee; the fourth to chair the social committee; and the fifth to chair the boys' and girls' welfare committee. The local improvement committee's mandate included representation of Mount Royal and Mount Royal Park (both north of Alberta Avenue), and Bellevue Addition, as well as the Highlands.

The first elected executive committee consisted of A. U. G. Bury, president; Carleton G. Sheldon, first vice-president; J. W. H. Williams, second vice-president; E. W. Morehouse, third vice-president; Mrs. G. McManus, fourth vice-president; and Herbert Slate, fifth vice-president. Leonard Humphreys was the first secretary, while C. Harvey Baker served as the treasurer. Bury and Humphreys were the representatives on the Edmonton Federation of Community Leagues Council (EFCL).

As would occur at most meetings during the 1920s, the proceedings ended with entertainment. On this occasion Miss Marjorie Cobbledick, Miss Topping, Miss Wells, and members of the Highlands Orchestra performed a musical program.

The first ordinary meeting of the community league was held in Highlands School on 1 March 1921, with over 200 present. "After greatly appreciated solo and encore by Miss Ethel McKenzie," the Minute Book reports, "Lieutenant G. Carman delivered an interesting lantern talk upon "The Trail of '98," followed by humorous songs by Mr. H. P Coles and friend and some infant ballet dancing by little Miss B. Coles." Membership was increased to 85 at this time.

It was announced at an executive committee meeting on March 18 that the community league could use Highlands School for its regular monthly meetings, and this remained the case for the rest of the decade. At the same

First members of the Highlands and District Community League 1 March 1921:	
Mrs. M.E. Anderson	Mr. and Mrs. Leeman
C. Harvey Baker	Mrs. A.J. Montgomery
Edward J. Bond	E.W. Morehouse
Mr. and Mrs. E.B. Brown	Mr. and Mrs. George McManus
Mr. and Mrs. G.R. Brown	Mrs. H.C. McNeil
W.F. Brown	Mrs. J. Oliver
A.U.G. Bury	Mr. and Mrs. R.A. Richards
P.F. Canniff	Mr. and Mrs. R. Seeman
James Clements	R. Sladden
H.B. Collins	Mr. and Mrs. Herbert Slate
O.W. Cunningham	Mr. and Mrs. C. Smith
Mr. and Mrs. H. Leonard Humphreys	G.W. Underwood
B. Jones	A.M Vail
S.C. Jones	Mr. and Mrs. Edward A. Ward
Mrs. W. Lammie	J.W.H. Williams

Gladys Griffith, teacher and assistant principal at Highlands School from 1914 until 1924. Photograph courtesy of Margaret Husband.

This photograph shows an early recess in the schoolyard of the early frame Highlands School.
Photograph courtesy of Margaret Husband.

meeting the question of establishing "some form of worthwhile awards for all-round manly and womanly conduct among the pupils of the Highlands School was introduced by Mr. Williams...." On May 31 this was extended beyond "Scholarship and all-round conduct" to include "one or more such [awards] to pupils of foreign birth." Also, it was decided that the parent-teachers' committee should consist of Carleton G. Sheldon, the chair, and Highlands Principal Wilmer J. Kelly and Vice-principal Miss Gladys Griffith, as well as residents Miss Phelps, Mrs. C. A. Anderson, Mrs. C. McGillivray, Mrs. Morrison, Mrs. F. Leeman, Mrs. E. H. Ward, Mrs. C. J. Thompson, and Mrs. Nye.

The meeting on April 5 was addressed by members of the city's board of commissioners and Mayor Duggan, who among other things promised to look seriously at the building of more plank sidewalks in the Highlands. Master Jack Peterson, "a talented young boy soprano," concluded the evening with song. Sidewalks and songs would dominate many a meeting after that.

On April 21, in anticipation of the coming summer programs, the name of the boys'

and girls' committee was changed to the "recreation committee" to broaden its mandate. "Wishing to continue the facilities always so liberally supported and heartily cooperated in by the late Mr. W. J. Magrath, Mrs. Magrath agreed [to] the continued use of the excellent Tennis Courts, Bowling Greens and Baseball grounds on her property...." The recreation committee undertook the maintenance of these areas. Plans also were made to make use of the EFCL "cinema machine" to show the Boy Scouts movie "The Lion's Cubs" at the next meeting. This meeting was largely devoted to this show, and led to a vote to support the purchase by the EFCL of such a projector.

Ada Magrath was devastated by the death of her husband. Dorothy Aird recalled that she would sit on her veranda beginning in the summer of 1921, and when the Highlands children were walking past would call them in for a visit in the mansion. About this time she also hosted what were called mission band meetings at the Magrath Mansion. A religious youth guidance group would gather for refreshments and watch lantern slide shows of scenes from the Magraths' trip to the Holy Land. These special viewings were usually held in an impromptu "theatre" set up in the upstairs hallway.

E. W. Morehouse had organized the local improvement committee by the end of April, with T. R. Seeman responsible for the Bellevue Addition, W. F. Brown for "Highlands central," E. T. Ward for Highlands East and Mount Royal, and Jesse Oliver for "Alberta Avenue and North." This committee thereafter would take on the persistent issue of adequate sidewalks throughout its district.

Still, little growth took place in the Highlands during 1921, with M. Ault obtaining the single permit, to build a "private garage" on Lot 10 Block 8 (11128 – 62 Street) on May 20. However, Hambley Confectionery Store (7599 – 112 Avenue) opened in the Bellevue section of 112 Avenue that year. This business would play a role in Highlands life until 1931, when it became the Park Grocery from 1932 until 1937, the James Warmington Grocery from 1938 until 1940, and the Parkview Red and White Store from 1940 until 1964.

During May 1921 the community league organized a Victoria Day tennis club dance, as well as a baseball game between single and married members. Both events raised money for baseball equipment for the local boys.

While the nearby industrial developments would become more important as a source of employment, the industrial stink sometimes vexed Highlands residents. "The matter of the nuisance again affecting this district on several recent dates was discussed and the Secretary was instructed to lodge complaint in the proper quarters," the Minute Book reported for the meeting on 31 May 1921.

Proximity to the exhibition grounds also could be a mixed blessing. "The question was discussed [on May 31] of the annual serious inconvenience caused to regular street car passengers from and to the Highlands by the fast practice of unloading such passengers at Agnes street to convenience the temporary Exhibition traffic in July..."

On June 7, the last meeting before the summer, the students at the school provided a concert of choruses and drills. The big event of that summer was the Sports Day held on August 13. Carleton G. Sheldon offered a $25 prize on behalf of the Humberstone Coal Company, while J. W. H. Williams offered to print the necessary handbills on behalf of the Western Veteran Publishing Company.

The Highlands has had its problems with vandalism over the years, due partly to its semi-isolated location, vacant lots, and wide spaces between houses and other buildings. At the executive committee meeting on 28 September 1921 Herbert Slate referred to "the practice of youths wanton destruction of street lights." Plans were put in place to get permission from Mrs. Magrath to allow use of the tennis courts for winter skating, possibly to find activities for the local youth that were more wholesome than throwing stones. In January 1923 a letter from the Superintendent of the Electric Light Department was read at the Highlands meeting, urging parents to control young people who were destroying community lights, and "also the matter of the danger of life and property consequent on false fire alarms of which this locality has not been innocent."

E. W. Morehouse reported to the annual meeting on October 4 that the city board of commissioners had made a "definite" promise "of necessary drainage and water service in this district to be installed as the next provision following that of Calder now in hand." Drainage, again, would occupy Highlands residents for years to come.

At the final meeting of 1921 President Bury reported that he and Herbert Slate had received a promise from the Edmonton Public School Board for "a fine standard Gymnasium equipment for the Highland School Community." The social program ended with a whist drive and dance.

Only four buildings were constructed in the Highlands during 1922. A. W. Plum of 11316 – 91 Street received a permit for a house at 11228 – 64 Street. On April 19 G. F. Young, of 11234 – 61 Street, obtained one for a house on Lot 11 Block 13, also on 61 Street. Then on

⚒ BUILDING PERMITS

A. W. Plum
11228 – 64 Street

G. F. Young
Lot 11 Block 13, 61 Street

⚒ BUILDING PERMITS

G. B. Holmes

Lot 32 Block 56

William Cooke

Store and dwelling

11204 – 61 Street

July 18 G. B. Holmes obtained his permit for a building on Lot 32 Block 56, valued at only $1,000. Also on July 18, William Cooke of Beverly received a permit for a store and dwelling on Lot 16 Block 12 (11204 – 61 Street).

At the annual meeting on 16 October 1922 thanks were offered to G. H. Davis "for his very efficient and happy control of the skating rink, tennis courts and bowling green." Bury was re-elected president, Leonard Humphreys secretary, and G. H Ward treasurer. C. A. Anderson now was chair of the parent-teachers' committee; W. McSweyn the program committee; Clarence Smith the local improvement committee; Herbert Slate re-elected to chair the recreation committee; and Mrs. Holgate the social and refreshment committee.

Efforts by the recreation and local improvements committees led to an agreement by city council "to apply the whole of the block east of 62ⁿᵈ street from north of 113ᵗʰ Avenue to the school boundary to these [playground] purposes, and report was made of current efforts to get in addition the west half of the block immediately south of [this area] for suitable layout by the hoped for co-operation of the Gyro Club in equipment, for children of ages to 13." During June 1923, 433 adults and children in the Highlands contributed to this project during the "Special Gyro Playgrounds Drive."

The first small branch of the Edmonton Public Library was established at Sissons Drug Store in July 1922 through the efforts of the league. This service apparently was at first very popular and heavily used. However, in November 1925 the league once again was asking for a branch at this location, suggesting that the service had ended.

As the winter of 1922–1923 came on, Herbert Slate pointed out the dilapidated condition of the existing skating facility and the need for a larger dressing room. He recommended extending the existing building for this purpose and renting a gramophone and amplifier for the use of the skaters. G. H. Davis was retained to supervise the winter skating, and was given the right to sell candy, soft drinks, and other treats to the patrons.

Also that October, Clarence Smith noted the need for neighbourhood street improvements north of Alberta Avenue, especially land "clearance" and sidewalks. Smith also reported the need for streetlights and fire alarms, "including one opposite Highlands School." Slate suggested that the league advocate for sidewalks for the students westward from the school along 113 Avenue and 114 Avenue, citing "the greatly increased school population." Alderman A. U. G. Bury, the league president, forwarded these concerns to the city's board of commissioners. However, at the 4 November 1924 meeting concerns remained about "the still unfinished condition of the School Children's sidewalk along 114 Avenue east to the school, including the lack of lights at certain dark corners."

Sidewalks were a constant topic of concern for Highlanders during the 1920s. Enid Hart and Jean Robbie remember the wooden sidewalks along the main commercial stretches of 112 Avenue and 118 Avenue, sections of which were elevated above any potential seasonal mud. The sidewalks along 66 Street and 67 Street were supported on a stilt-like structure to elevate them above the marshy ground in that part of the neighbourhood, which could be under up to three feet of water in the spring. Dorothy Aird describes how it always was an adventure making her way to school with her fellow pupils. She would walk about eight blocks, "but everyone had shortcuts."

There were lots of sloughs to play in. They had something they called "rubber ice." This was when the slough would start to freeze and they could run and slide across the ice like they were on a roller coaster. Of course, most kids would fall in.

On November 7 a whist drive and dance were held, with prizes provided by Mr. Moffatt of the Canada Candy Company, and Sissons Drug Store. Mayor Duggan presented the prizes to the winners. Such events continued to brighten the winters during the 1920s.

On November 21 the local improvement committee reported installation of a water hydrant on Alberta Avenue, as well as an extra streetlight. Mrs. Ash then requested further efforts to get more streetlights along Ada Boulevard. The recreation committee announced plans for two weekly band nights at the skating rink, although it later decided to purchase a gramophone and amplifier as a cheaper alternative. However, Frances Martell recalled that on some memorable occasions a live band played in the middle of the rink, with skaters swirling around it.

At an executive committee meeting held in the home of Clarence Smith, Herbert Slate reported that a ladies' aid society formed to promote "boys work" had solved the problem of dressing rooms by purchasing the "Ladies' Club House" located near the east end of Ada Boulevard. This had been moved to the rink and was being renovated for the winter skating.

By December 1922 monthly socials were being held, frequently involving the popular whist drive and dance. While every effort was being made to raise funds, by December 1922 the league was in default to the EFCL. This would persist for several years.

On 2 January 1923 a list of desired improvements was drafted to send to the city's

Highlands United Church as it appeared about 1932. City of Edmonton Archives Photo EA-160-866

board of commissioners. In addition, this letter pointed out "the pressing need of attention by macadamizing, cinder ash or asphalt of the whole of 112 Ave forming sides of the main street car track through this district to at least the end of the line from East End Park pavement and also as affecting travel facilities of our residents, [and] treatment by filling in and straightening of [the] car line over present Penitentiary ravine."

Churches were continuing to grow in the Highlands. The Presbyterian Church of Canada obtained a permit for its manse at 11309 - 63 Street on 21 June 1923. On July 21 the Highlands Methodist Church (6322 - 113 Avenue) received a permit for a church basement located on Lots 1–2 Block 3, beside the frame Methodist church. This was the beginning of the current Highlands United Church, and the first step in realizing a community dream of a brick church in the neighbourhood. The brick and cement basement beside the little white Methodist church, 52' x 78', served as a church until "the top" could be added later. Rev. T. C. Buchanan, Superintendent of Missions, laid the cornerstone on 15 August 1923, and the first services were held

⚒ **BUILDING PERMITS**

Presbyterian Church manse
11309 - 63 Street

Highlands Methodist Church
6322 – 113 Avenue

in the basement church on November 11. The old frame church remained in use as a Sunday School and for boys' and girls' clubs after this.

Construction during 1923 also included a house on Lot 10 Block 6 (11340 - 62 Street), for which S. G. McCormack took out a permit on May 15. John L. Bond took out a permit to build a "private garage" for his 1913 house at 11127 - 63 Street. Apparently the Alex Cormack residence at 11231 - 65 Street was finished in 1923 as well. This house remains a nice example of the post-war dwellings being built in the Highlands during the 1920s.

The league raised funds for sweaters for the boys' hockey teams by holding the usual whist drive and dance at Highlands School that January. Most of the Highlands effort and expense were directed at operating the skating rink during the 1920s. Such efforts were beginning to take a toll on volunteer time and energy, but it is hard to exaggerate the importance of skating in the Highlands, especially among the girls.

Enid Hart and Jean Robbie recall that winters were largely for skating to recorded music at the rink - until 8:30 on school evenings, and until 10:00 on Friday and Saturday nights. "Then everyone came - even the boys." Many of the boys, however, reserved their enthusiasm for hockey, which was played on Saturday nights.

Otherwise, the boys loved to tempt the steep daredevil hills in the river valley on skis or toboggans before these were taken over by the golf course at the end of the decade. In the winter kids would ski, toboggan, or walk right out onto the river ice.

When the EFCL decided to transfer funds to hire a paid secretary, the Highlands group began to drift away from the Federated

Council, viewing this as an unnecessary expense. The rift would soon become more acrimonious, with the Highlands league consistently opposing the council on this and other funding issues. The Highlands Community League stopped and renewed its membership payments on several occasions.

Improvements in the district resulting from advocacy by the league in 1923 included installation of water and sewer mains on 71 Street and 72 Street north of 112 Avenue. Application also was made for further sewer installation on 66 Street, north of 112 Avenue. Brushing and sidewalk construction was commenced along the north side of 114 Avenue, from the East End Park to 62 Street at the school. Further east, development was beginning to progress slowly with the grading of 54, 56, and 59 streets between 118 and 120 avenues. Also, 65 Street was to be improved by being opened and graded from 112 to 118 avenues, and sidewalks constructed on its east side from 112 Avenue to 118 Avenue. Streetlights were installed throughout the neighbourhood as a safety measure, including along 62 Street in front of the school and between 114 Avenue and 118 Avenue. Two fire alarms were installed at the east ends of the main thoroughfares of 112 Avenue and 118 Avenue. A "danger signal" was installed on 112 Avenue opposite the park, where a recent accident had occurred. Application also was made to replace boulevard trees that had been destroyed by the opening of the Highlands.

The community league meetings at the school continued to be a focal point of local entertainment and debate during 1923. At the meeting on February 6, with the weather especially cold, much of the evening "was devoted to the enjoyment of real musical treats in

---

⚒ BUILDING PERMITS

S. G. McCormack
11340 – 62 Street

soprano, contralto and bass solos and duets by Mr. Andrew Slater and party." Fred McNally, principal of the Normal School, presented information on "the New Curriculum" at the March meeting. Miss Reeves addressed the April meeting on behalf of the Horticultural and Vacant Lots Association, announcing a plan to plant up to 4,000 boulevard trees during the upcoming Arbor Day week in Edmonton. Volunteers came forward to help plant these birch trees, to be taken from a plantation located outside the city. Professor W. H. Alexander and the Rev. R. Lorne McTavish debated the proposed repeal of prohibition before the general meeting on October 2.

Like other leagues, the Highlands and District Community League provided a great deal of volunteer service in their immediate area. League volunteers worked at brushing and clearing the full block located south of the school, planned as a playground with the assistance of the Gyro Club. The local improvement committee also worked to clear the half block between the streetcar line and 113 Avenue, a southern extension of the playground lots. This committee was very active in this type of work throughout the 1920s.

The Highlands Bowling Club house was moved from the original location near the tennis court to the new recreation block, "anticipating of its use in connection with the new and enlarged skating and hockey open air arena proposed...for the coming winter" of 1923–1924. At the general meeting on October 2 plans were put forward for the new community skating and hockey rink on Block 13 south of the school. Plans also were made at a subsequent meeting to have E. J. Bond move the old rink shack to the new location. William J. Beecroft took over as caretaker of the

rink in November 1923. The rink was a vital part of the Highlands, and during the winter of 1924–1925 hockey was played on Monday and Thursday evenings and Saturday afternoons, with other times set aside for public skating.

At the December 4 meeting it was announced that President A. U. G. Bury, Secretary H. Leonard Humphrey, Treasurer Wilmer J. Kelly and Recreation Committee Chair Clarence Smith had been appointed trustees and as such had signed the contract to take over the new recreation grounds located on the western half of Block 12 and Block 13, Highlands Survey, along with the skating rink, on behalf of the league. All work on the property was to be undertaken by Highlands residents. The contract would end on 31 December 1928. Andy Hollands, a Highlands teen, offered to present a minstrel show to raise further funds for the project.

A little more construction took place during 1924. F. Urquhart, who lived at 6210 Ada Boulevard, was issued a building permit for a house on Lot 10 Block 7 (11242 – 62 Street), on 25 March 1924. Mrs. J. L. Wright of 11242 – 64 Street, then obtained a permit for a house on Lot 17 Block 2 (11227 – 64 Street), built by William F. Brown. On May 5 A. M. Vail, who lived at 11223 – 64 Street, obtained a permit for an addition to his own house, also constructed by William F. Brown. On June 12 Mrs. E. Wakeman, who lived at 6318 Jasper (111) Avenue, took out a permit for a house valued at $4,000 on the west 46 feet of Lot 22 Block 9 (6270 Ada Boulevard), to be built by Muttart and Wright.

On July 16 May Griffith, who was living in the Gibbard Block at the time, received a permit to build a house on Lot 22 Block 24 (11212 – 64 Street). On 22 October 1924 she received another permit for a dwelling on Lot

BUILDING PERMITS

F. Urquhart
11242 – 62 Street

J. L. Wright
11227 - 64 Street

A. M. Vail addition
11223 - 64 Street

🔨 BUILDING PERMITS

E. Wakeman
6270 Ada Boulevard

May Griffith
11212 – 64 Street, and
11217 - 64 Street

George F. Jeffery
11209 - 64 Street

3 Block 2 (11217 - 64 Street), to be built by William F. Brown.

The Highlands School remained a centre of neighbourhood entertainment and debate during 1924. On February 5 Misses G. and M. Griffith, Mrs. D. Horn, and Mr. Roy "rendered vocal selections...." In April Dr. N. Burton Logie, from the University of Alberta medical faculty, presented a lecture on "Race Psychology as applied to this generation...." Senator William Griesbach addressed the November meeting on "Early Days in Edmonton." The December meeting heard Professor A. L. Burt on "the Unity of Canada."

By the 1924–1925 season some noteworthy changes had occurred in the community league executive. Carleton G. Sheldon now was president; H. H. Parlee, first vice-president and chair of the parent-teachers' committee; Andrew Hollands, second vice-president and chair of the program committee; Clarence Smith, third vice-president and chair of the recreation rommittee; J. Price, fourth vice-president and chair of the local improvement committee; W. J. Kelly, treasurer; and J. L Humphrey, secretary.

While the rink remained at the centre of activities for many of the Highlands youth, things did not go smoothly at all times. At the meeting on 3 March 1925 Clarence Smith resigned as caretaker, "stating that the janitor and he had been unable to cope with the younger element, at the rink and that nothing could be done unless the offenders were barred from the place absolutely." Smith was requested to reconsider his resignation, and given power by the executive to bar the local bad boys, including Bruce and Gordon Matheson, Harold Shortridge, and Wilson Harris. When the parents did not respond, Smith resigned in frustration.

The community league first organized and entered boys' and girls' baseball teams from the Highlands in the appropriate city league in the spring of 1925.

Only one house received a permit in the Highlands during 1925. George F. Jeffery of 11322 - 62 Street received his permit for a dwelling on Lot 2 Block 2 (11209 - 64 Street) on August 21 of that year.

The Edmonton Public School Board was discussing plans to close the Highlands Junior High School that spring as well, and Carleton G. Sheldon, H. H. Parlee, and J. W. H. Williams were appointed to attend the next board meeting to protest on behalf of the community. In March 1926 the league protested this move of the high school to Eastwood School once again, urging that the unoccupied rooms in the Highlands School be used as high school accommodation.

At the September 1925 meeting a proposal by Christopher J. Yorath, president of Northwestern Utilities Ltd., to bring natural gas to the neighbourhood was put before the community league. Carleton G. Sheldon and H. H. Parlee were delegated to meet the company to further this idea. This committee reported to the October 6 league meeting that the project would cost $40,000, and that the expectation was that the Highlands would provide 175 consumers willing to deposit ten dollars each, in addition to their contracts with Northwestern Utilities. Yorath described natural gas service to the Highlands as probable under this arrangement. Already plans were being drawn up for natural gas lines into the district located east of 82 Street. Sheldon and Parlee were delegated to advocate further for the extension of gas service to the Highlands, and at the March 9 meeting a motion was passed to form a committee to meet city council and Christopher Yorath "to press our claim for extension of gas line to Highlands."

By March 1926 streets and roads in the Highlands had deteriorated, and their anticipated upgrading had not been realized. This concern became more acute with the advent of spring. The community league noted that there were many complaints, particularly about "the terrible condition of streets east of Borden Park." Adam J. Davidson, Harvey Baker, and Robert W. Grierson were delegated to cooperate with the nearby Swift's company plant and city council to organize improvements through "proper drainage by using cinders or some such porous material." Special attention was focused on 112 Avenue and Alberta Avenue, as well as streets going through the neighbourhood south of Alberta Avenue to Ada Boulevard.

There also were concerns about the condition of the pavement near Concordia College, and a delegation was struck to advocate that city council deal with this part of Ada Boulevard. The new streets committee requested that the sidewalk along 63 Street be surfaced as well. Ada Boulevard was slumping and cracking above the Standard Mine, and demands were made for the repair of this route. The section of 63 Street between Jasper (111) Avenue and 118 Avenue also needed to be graded and drained. Finally, in its petition to the board of commissioners, tabled with city council on March 20, the league stated "[that] all of the streets east of Borden Park up to 61st Street be at least drained and brushed and a narrow portion of the street graded between Ada Boulevard and 118th Ave., especially 61st Street."

During the 1920s Ada Boulevard remained fairly rough along its eastern and western sections. Between 60 Street and 55 Street it passed fenced-in pastures and agricultural properties.

To the west a wooden bridge spanned a deep gully between 65 Street and 66 Street. Enid Hart and Jean Robbie remember how kids would slide down the hill under the bridge on pieces of cardboard during the winters. Narrow extensions of the bridge planking extending beyond the handrails tempted the more daring to walk along this dangerous margin. This lasted until the Second World War, when the gully was filled in.

The community league executive for 1926 was elected at the November 1925 meeting. H. H. Parlee was the new president; F. G. Brown, chair of the parent-teachers' committee; M. Cryderman, chair of the program committee; D. A. Morrison, chair of the local improvements committee; H. Pettis, chair of the sports committee; R. A. Bullock, secretary; and W. J. Kelly re-elected treasurer.

By the mid-1920s the drowsy real estate market was beginning to erode the Highlands value restrictions. On 1 February 1926 T. R. Dando of Beverly obtained a building permit for "repair" to a dwelling on Lot 7 Block 2, Highlands Survey (11239 – 64 Street), valued at $800. Then on 29 March 1926 he obtained another permit for "repair" to a dwelling on Lot 8 Block 2, Highlands Survey (11245 – 64 Street) valued at $1,400. At its March meeting the community league took issue with these permits, describing the houses as having been "moved onto 64th Street." "It was pointed out that the houses in question did not comply with the restriction re buildings in the Highlands." These infractions appear to have been the beginning of the end for the caveat. A committee was struck and given the task of meeting with Dando.

Apart from the Dando houses, Herbert Baker was granted a permit to build a house at 6319 Jasper (111) Avenue or Lot 18 Block

---

⚒ BUILDING PERMITS

T. R. Dando renovation
11239 - 64 Street and
11245 – 64 Street

Highlands United Church. Dorothy Husband and Audrey Hibbert were the first two infants baptized in this new church. Photograph courtesy of Margaret Husband.

BUILDING PERMITS

Herbert Baker
6319 – 111 Avenue

W. J. Bancroft
11228 - 61 Street

William F. Brown
11108 – 64 Street

F. G. Dear
11142 - 63 Street

Herbert Baker
6274 Ada Boulevard

1, Highlands Survey on 22 March 1926. This house was directly across the street from his former residence at 6318 Jasper Avenue (later called the Marshall Residence). W. J. Bancroft also received a permit to build a house on Lot 12 Block 12 (11228 - 61 Street) on May 11. No other houses were built in the Highlands in 1926.

The community league executive for 1927 included H. H. Parlee, president; W. McSweyn, first vice-president; Adam J. Davidson, second vice-president and chair, local improvements committee; Mrs. H. H. Parlee, third vice-president; R. A. Bullock, secretary; and W. J. Kelly, treasurer.

At least six buildings were added to the Highlands during 1927. William F. Brown obtained a permit to build a house valued at $4,500 on Lot 29 Block 23, a corner lot located at 11108 - 64 Street. F. G. Dear, living in the Hecla Block, received a permit for a house on Lot 10 Block 1 (11142 - 63 Street).

Herbert Baker, who was then living at 6318 Jasper (111) Avenue, received a permit to build an eight-room house on Lot 23 Block 9 (6274 Ada Boulevard). He had purchased the lot in 1913, but did not build for several years.

Herbert Baker was born in Yorkshire, England in 1866, and immigrated to Canada in 1882, where he worked for the Massey Manufacturing Company and its successor Massey-Harris. He moved west to Winnipeg, then to Edmonton in 1910 as the company manager for northern Alberta. Baker retired in 1925, when he entered local politics. He moved into his new house in 1928, living there until 1943. Baker was elected alderman from 1927 to 1933, during which time he promoted the longstanding dream of the Highlands Scenic Drive, also known as Baker's Folly (so-called because it was so unstable that it was used for only a couple of years).

In 1927 the Highlands United Church also was given clearance for an addition to the church on Lot 1 Block 3 (11305 - 64 Street). Plans for construction of this church had begun in 1923, when a cornerstone was laid for what was then called the Highlands Methodist Church. (It became the Highlands United Church following church union in 1925.) Much of the work on the original structure had been done by 1926, with additions made in 1927 and 1953.

Frances Martell, who sang in the Highlands United Church junior choir as a young girl, recalls the first church as "just a clapboard building on the corner." She also recalls how the new church held services in the basement for years, until the building could be completed. Dedication services were held on 11 December 1927.

W. G. Blakey, a prominent Edmonton architect, was the designer, while Pheasey and Batson were the contractors who built the church, valued at $12,000. The Blakey design is similar to his Gothic Revival style Christ Church Anglican, built six years previously. A new entrance, built in 1953, has changed the original façade.

The attractive clinker brick William Brown Residence (11108 – 64 Street), also built in 1927, remains a reminder of one of the earliest and most influential of Highlands builders and promoters. On 19 April 1912 William F. Brown, of 624 15 Street, obtained a building permit for a frame house on Lot 23 Block 23, Highlands Survey, on West Houston Street, valued at $4,000. He was the first occupant listed in 1913 at this house at #1804 Houston Street (11150 – 64 Street). This house was the first of many that he would build in the coming decades.

W. F. Brown & Co. in 1912 was advertised as "Financial, Insurance and Real Estate Agents, Practical Home Builders." Company offices were located in Room 11, Orpheum Arcade (Orpheum Arcade and Orpheum Theatre), 42 Jasper Avenue East. Brown also was with Triple Realty Company.

Will Brown's daughter, Marjorie Hammond, described how he taught school in Strathrow, Ontario, and owned a store in Mount Bridges, Ontario, before moving to Edmonton. Arriving during the boom years, Brown began to buy land on Jasper (111) Avenue as well as some farmland as speculative ventures. His wife, Mabel Edna Brown, died in 1963, and he moved to Calgary to be with his daughter Marjorie until his death in 1967.

Finally, George H. Van Allen, a significant supporter of the Highlands socially and politically, occupied his residence at 6326 – 111 Avenue in 1927, apparently the year in which this distinctive pebbledash and clinker brick finished dwelling was constructed. After studying law at the University of Alberta before the First World War, Allen was admitted to the bar in 1915. He represented Alberta as counsel before the Royal Commission studying grain

freight rates during 1923 and 1924. After moving into the Highlands George Van Allen also took on many neighbourhood responsibilities. As president of the Highlands Golf Course he initiated a relief labour project to widen the fairways on the east nine holes. Building upon his many local connections and widespread popularity, Van Allen was elected Liberal MLA, and served from 1935 until his death in 1937. After his death, the family remained in the house until 1941, when his widow Ruby moved to Vancouver to be closer to her family.

In October 1927 Adam J. Davidson reported that the local improvement committee required strong support for its demands that the city drain and gravel 112 Avenue from the pavement at 75 Street to the end of the streetcar line. In November Davidson reported that he felt this work would be done by the fall, as far east as 50 Street. The league then requested that two streetlights be placed on this newly paved stretch. Early in 1928 the condition of 114 Avenue between 62 Street and 63 Street also was felt to be "deplorable...broken glass and rusty jagged tine being very much in evidence."

Little success seems to have resulted from league advocacy on many of these concerns. Nevertheless the league soldiered on, requesting city grading on 113 Avenue between 62 Street and 64 Street, as well as the need for a cinder sidewalk on the north side of 113 Avenue between 64 Street and 65 Street, again to facilitate school children during inclement weather.

The community league executive elected for 1928 included Adam Davidson, president; F. Urquhart, first vice-president and chair of the parent-teachers' committee; Mrs. H. H. Parlee, second vice-president and chair of the

Eda Owen, the "weather lady," reading her meteorological instruments in the Highlands, 1935. Glenbow Archives Photo ND-3-6913a.

program committee; J. Price, third vice-president and chair of the local improvement committee; Mrs. E. J. Bond, fourth vice-president and chair of the social committee; S. G. McCormack, fifth vice-president and chair of the recreation committee; Frank Slate, secretary; and W. J. Kelly, treasurer.

Again, very little construction took place in the Highlands during 1928. W. J. Rose received a permit for a garage at his house at 11212 - 64 Street. Mrs. Marion P. Hall, who lived at 11223 - 64 Street, obtained a permit to build a house and garage on Lot 1 Block 9 (11023 - 64 Street), to be built by Muttart and Wright. Still, the Highlands community continued to grow in population as more children were born. The Highlands School was expanded to include intermediate grades in 1928, thus alleviating the shortage of classrooms resulting from neighbourhood students continuing into the higher grades.

The Owen Residence (11227 - 63 Street) became one of the principal social hubs in the

Highlands during the 1920s and 1930s. Eda Owen, Canada's first female weather observer, lived in this modest wood-frame foursquare house built by Highlands lumberman Garnett M. Meiklejohn. Eda came to Edmonton in 1908 with her husband, Herbert, a retired sea captain. When he became a weatherman in 1915, they moved to the house, and it became a Dominion Meteorological Office. Meiklejohn owned the house until 1918.

The Owen house was a landmark with its 60-foot red-painted wooden scaffold tower mounted on the roof to hold the rotating wind gauge. A meteorological instrument platform also was affixed to the home's rear dormer, and other equipment was installed in the front room and backyard, until the house virtually bristled with instrumentation. The devices eventually in use included terrestrial radiators, moisture meters, maximum and minimum thermometers, and self-recording rain and snow gauges. The Owen Residence was carefully restored by Sandra and Jim Storey, who purchased it in 1980, and it was designated a Provincial Historic Resource in March 1994.

When Herbert enlisted during the First World War, Eda took over his duties, taking daily readings from her meteorological instruments and sending them to Toronto. Herbert died in a prisoner of war camp in 1917, and Eda became the weather station manager, making her the first woman to hold such a post in Canada. Eda's daily routine began at 5:40 in the morning with readings and telephone reports. Over 140 weather stations contacted her daily, and she sent two daily and one monthly report to Toronto.

During the 1920s and 1930s, a time hungry for unusual news, Eda's weather observatory became a popular meeting place for academics, exploration groups. and globe-trotting aviators passing through Edmonton. Pressure from American military authorities in July 1943 forced its closure during the so-called friendly invasion of the city by US military personnel, many of whom worked on the Northwest Staging Route, the series of airstrips and radio ranging stations built in conjunction with the Alaska Highway. Eda Owen later moved to Calgary, where she died in 1957.

In May 1928 E. J. Bond, W. J. Kelly, and F. Urquhart formed a committee responsible for future plans for the Highlands Bowling Club. The most immediate idea involved the allotment of three lots within Block 13, located at its southeast corner and angled by 61 Street and 113 Avenue. This allotment included part of the land the community league had leased from the city for several years. The league hoped to renew the lease for another ten years, to allow the bowling club to operate on the site.

As throughout the decade, several issues continued to dominate the concerns of Highlands residents: the need for sidewalks, paved or graded streets, adequate lighting, the restoration of sidewalks removed by the city near the Highlands School, and general clearing, such as the removal of "surplus dirt and filth now covering a large portion of the cement road known as Ada Bld." Presumably this dirt had resulted from the work being done on other roads at the time. Times were tough for the Highlands and the city, and sometimes community residents had to step up to make sure its sports and social life continued as well as possible.

Alderman Harvey Baker, for example, personally covered the cost of cindering the skating rink site so that it could be used for

tennis during May 1928. As a city alderman Baker also championed keeping open Highland Drive, also known as Baker's Folly. This rough gravel road provided a shortcut from Jasper Avenue and 82 Street to the Highlands by way of a steep descent to the river valley on the Premier Mine Road, and ascent to Ada Boulevard at 68 Street. It was so unstable that it only was used for a couple of years during the 1920s, according to Enid Hart and Jean Robbie.

As late as September 1928, 115 Avenue east of 64 Street "was under cultivation at certain points," as the minutes stated. The league approached the city to have 115 Avenue opened up through to 62 Street. However, some houses were being built just to the west along 65 Street, such as the little house that is still standing at 11150 – 65 Street, built in 1928.

Once again the city commissioners were requested to improve pedestrian accessibility by providing sidewalks on the west side of 60 Street from Jasper (111) Avenue to Ada

Eda Owen climbing her weather tower in the Highlands, 1929. Glenbow Archives Photo ND-3-4520e.

The Husbands just before their move from the McLuhan house in March 1956. Photograph courtesy of Margaret Husband.

Boulevard, as well as the west side of 62 Street and both sides of 65 Street.

During the 1920s Ada Boulevard east of 60 Street to 55 Street was fenced in and racehorses were kept in the pastures. "Lots of people also had chickens and cows," Enid Hart and Jean Robbie later recalled. "Living in this area was like living in a rural setting but with all the conveniences of a city," Dorothy Aird adds. "The Gimby barn had a large pulley system to lift the hay up to the loft. The bigger boys especially liked to play with this pulley system."

A storm drain also was requested at the corner of Jasper (111) Avenue and 62 Street to permit travel following rain. During 1928 the Edmonton Radial Railway on 112 Avenue had been rerouted between 72 Street and 75 Street, with that section then being graded and graveled to improve access to the Highlands and the rest of east Edmonton. The league continued to press for the completion of the rest of 112 Avenue to the end of the ERR line. Lights also were demanded for Ada Boulevard as far east as 50 Street, which were described as a road that was "extremely dangerous to night travelers."

The skating shack was moved to the lane between 61 Street and 62 Street directly opposite its previous site and placed on a cement foundation. Water and sewer were added to the shack at the same time. After this the hockey, skating, and bowling clubs shared this facility as appropriate to the seasons.

In October 1928 Adam Davidson reported on improvements in the Highlands, and noted that some progress had been made. He could point to the newly graded roads and boulevarded streets, and especially the bituminous sidewalks and new catch basins on 112 Avenue, as

well as the rerouting of the ERR streetcar line on that avenue. Also, Ada Boulevard had been extended from the end of pavement eastward to 50 Street.

Much credit for these improvements was given to the fact that both Mayor A. U. G. Bury and Alderman Harvey Baker had actively advocated for the community league and the Highlands itself. That month Alderman Baker addressed the league meeting, noting that many improvements were required and merited in the Highlands, and that "previous years have seen little accomplished in this direction, while other parts of the city have received many favors." Of course, the annual civic election was looming on the horizon by October.

The community league executive for 1929 included A. J. Davidson, president; M. MacLeod, first vice-president; Mrs. H. H. Parlee, second vice-president; J. Price, third vice-president; Mrs. Seller, fourth vice-president; S. G. McCormack, fifth vice-president; W. J. Kelly, treasurer; and J. Leonard Humphreys, secretary.

The periodical debate of the Lord's Day Act arose at the 22 November 1928 meeting, where it was decided to not allow Sunday skating on the Highlands rink. This seems to have continued until the 1930s. Sunday skating was discussed at the annual meeting on 7 November 1935, and "the need for a caretaker there on Sundays as a great number skated there altho' the Rink was not open." A motion was passed then to keep the rink open on Sundays for two hours in the afternoon.

The energetic support for the hockey team paid off during the 1928–1929 season. On 12 April 1929 a banquet honouring the team was held at the Highlands School. The Highlands and District Community League boys' team won the Federated Leagues Cup for Senior Hockey that year. Mayor Bury presented the cup to the team, and following the banquet dancing and the ever-present whist were enjoyed.

Hockey was the most popular game among boys in the Highlands during the 1920s. On 30 November 1929, for example, the *Edmonton Journal* reported that the Highlands United Church was organizing its Wolves hockey team at "a snappy meeting" which opened with a prayer, included a devotional period and a talk on the life of David Livingstone, and concluded with a game of ships and sailors. A model airplane club was associated with the Wolves.

The community league executive elected for 1929 included Malcolm Macleod, president; Ross, vice-president; Manley R. Cryderman, chair of the finance committee; A. J. Davidson, chair of the local improvements committee; S. McCormack, chair of the sports committee; J. Dalziel, chair of the social committee; R. Smith, secretary; and W. J. Kelly, treasurer.

Many of the same people continued to take a lead in keeping the social organization of the Highlands active, forming a core of conscientious participants in the pursuit of community interests and well-being. "Mrs. Malcolm Macleod was elected president of the ladies' aid of the Highlands United Church at the annual meeting of that organization," the *Edmonton Journal* reported on 4 December 1929. "Mrs. Tappenden was in the chair and others appointed to the executive for the year were: hon. presidents, Mrs. W. J. Magrath and Mrs. W. H. Haggith; vice presidents, Mrs. Fredrick Tappenden, Mrs. Chambers, Mrs. W. A. Atkinson and Mrs. P. W. Gimby; recording secretary, Mrs. C. A. Anderson;

corresponding secretary, Mrs. Emmerson." Such notices substantiate the intersection of the principal Highlands groups.

Violet Macleod, daughter of Malcolm and Loretta Macleod, recalled that her parents, and those of many of her friends, were very active in the Highlands United Church, and that her father taught a young men's Bible group in addition to his wife's work with the ladies' aid. Violet attended the Christian Girls in Training meetings at the church. "They had a good Sunday School," she stated. "Church was very important in their lives – it was the centre of the community."

Dorothy Aird observed during an interview for the Highlands Historical Society that not everyone rejoiced in the tightly knit leadership within the Highlands. She noted that in some ways the neighbourhood resembled "a company town," with a certain elite represented by the Magraths, Holgates, and Dr. Atkinson directing the fortunes of the district. Some Highlanders from the margins were left feeling somewhat excluded, feeling like "serfs" as the more influential and prosperous left their imprint on the community through their direction of almost all social and church events. Dorothy Aird especially recalls some

The Felix Frederickson residence at 11342 – 67 Street, 1941. City of Edmonton Archives Photo EA-160-661.

🔨 BUILDING PERMITS

A. J. MacKay

11216 - 61 Street and
11220 – 61 Street and
11212 – 61 Street

F. Frederickson

6420 Ada Boulevard

G. F. Jeffery

11220 - 62 Street

general resentment of the Holgates, who remained somewhat more aloof than most.

Dances remained the mainstay of local entertainment among young people. Notices of such events were common. "Miss Violet Hillaby was hostess at an attractive dance ... at the residence of her parents, Mr. and Mrs. W. H. Hillaby, the Highlands," the *Edmonton Journal* reported on 22 November 1929. "Balloons and streamers in shades of mauve and yellow decorated the rooms."

Also on November 22 the *Edmonton Journal* reported that Mrs. W. J. McGrath had opened her home to the Central Women's Christian Temperance Union. "A very interesting affair was held Thursday afternoon when Mrs. W. J. McGrath graciously placed her beautiful home at the Highlands at the disposal of Central W.C.T.U. for a parlor meeting. Mrs. R. A. Richards, convener of parlor meetings, assisted Mrs. McGrath in receiving the guests. Mrs. J. H. Black, social convener, was in charge of the tea room.... Mrs. Willing and Mrs. Till accompanied by Mrs. Eastham contributed several delightful solos during the afternoon. Rev. Russell McGillivray spoke on the different phases of W.C.T.U. work with special reference to the new department of Peace and Goodwill.

Only five building permits were issued for the Highlands during 1929. A. J. MacKay took out a permit to build a dwelling on Lot 14 Block 12 (11216 - 61 Street). On April 24 he received another permit for another dwelling on Lot 13 Block 12 (11220 - 61 Street). A third permit was issued for a MacKay house on Lot 15 Block 12 (11212 - 61 Street) on May 29. F. X Frederickson, who lived at 11342 - 67 Street,

took out a permit on May 31 for a house to be built at 6420 Ada Boulevard. Walter Husband's sister Maude married Arthur Jackson, and they moved into this, their second Highlands house, with their two children in 1930. Finally, G. F. Jeffery, of 11322 - 62 Street, received a permit to build a house on Lot 13 Block 7 (11220 - 62 Street) on June 8. This little clinker brick and stucco Arts and Crafts residence was completed in 1930.

The story of the Highlands during the 1920s was essentially that of a self-reliant community striving to maintain the quality of its pre-war dreams of genteel and gracious "country living" within the city. The main instrument of this effort was the Highlands and District Community League, and the effect of several of its influential members like Mayor Bury and Alderman Baker. Highlands men and women like the Parlees and Browns worked hard to keep the community league a vital part of advocacy for the neighbourhood. The victories sometimes seemed small and hard won, but Highlanders knew that their city and community had experienced great times in the past and felt that they would experience such times again.

The new Canadian National Railway station opened to much fanfare and huge crowds on St. Patrick's Day 1928. Few buildings had risen during the 1920s, especially when compared with the boom preceding the war. For many, this event heralded what they hoped would be a more prosperous future, but these hopes would be dashed as the economic stagnation of the 1920s culminated in the beginning of the more traumatic Great Depression in October 1929.

11
Weathering the Great Depression, 1929–1939

The cheery glow of the first neon signs on Jasper Avenue would belie their optimistic promise as the Wall Street crash soon slammed the world on Black Thursday, 24 October 1929. The shock waves of this financial collapse soon reached Edmonton, and the Canadian west slipped into another decade of even greater economic distress.

During the infamous Dirty Thirties, made still worse by a widespread drought, soup kitchens came to symbolize the difficulties of the unemployed. Those desperate men lucky enough to secure government "relief work" on city streets were provided with barely enough to feed their families. Relief became an urgent and constant concern of the Highlands and District Community League during the depression. Its meetings frequently ended with petitions to the city to provide relief work, and during the worst years the league established its own relief committee to assist in providing necessities and finding work. Free tickets for the skating rink also were provided to families on relief.

Stuart Pearce, who grew up in the Highlands during this time, later recalled how many neighbours grew vegetable gardens, and that his father had such a garden, won prizes for his flowers, and also built a greenhouse at the Pearce house at 11448 – 67 Street. For a fee of one dollar the city of Edmonton also allowed Highlanders to plant vegetables on vacant lots along 111 Avenue during the 1930s. Stuart Pearce recalled that the Highlands kids liked to play "rabbit" and help themselves to the carrots.

Violet Macleod remembered in later years that the Highlands had not been hit quite as hard as some other city neighbourhoods. Malcolm Macleod, her father, managed to work through the depression. "Everyone helped everyone," she observed. "Relatives would all hand down clothes." Violet also remembered that many men were riding the rails, and "there always would be men off the trains, 'tramps,' who would knock on the door for food." Mrs. Macleod would make sandwiches and Vi would serve them on a little table set up in the back

yard. The railway was not that far away, and word got around about the kind lady in the Highlands, so many men would hop off and walk into the neighbourhood and make a bee-line for the Macleod house. Others recall that some men squatted near the valley gravel bars to pan for gold, sometimes coming up to the community to ask for, or offer to work for, meals.

On 20 December 1932, crowds of distraught people converged on Market Square in the city centre to protest their dilemma, only to be dispersed with violence. Perhaps in response to these shocking events, the community ceague passed a resolution on the relief issue to be presented to city council the following April.

Edmonton Journal delivery boys for The Highlands and Beverly gather at the paper shack to start their rounds, 1930. Glenbow Archives Photo ND-3-5172.

RESOLUTION ADOPTED BY HIGHLANDS & DISTRICT COMMUNITY LEAGUE
TO BE SUBMITTED TO EDMONTON CITY COUNCIL

WHEREAS we believe that the most valuable asset of the Country is the self-respect and ecconomic (sic) independence and initiative of our people

AND WHEREAS we believe that the Country's supreme duty is to preserve these human qualities in adults and to develope (sic) them in the young

AND WHEREAS we believe that the system of Direct Relief is destroying these qualities in our people and preventing their normal development in young people

AND WHEREAS we believe that in a land of plenty like our own every person has the inalienable right to the necessities of life

AND WHEREAS we believe that receiving these necessities from organized society every person should make voluntarily or by compulsion an adequate contribution towards the common good

WE THEREFORE urge upon our CITY, PROVINCE and DOMINION authorities that all able-bodied persons receiving relief be required to contribute services in proportion to the relief given

AND FURTHER we offer our support to the elective representatives of the city of EDMONTON in their endeavors to provide work for the unemployed who seek relief. We realize that this work would need to be such as would not be undertaken under ordinary Capital expenditures at this time but believe that the City Commissioners would suggest work to be undertaken in the Parks and other places that would add to the beauty and health of our city

AND WE RESPECTFULLY suggest that if extra financing be necessary to provide material and equipment that the unsold Bonds of the City be offered to the Contractors in payment. The Relief Administration to furnish all the labor required for such Contracts

Adopted 7th April 1933

The provincial government set up relief labour camps for single young men during this period. While the Highlands could not escape the wave of problems sweeping over the land, and although the community did its best to engage with the issues of the day, many residents would be reduced to simply holding on as best they could during the mid-1930s. On the whole the Highlands remained a fairly inward-looking community.

Throughout the Great Depression, the prairies saw the rise of radical new political philosophies like the Co-operative Commonwealth Federation and the Social Credit movement. The Communist Party voice became more vociferous and grew in popular appeal. Everywhere, people were seeking a solution to their distress, and religious movements became ever more popular among the hopeless as well as among traditional adherents. The role of the churches was further reinforced in the social and spiritual lives of Highlanders.

City businesses and industries were unable to sustain much building during the 1930s. Many buildings were modified and converted into other uses as businesses faltered or failed. During the decade many houses in the Highlands would be rented, while others would be divided into suites. The Canada Safeway grocery store (6414 – 112 Avenue) was an exception when it opened in 1930. The Safeway would operate at this location until 1960, when the Canadian Imperial Bank of Commerce moved in with a Highlands branch that remained there until 1994. As the Highlands drew further into itself, its tightly knit families, friendships, and community organizations proved even more important.

Social groups like the Highlands United Church ladies' aid society and the Highlands and District Community League would continue to play an even more important role in the communal life of the Highlands. On 30 January 1930 the *Edmonton Journal* reported that the ladies' aid society had presented a delightful Burns' Night program for over 100 guests. Mrs. E. J. Bond convened this affair, with the Rev. W. J. Haggish as chairman. It featured a talk on Robbie Burns by Major A. C. Grant. Robert Stoker played the bagpipes, while others provided a vocal musical program. At the conclusion Mrs. Malcolm MacLeod convened a social hour, including a tea table "attractive with Scottish thistles and plaids."

On June 27 the ladies' aid presented a garden party that involved many Highlanders. Held on the United Church lawn, the party was organized by Mrs. J. L. Anderson and Mrs. Robert W. (Allie) Grierson. Mrs. B. A. Holgate and Mrs. Fred Williams were in charge of "a candy booth in gay summer dress," while Mrs. J. W. H. Williams and Mrs. Hunter ran the ice cream booth. Mrs. Herbert Baker set up "a photograph bureau." The *Edmonton Journal* reported that "An extensive foreign exhibit will be in charge of Mrs. W. H. Haggith and Mrs.

Fred and Margaret, the Husband twins, celebrate their fifth birthday with their friends Don and Joyce Cobbledick, their cousin Helen McDonald of Ottawa, all blowing up a storm. Photograph courtesy of Margaret Husband.

91

The view west along Ada Boulevard from 64 Street, 1934.
City of Edmonton Archives Photo EA-160-1077.

W. A. Atkinson." Of course there was also a musical program, including orchestral music. "Mrs. Stanley Emmott will supply amusement through the medium of a bran tub" (an English tradition in which small wrapped gifts were buried in a barrel or tub full of bran).

Later in the summer, the Highlands United Church, which maintained an important position in the community's social life during the interwar years, arranged a Sunday School picnic. On Wednesday afternoon, July 9, "a gala outing" was held on the community grounds to close the season's activities. Competitions were held for the various age groups of boys and girls in the three-legged race, peanut race, and free-for-all, after which a lunch was served on the church lawn.

Construction in the Highlands declined even further with the onset of the depression. In 1930, for example, only two building permits were issued for the neighbourhood. On May 10 A. W. Thomas, who lived at 11320 – 65 Street, obtained a permit to build a house on Lot 21 Block 24 (11220 – 64 Street). Then on August 1 A. G. McKay was given a permit to build a garage at 11215 – 61 Street.

The Highlands and District Community League remained a vital part of life in the Highlands. At an executive meeting on 13 January 1930 it was decided that A. J. Davidson should investigate the feasibility of getting a bridge connecting Jasper Avenue "via the Saskatchewan riverbank" east of 82 Street to Ada Boulevard. Davidson was further advised to request that the city commissioners provide support for lighting along Ada Boulevard between 50 Street and 60 Street. The executive also passed a motion to request a cement sidewalk along the east side of 62 Street from 112 Avenue and the existing sidewalk in front of the school. The tennis club was in financial difficulties by 1930, and the Highlands league held several events to raise funds to support its work that February.

At the 29 March 1930 executive meeting at the Davidson Residence, Carleton G. Sheldon reported that plans were in place for another coal mine in the Highlands area, "and in view of the consequences elsewhere of such operations upon surface properties," he was requested to draft a letter to city council opposing this mine. By 1934 the Edina Coal Mine was operating, to the consternation of the Highlands and District Community League, which petitioned the city engineer to provide maps allowing them to determine under which block the mine was operating.

The demands upon such social agencies as the Edmonton Creche were growing greater, but a request to the league for assistance found no such funds available. A letter of thanks also was drafted for William Beecroft, who personally had cleared out "part of the park-like portion of the Community Play centre." On October 30 the tennis club was granted permission to move the fence around the skating rink south to allow for two more tennis courts. During the winter of 1933–1934 an eastern section of the rink would be added for "fancy skating." The Highlands skating rink struggled financially during the 1920s and 1930s. During the winter of 1934–1935 the Bellevue community opened its own rink, taking away additional support and revenue.

The community league executive for 1931 and 1932 included Malcolm Macleod, president; Carleton G. Sheldon, vice-president; A. J. Davidson, public affairs committee; Sam G. McCormack, sports committee; James A. Ross, finance committee; Mrs. Carleton G. Sheldon, social committee; M. H. Gilmour, secretary; and W. J. Kelly, treasurer.

At the 31 January 1931 executive meeting it was decided to request that the Rat Creek Ravine be filled in permanently and the banks planted to beautify an improved connection with Ada Boulevard. The city commissioners and city council were then petitioned by a delegation to carry out this requirement for an adequate connection with the Highlands following the main route along the river escarpment. Dissatisfaction with the Edmonton Federation of Community Leagues had reached the point where the Highlands group was threatening to withdraw, and only a personal representation from the community league council on February 18 persuaded members to reconsider and agree to pay dues to the parent organization.

E. E. Hyde made a presentation to the executive committee on 10 February 1931, pointing out the overcrowding at Eastwood School, which most Highlands students attended, as well as at Highlands Junior High School. The Cromdale, Eastwood, and Alberta Avenue leagues then were invited to cooperate in holding a public meeting on February 18 to discuss the need for a new Highlands school. The meeting was addressed by Hyde and Elmer Roper, who outlined the problems. A motion was passed in support of the Edmonton Public School Board's high school building program, and James Ross was delegated to press the issue with the Edmonton Federation of Community Leagues.

The executive committee met on 16 October 1931, and following recommendations by the town planning committee, voted to petition the board of city commissioners to support extension of 112 Avenue along the ERR tracks at the south edge of Borden Park from the east switch to Pine Place, with a road 80 feet wide. It also was asked that road grading on this section, "followed with gravel when convenient," be undertaken in the fall as a relief work project. The need to gravel 62 Street between 112 Avenue and 118 Avenue was raised, as was the poor condition of sidewalks along 112 Avenue. At this annual meeting James Ross reminded the members that "this was a League for all the district and we are interested in everyone within reach of this district who would identify themselves with our activities." As such, at its annual meeting in October 1931, the league petitioned in support of Park Addition in its application for extension of sewer and water.

In 1931 only five building permits were issued for the Highlands. On 27 March [Zola] M. Ferguson obtained a permit for a house on Lot 6 Block 2 (11233 – 64 Street). On 29 April R. Jennings, who lived at 11120 – 66 Street, obtained a permit to build a house on Lot 12 Block 1 (11128 – 63 Street), to be constructed by R. H. Rae, and valued at $5,000. Three other permits were issued along what was still designated Jasper Avenue (now 111 Avenue), between 60 Street and 63 Street. On May

BUILDING PERMITS

Zola M. Ferguson
11233 – 64 Street

R. Jennings
11128 – 63 Street

21 Charles F. Card received his permit for a residence on the east 50 feet of Lot 1 Block 9 (6335 Jasper Avenue); on October 7 J. Marshall obtained a permit for a residence on parts of Lots 21–22 Block 9 (6260 Jasper Avenue; on December 15 R. H. M. Gilken received a permit for a garage at his house at 6013 Jasper Avenue.

In 1932 only two building permits were issued in the Highlands. On April 28 F. Schroffel, a building contractor, obtained a permit for alterations to a house located on Lots 10-11 – now Lot F - Block 9 (6205 – 111 Avenue). John Truesdale then obtained a permit for a dwelling on Lot 7 Block 18 (11128 - 60 Street).

The Highlands Beauty Parlor seems to have opened at 6510 - 112 Avenue during 1932, operating at this location until 1955. The Highlands Barber Shop also operated here between 1934 and 1942. After 1955 Highlands Shoe Repair took up this location.

By 1932 the community league was operating a relief committee, which on February 3 reported four cases. Three received relief and the fourth was given work. The Margaret Marshall Residence (11119 - 62 Street) is also a visible reminder of the charitable social work undertaken by one Highlander. Margaret Marshall, who worked at the *Edmonton Journal* during the depression years, founded the Sunshine Club at that newspaper. Regular columns promoted relief projects, and reported on activities, and parties and gifts given to children in need. It also helped find work for the unemployed, a group that increased dramatically with each year during the 1930s. In 1930, 1,500 hampers were provided for those in need, some of them in the Highlands itself. After leaving *The Journal*, Margaret Marshall was employed by the City as a "lady officer," responsible for inspection of municipal relief and an "investigator" for city hall.

The Marshall Residence at 6318 - 111 Avenue was the home of another socially prominent Highlander. Originally built as a four-square by C. L. Freeman in 1914, the house was occupied by Herbert Baker from 1915 until 1928, when he moved to his new home on Ada Boulevard. It was then bought in 1929 by Daisy-May Marshall, wife of Robert Colin Marshall, former alderman (1917) and mayor (1919) of Calgary, and later MLA (1921–1926). After moving to Edmonton he worked for Crown Paving Co. Ltd. Following a fire at the house, Marshall rebuilt it in the early 1930s, which accounts for its unique design. Daisy-May Marshall lived in the house until 1962, and during that time she served as president of the Alberta Chapter of the Imperial Order of the Daughters of the Empire between 1924 and 1948. In 1935 she was made a Member of the Order of the British Empire.

Community league complaints regarding ERR service also continued in 1932. There were protests about the long time spent on the streetcars pending construction of the new bridge over Rat Creek. Alderman Baker also was promoting a "scenic driveway" along the top of the river valley on Ada Boulevard, and the league wrote to the mayor in strong support of this initiative. On July 9 a special executive meeting was held at the Davidson Residence to plan a protest to the Edmonton Public School Board's proposal to remove grade 9 classes from the Highlands School. At the end of the year the annual meeting could look back on successfully gaining adequate streetcar services during the rebuilding of the Rat Creek Bridge, gravelling lanes and other routes through the neighbourhood, and cooperating with the city in finding relief for "needy persons in the District." The troubled relationship with the EFCL culminated with a motion to withdraw from that body at the final executive committee meeting held at the Davidson Residence on 25 November 1932.

The league executive committee for 1933 saw Malcolm Macleod returned as president; James Ross as vice-president; Carleton G. Sheldon as second vice-president; M. H. Gilmour as secretary; W. J. Kelly as treasurer; Sam Mc-Cormack, sports committee; A. J. Davidson, local improvements committee; Paul Knepp, grounds and social committees. At the 19 October 1933 annual meeting A. J. Davidson would report community "activities somewhat curtailed owing to depression." This lack of activity was offset somewhat by the even greater interest in sports among young Highlanders. The girl's baseball club placed third in community league competition, with other teams in lawn bowling, basketball, swimming, and football participating enthusiastically as well.

When the league elected a new slate of officers for 1934, it included James A. Ross, president; Carleton G. Sheldon, first vice-president; Malcolm MacLeod, second vice-president; M. H. Gilmour, secretary; W. J. Kelly, treasurer; Sam McCormack, sports committee; A. J. Davidson, local improvements committee; and full time representation on the tennis, bowling, and baseball clubs. The same slate was returned for 1935.

By 1933–1934 the league was largely in the hands of the executive committee, with little other attendance at meetings. Perhaps this was due to the pressing needs imposed on residents by the depression. At the annual meeting in 1933 the membership secretary

Twins Margaret and Fred Husband in their yard in 1934. Photograph courtesy of Margaret Husband.

attributed the low attendance to the effectiveness of the executive committee, since "nobody comes to criticize their work or fight with them." Leonard Humphreys recalled "the days when we had Bees to make boulevards and plant trees. He thought that we should have more Public Meetings to stir up local interest." Still, things remained sluggish during the decade, and if not for the enterprise of the league executive committee, the local ladies' aid societies, and other church groups, little likely would have occurred during these days of economic doldrums.

James Ross reported during the annual meeting at the end of 1934 that "the Depression curtailed our activities considerably and conditions existed both Socially and in business which were of grave anxiety to us all." He suggested a greater effort be made to cooperate with the EFCL in the face of municipal community needs. Ross also successfully suggested that a motion be passed advocating that the city approach provincial and federal governments for grants in lieu of taxes "on the considerable properties operated by them here free of all Taxes." At the same meeting A. J. Davidson reported that little had been accomplished through the civic improvement committee "owing to the lack of money." However, he reported that "gravelling and grading on streets and lanes had been completed where asked for. Trees had been planted all round the Community and School Grounds and were growing." Plans were in place to build a new bowling club house on the existing foundation. So the league could look back on some successes.

The year 1935 was difficult as well, but the league improvement committee could point to more grading and gravelling, especially along 112 Avenue, 61 Street, and 62 Street. "In spite of General Conditions," the league Minute Book reported, "we have gone ahead enlarging our Skating Rink and Tennis Courts, and have helped the Tennis Club to function this Season. The Bowling Club was granted additional ground and they are building another Bowling Green. Other community clubs have done equally well under our patronage."

From 1933 to 1935 virtually no construction occurred in the Highlands. On 4 May 1933 E. T Love received a permit for repairs to his residence at 11108 – 64 Street, to be carried out by the contractors Campbell and McDonald. No permits at all were issued during all of 1934 or 1935.

The community league executive committee for 1936 was made up of James Ross, president; G. H. Van Allen, first vice-president; Carleton G. Sheldon, second vice-president; Malcolm Macleod, third vice-president; Robert Walter Grierson, fourth vice-president; Herbert Baker, fifth vice-president; M. H. Gilmour, secretary; W. J. Kelly, treasurer; S. J. McCormack, sports committee; A. J. Davidson, local improvement committee.

In 1936 Fred John Mitchell received a building permit to build a house on Lot 18 Block 10 or 6128 Jasper (111) Avenue, to be built by F. Schroffel. The city had acquired this lot among many Magrath Holgate properties through tax forfeiture in 1922, and Mitchell purchased it later that year. Mitchell was born in Stratford, Ontario, in 1893, moving to Edmonton in 1914, where he spent the next three decades working in the coal business. Fred Mitchell also remains one of Edmonton's longest serving councillors (1941–1964). He frequently acted as deputy mayor, and took on the responsibilities of mayor for five weeks in 1958 following the resignation of Mayor William Hawrelak. Mitchell lived in this house until his death in 1979.

William Boytzum also obtained a building permit for a garage and alterations to his property on Lot 13 Block 27 (6401 – 118 Avenue) in 1936. Another Highlands landmark also appears to have been completed during 1936, the log house sitting on three corner lots at 11305 – 68 Street. Meanwhile, Highlands and District Community League concerns were mostly focused on further development of the rivertop scenic drive, extra streetcar service, and the need for relief work, especially in the east end of the neighbourhood.

In 1937 Mrs. B. L. Cryderman received a permit for alterations to her house on Lot 3 Block 8 (11135 – 63 Street), to be completed by the contractor J. McKay. This appears to have been the only building activity in the Highlands during that year.

⚒ BUILDING PERMITS

E. T. Love
11108 – 64 Street
"Repairs"

Fred John Mitchell
6128 – 111 Avenue
"Repairs"

The Highlands School Girl's Softball team were successful competitors, seen here on 31 August 1936. City of Edmonton Archives Photo EA-160-1594.

The league Minute Book reported in November 1937 that "The Scenic Drive was now all but completed except for protective fencing, thanks to the persistence of ex Alderman Baker." Old telephone poles were recycled for this protective fencing. James Ross "noticed that in the deep gravel cut in the Scenic Drive, the Volcanic ash, ironstone and petrified wood... made an interesting study," and concluded that "This is possibly the only piece of work done by Relief, which represents some gain to this District."

By 1937 more workers at the packing plants were living in the Highlands. James Ross as president of the community league supported the growing requests for a bus line to join at 83 Street and service the area to the north near these plants. The city later let tenders for three new buses to try out this idea, which met with some success.

Two of the girls' baseball teams, a junior team and a community team, were organized in 1937 and did quite well. The Redheads, the junior team, won the provincial title that year. The community team was not able to complete the season because of a ban necessitated by an outbreak of infantile paralysis. A new bowling green was laid out in 1937.

Several new executive members replaced the old guard on the community league for the year 1938: W. R. Churchill, president; E. Goodenough, first vice-president; E. R. Booker, second vice-president; James Ross, in the new position of past president; G. Bayley, secretary; W. J. Kelly, treasurer; Mrs. T. Wigston, social committee; S. G. McCormack, recreation committee; A. J. Davidson, local improvements committee; M. H. Gilmour, educational committee.

BUILDING PERMITS

Mrs. B. L. Cryderman
11135 - 63 Street
Alterations

⚒ BUILDING PERMITS

Dan Balks
11325 – 57 Street

H. C. Newlands
11129 - 61 Street
Alterations

James H. Thewlin
11120 – 63 Street

John Bank
11324 – 54 Street

George Prudham
11216 – 60 Street
"Repairs"

J. H. Davies
11124 – 63 Street

A. R. Carter
11134 – 63 Street

A. E. Newton
11118 – 61 Street

M. M. Dunsworth
11239 - 63 Street
Addition

William Boytzum
6401 – 118 Avenue
Alterations (cancelled)

At the first executive committee meeting of 1938, reminded of EFCL fees that were in arrears, the Highlands group voted once again to leave the parent body. A few days later this decision was overturned.

During the year concerns about the condition of 112 Avenue surfaced again, especially the need to open up the avenue between 82 Street and 84 Street, and the need for grading between 61 Street and 63 Street, a stretch of road constantly causing concerns for the Highlands residents. The board of commissioners turned down these requests because of lack of funds.

In 1938 more construction took place, notably in the eastern part of the Highlands. On April 19 Dan Balks received a building permit for a dwelling at 11325 – 57 Street. H. C. Newlands then obtained a permit on April 23 for additions and alterations to his house on Lot 3 Block 18 (11129 – 61 Street). Rosana M. Thomas obtained a permit for a garage at her home at 11228 – 64 Street on June 3. James H. Thewlin obtained a permit for a house on Lot 14 Block 1 (11120 – 63 Street) on July 14. John Bonk, who lived in Beverly, received a permit on August 24 for a house on the east part of Lot X (11324 – 54 Street) with "no...sanitary features," and valued at $1,000. George Prudham obtained a permit for repairs to a house on Lot 14 Block 17 (11216 – 60 Street) on September 6. On September 16 A. J. Davidson, who lived at 5650 Ada Boulevard, received a permit for a dairy barn to be built on Lot Y, near 56 Street and Jasper (111) Avenue. Finally that year, on September 28 J. H. Davies obtained a permit for a house on Lot 13 Block 1 (11124 – 63 Street), to be built by the contractor D. N. Hayden.

In 1939 five permits were issued for the Highlands. A. R. Carter, who lived at 11223 – 64 Street, obtained a permit on April 20 to build a house on Lot 11 Block 1 (11134 – 63 Street), to be constructed by R. H. Rae. A. E. Newton was issued a building permit for a house on Lot 11 Block 11 (11118 – 61 Street) on August 11. On September 1, the day war was declared in Britain, M. M. Dunsworth, who lived at 11239 – 63 Street, was issued a permit for an addition to his house. On September 11 William Boytzum received a further permit for alterations to his house on Lot 13 Block 27 (6401 – 118 Avenue). This building permit was later cancelled. With the onset of the Second World War the pace of construction would accelerate, as there was an increased need for housing.

During the 1930s the Highlands Golf Course was established as one of the most significant institutions in the neighbourhood, a position it continues to hold to this day. Development of the course seems to have resisted the general malaise that had an impact on other activities during that period.

Plans for the golf course had been in the works for some time, and things began to take off by 1928. H. H. Parlee addressed the Highlands and District Community League about a proposed golf course for the Highlands at its annual meeting on October 2 that year, observing that some difficulties had arisen over several lots that were under dispute. "However next spring should see the preparation of course underway." The league Minute Book reported over-optimistically "possibly that a few holes will be ready latter part of August."

The Minute Book continued: "Major Pierce, an authority on laying out golf courses, has been consulted – is favorably impressed with site." Plans called for 120 acres of land, a 6,000-foot fairway, and the intention to lay out nine holes on the west end of the links

first, from 66 Street west. The east nine holes were felt to offer more hazards "and would prove discouraging to beginners in the game." It was hoped the course would be open by August 1929, despite the problems with land assembly.

The *Edmonton Journal* reported on November 26 that, following years of negotiations dating back to the early 1920s, the final dispute between the city and what remained of Magrath- Hartt Limited over three blocks in the Highlands had been concluded. Litigation had been threatened several times, although "the final settlement was an amicable one." Commissioner David Mitchell reported that an "involved dispute" between Magrath- Hartt and Magrath-Holgate had been settled. The company finally agreed to quit claim to Blocks

X, Y and Z, some 81 acres, on the Highlands Survey. The city left about 14.27 acres in Block Y with the company, following provision for the extension of Jasper (111) Avenue through the block.

The property dispute dated back to the 1913 collapse, when the property had reverted to Edmonton for tax defaults. However, the company repurchased the land in 1920 for $6,420, $1,250 of which was paid up at the time of sale. When the balance remained unpaid, the city began legal action against the company, while Magrath- Hartt launched a counter claim that the city had encroached upon its previously owned property at Jasper Avenue and 96 Street. The company also charged that the city had allowed sewage to cause damage to its riverbank property. The

The Highlands Golf Course clubhouse as seen in 1946 from the present location of the Wayne Gretzky Drive.
City of Edmonton Archives Photo EA-160-1880.

upshot of this long legal wrangle was that under the 1929 settlement, provision was made for the exchange, "value for value," of eight lots on Block B, Bellevue Survey, "on a hillside," for municipally owned lots elsewhere. This agreement gave the city complete control of property that was at the time under lease to the Highlands Golf Club.

The Highlands club's first lease with the city was for 21 years, with a 20-year option to renew. The lease was quite fair, with no rental payment for the first two years, followed by a lease rate of $6 per acre (only about $408 annually). However, the club was required to expend $20,000 to construct the course and build a clubhouse.

Construction of the Highlands Golf Course commenced during the spring of 1929 around the Premier Coal Mine, which operated between 1920 and 1937. A nine-hole course was completed on the western part of the property that fall. (The eastern nine holes were completed and used during 1931.) The

original nine holes reflected the history and topography of the course: Breakaway, Hillside, Cacanny, Westward Ho, The Plateau, The Toboggan, Tipple, Shorty, and Hame. Mayor A. U. G. Bury, another leading light in the Highlands, turned the first sod in 1929.

Play began during the spring of 1930, under its first board of officers, names very prominent in the early development of the Highlands. H. H. Parlee was the first president; Dr. W. A. Atkinson the first vice-president; W. F. Brown the first secretary-treasurer; George H. Van Allen, R. C. Marshall, and H. L. Humphreys the first directors. Tom Henderson was the first club greens superintendent. One hundred shares were authorized, and the first season's green fees for shareholders were $35 for a shareholder and his wife.

The Men's Club Championship was known as the Parlee Cup during the first season of 1930, with an entrance fee of one dollar, and a qualifying round of eighteen holes. The Ladies' Club Championship was the Van

Allen Cup, while other competitions of that season included the Kirkland Cup (the Men's Handicap Match Play) and the Dr. Atkinson Cup (Ladies' Medal Handicap). The Robert MacDonald Trophy was awarded for the men's novice handicap competition, for men with a handicap of 25 or over. The R. C. Marshall Trophy was for women with a handicap of 30 or over.

During 1932 the Highlands Golf Club saw the inauguration of the President versus the Vice-President teams. Interclub competitions began that year as well as the introduction of mixed foursomes. The Spring Teas at the beginning of each season remained an important part of the Highlands social season, with other more regular Friday gatherings in the clubhouse.

The Highlands opened its larger new clubhouse in 1938, enlarging and refurbishing the original building at a cost of $5,000, a significant sum at the height of the depression. The famous Martell brothers, golfing celebrities in the Highlands and well beyond, helped mark the occasion by defending for the third time their hold on the Challenge Trophy.

The club continued to flourish during the depression years, partly because of its dedicated board and members, and partly due to the presence of Highlands luminaries like the Martells and Head Professional Alex Olynyk.

Louis and Edna Heard moved to the Highlands in 1939, buying their house from A. U. G. Bury in 1946, and residing at 11122 – 62 Street from that year until 1984. Louis Wesley Heard, born in Saskatchewan in 1909, was a former banker and chiropractor who later was elected to represent Beverly constituency for the Social Credit government, a position he held for eighteen years.

Edna became well known for calling on new Highlanders and welcoming them with one of her apple pies. She recalls that the Cozy Corner (11204 – 65 Street) was the teen hangout during this time, mostly patronized by the boys who liked to play cards in the back. No smoking was allowed, though. Pete's Grocery, formerly Stone's Meat Market, "was where everyone dealt." She would phone Pete's for her groceries, have them delivered, and put them on a tab until the end of each month. The Highlands struck her as very like one of the many small towns in which she had lived, with its churches, a plumber, hardware, dress shop, beauty salon, grocery store, bakery, drugstore – "all within easy walking distance." The kids could not buy cigarettes "as everyone knew them." Jamison's Coffee Bar, with its round counter, was another regular neighbourhood hangout from 1947 to 1964.

The Cozy Corner holds a special place in the memories of Highlanders. John Glasgow first opened the spot in 1939 as Johnny's Confectionery, selling it the following year to John W. Eccleston, who renamed it the Cozy Corner. This it remained until sold in 1960, when it became the Tip Top Café. The little gathering spot reopened in 1965 as the Highlands Coffee Shop, after remaining vacant in 1964. Apparently it had also operated briefly as the Tin Ton Café in 1963. In its heyday the Cozy Corner was known affectionately among many Highlanders as Eccy's or the Coz. It became Chickies Antiques in 1997.

Between the world wars, many Edmonton subdivisions were cancelled. The building boom, fuelled by railway and real estate speculation, had left behind a vast urban area, only the core of which had been developed. Following the collapse of world markets in

1929, the Great Depression saw the sale of city land come almost to a complete halt. The city of Edmonton would remain the major landowner until after the Second World War. Even the Highlands saw a substantial number of lots return to the city. By the time hostilities broke out in Europe, Edmonton Real Estate Board membership had declined once again to a mere 46 agents. However, during the Second World War Edmonton grew rapidly and was drawn further into the wider political and economic world. The wartime search for strategic reserves of oil soon would pay off, and the city would enter a new period of prosperity.

Newspapers began carrying more alarming and ominous stories of the rising tide of violence in Europe and Asia during the late 1930s, and many accepted the inevitability of the coming war. On 2 June 1939, King George VI and Queen Elizabeth visited Edmonton, and thousands of men, women, and schoolchildren crowded bleachers along Kingsway Avenue, renamed in honour of the royal visit. Many rightly viewed this Canadian tour as an omen of the impending war. Many of the young people waving a sea of Union Jacks as the royal entourage passed would be called on to make the greatest sacrifice for their country.

12
Life on the Home Front, 1939–1945

Life in Edmonton was largely directed towards the war effort following its outbreak in September 1939. The Prince of Wales Armouries once again became the heart of the city, as a makeshift community of tents and barracks sprang up outside its brick walls to accommodate the thousands of men rushing to join up and serve the country. Thousands of other servicemen would pass through the Manning Depot barracks located at the exhibition grounds. Enid Hart remembers sleeping in the screened porch during the summer and fall, like many Highlanders, and being wakened by newsboys running through the district announcing the outbreak of war in September 1939. Like her neighbours, she had little idea at the time how profoundly the war would affect her life.

Alberta's contribution to the war was significant. Albertans served in every theatre of war in such distinguished units as The Loyal Edmonton Regiment. Although Edmonton was far from the major theatres of war, it played a significant role in the global air war and North American continental defence. The most immediately visible effect came with the British Commonwealth Air Training Plan (BCATP) facilities hastily constructed throughout Alberta to provide the technicians and aircrews needed for the Allied air forces. An Air Observer School and Elementary Flying Training School were established in Edmonton. More importantly for the Highlands, Borden Park became the site of the RCAF Manning Depot, and many men from the Commonwealth were barracked there during training with the BCATP. Enid Hart and Jean Robbie recalled years later that many Saturday night dances were held for the young airmen, and many of the older girls in the Highlands would skip regular Saturday night skating to attend these dances.

At the airport, Aircraft Repair Ltd., later to become Northwest Industries, restored Allied planes damaged during the war, employing many Edmonton men and women. The federal government took over control of the city's airport, Blatchford Field, which was rapidly

Fred Husband playing the trombone. Fred joined the Edmonton School Boys Band at the age of twelve, and played in the School Boys Alumni Band, Lions Big Band, and in a Dixieland band for decades.
Photograph courtesy of Margaret Husband.

deeper role on the home front, while American cultural influences grew more pronounced, partly through the demand among US military personnel and employees of construction companies. The many young men who were in the city training at the British Commonwealth Air Training Plan crowded the cafes and dance floors, jitterbugging and swinging to American big band music. Big bands like the Tommy Dorsey Band inspired many Highland kids like Fred Husband, who played a trombone for the Edmonton School Boys Band, which he had joined just before the war.

During the war years the city grew rapidly, from 90,419 in 1939 to 111,745 in 1945, as it was drawn into the continental and international political and economic world. Most importantly, the wartime search for strategic reserves of oil would soon pay off.

Highlanders would be pinched by wartime constraints like the rest of the country. Many would have to line up at the Safeway store on 112 Avenue with ration coupons for their sugar allocation. But they would also sacrifice more tragically in the loss of boys from the neighbourhood as war casualties. Fred and Edith Pearce lived for many years in the Highlands, raising their family there. When the war came their son Stuart enlisted, and he recalled in a later interview the loss of several of his boyhood friends. His pal Curt Moffat, who had grown up at the family home at 11141 – 63 Street, was a schoolmate who would be killed during his first flight as an air gunner in 1943. Dick Morrison and Rod Matheson, son of Captain Matheson, two neighbours from 67 Street, and Newton Van Allen, were other friends who died during the war. The war seemed to touch everyone. During an interview Enid Hart recalled that her brother

expanded to serve the thousands of Lend-Lease fighters and bombers being ferried to the aid of the Russians through the Northwest Staging Route. A housing shortage developed very quickly, especially after the "friendly invasion" of American personnel in early 1942. Neighbourhoods like the Highlands provided rental space for many wartime visitors. For example, the Davidson Residence divided its second floor into suites, while the family continued to occupy the ground floor. Edmonton, as "the Gateway to the North," became the supply, communications, and transportation centre for the Alaska Highway, Northwest Staging Route, and Canol Pipeline projects. During peak activity, over 33,000 Americans were in Alberta, north-eastern British Columbia, and the Yukon Territory.

Popular culture changed in Edmonton between 1939 and 1945, and these changes were accelerated during the "American occupation" of 1942–1945. Religion seemed to play an even

Ian, who had enlisted in 1940, was killed in the war, as well as Jean Robbie's cousin.

In 1948 Rev. T. R. Davies oversaw the installation of a stained glass window comprised of fragments gathered from bombed churches in Europe as a memorial in the Highlands United Church. The new Highlands Community League Memorial Centre that was finally completed after the war was named to honour "local soldiers who were killed in action in WWII."

Several British children were among the thousands who were evacuated to safe homes throughout the Commonwealth during the war. Enid Hart and Jean Robbie noted that a family named Peeks who lived in the Magrath mansion's carriage house hosted one such young evacuee, and Jean Robbie remembered a little boy from Lancaster living in the house next door to her.

In 1939 the newly married couple Henry and Frances Martell moved into the Magrath carriage house, the former stable. Henry Martell, then with the Edmonton Police Department, and another policeman lived in the carriage house. The Magrath coach house, or carriage house (6229 – 111 Avenue) was designed by E. W. Morehouse when designing the Magrath Mansion, and was designed to complement the mansion. The coach house originally was approached through the mansion's porte-cochere. Harry Cox, the family chauffeur, lived here from 1914 until 1924, after which the Magraths, in less prosperous circumstances, rented the coach house to tenants. Ada Magrath, W. J. Magrath's widow, saw the property revert to the city in 1933.

The interest of community organizations remained focussed on the immediate neighbourhood as the war began. At the annual meeting of the Highlands and District Community League on 26 October 1939, the main concern remained petitions to gain adequate sidewalks, and gravelling on 62 Street. The Highlands Lawn Bowling Club remained active, presenting carnivals in the district to raise funds. While there had been no baseball teams that summer, the hockey team reached the semi-finals. On 11 January 1940 plans for a new and larger community hall were discussed, and these plans would become a subject of much debate. It would be some time after the war ended before such plans could be realized. On 24 April 1940 the league voted to abandon plans for a new hall, and to refurbish the old one after raising it on ten cement blocks. The league voted on 10 April 1940 to incorporate as a society. On 1 November 1940 the formation of the Bellevue Community League was announced, and the Highlands group recommended to the Federation that the boundary between the two be located at the centre of 68 Street. At its final meeting that year it petitioned the ERR for improved service to

An early photograph of the Magrath Mansion, showing the carriage house in the background. Glenbow Archives Photo NC-6-2143.

McLuhan Residence, 1912 11342 – 64 Street. Photo courtesy of Van Tsiclas.

BUILDING PERMITS

A. J. Davidson
5650 Ada Boulevard
Alterations

William A. Allen
11107 – 63 Street
Alterations

May John Bible
11234 - 64 Street

J. H. Merrick
6331 - 111 Avenue

William Husband
11342 – 64 Street
Alterations

A. U. G. Bury
11122 - 62 Street
Alterations

the district on Sundays and holidays. This remained a continuing concern during the war, as the ERR, like other municipal agencies, suffered from lack of funds. In May 1943 the league complained of the "disgraceful condition of the shelter at the end of the Highlands line...." Under president Earle Hay, the league increased its membership considerably during the early war years.

In 1940 several Highlands property owners were issued building permits to alter or repair their homes. Some of these alterations were directly related to the wartime demands for increasingly scarce housing as more people were attracted to the city with its military training facilities and home front industry. A. J. Davidson, for example, undertook alterations to his home at 5650 Ada Boulevard in 1940, and on 24 April 1941 he received another permit for further alterations. During the wartime housing crisis the second floor of the Davidson Residence was divided into suites, with the family occupying the main floor. The appearance of the Davidson house, like several others, changed at this time, as half the veranda was enclosed and the balcony on the second floor was converted to living space.

In April 1940 William A. Allen undertook such alterations to the house on Lot 16 Block 8 (11107 – 63 Street), valued at $1,000. On 25 May John Bible received a permit to build a home and garage on Lot 18 Block 24 (11234 - 64 Street). J. H. Merrick, who lived at 11154 - 66 Street, received a permit to build a house on Lot 2 Block 9 or 6331 Jasper (111) Avenue. William Husband received a permit to carry out a substantial improvement on his house at 11342 - 64 Street in 1940 (later better known as the McLuhan Residence) on September 24.

A. U. G. Bury undertook alterations to his newly purchased home at 11122 - 62 Street, under a permit issued on 14 November 1940. Bury had lived at this location since 1919, renting it for two decades and purchasing it in 1939. He was a very influential political and social influence in the Highlands for many years.

Ambrose Upton Gledstone Bury was born in Ireland in 1869, where he received an MA from Trinity College, Dublin, in 1890. After practicing law in Ireland, he immigrated to Canada, arriving in Edmonton in 1912, and being called to the Alberta bar the following year. He was following his sister Evelyn and her husband Quint Owen, who had come to Edmonton in 1903. Bury had a distinguished political career in Edmonton, serving as an alderman from 1922 until 1925, mayor from 1927 until 1929, Member of Parliament for Edmonton East during 1925–1926 and 1930–1935, and a district court judge from 1935 until 1944. His wife Margaret died in 1946, and he sold his house and moved to Ottawa, where he died in 1951.

The Highlands Golf Course remained very active during the war years, and began to print and distribute the *Highland Golfer* in

The streetcar ride to the Highlands did not always go well. Here the ERR car is wedged into the wye at 78 Street and 112 Avenue, the front heading for 78 Street, and the rear for 112 Avenue.
City of Edmonton Archives Photo EA-160-616.

1939. This newsletter served to inform Highlanders of not only golf competitions, but also curling results, skating events, and ski meets. Lively notes and poems of local interest spiced up the newsletter as well. The Junior Girls Club, the first of its kind in the city, remained popular, as did the women's "swing club," with Professional Henry Shaw giving lessons in all seasons. Alex Olynyk, the head professional, enlisted in 1940, and Muzz Kozak took over his duties until the war ended.

In 1941 the Canadian Ladies Golf Union organized a funding drive to buy a Spitfire for the Allied cause. The sum of $25,000 was required for this, a considerable goal in 1941. Many social events had to be organized by the Highlands Club before the national goal was finally met, and the Spitfire was allocated to fly in the North African theatre of war during 1942.

Mrs. J. Watson won the City of Edmonton Ladies Amateur Championship in 1942. During the "friendly invasion" of American military personnel, many played on the Highlands links. Some recall many offers to build an escalator down to the clubhouse!

In 1941 construction picked up as the war progressed and the demand for housing increased. Coal mining remained an important part of Highlands life, and the little "miner's shack," built in 1941 at 11306 – 50 Street, and still to be seen at this location, is a reminder of this fact. On 26 March Mrs. E. M. Mould received a permit to build a house on Lot 4 Block 9 or 6319 Jasper (111) Avenue, a $5,000 residence to be built by W. A. Sheppard. John Bonk built a garage at 11718 – 54 Street in May, and upgraded another property along 54 Street. On May 15 S. Graham, who lived at 6240 Ada Boulevard, received his permit to

🔨 BUILDING PERMITS

Mrs. E. M. Mould
6319 – 111 Avenue

S. Graham
11134 – 64 Street

J. R. Ash
11130 – 61 Street

Ernie Poole, seen here in 1931, delivered bread in the Highlands and Beverly for McGavin's Bakery.
City of Edmonton Archives Photo EA-160-1451.

BUILDING PERMITS

J. J. Butchart
11121 - 63 Street

J. H. Guenette
11210 - 53 Street

J. A. Taylor
11242 – 61 Street

A. J. Brown
11150 - 64 Street

Mrs. F. E. Gray
11128 – 64 Street

build a house on Lot 25 Block 23 (11134 – 64 Street), built by contractor R. H. Rae. On July 2 J. R. Ash of 11232 – 70 Street received a permit for a house on Lot 9 Block 11 (11130 – 61 Street), designed by architect John Martland, and built by Steve Hrudey, a contractor who would become a major builder in the Highlands. J. J. Butchart, of 11142 – 63 Street, also received a permit for a house on Lot 1 Block 8 (11121 – 63 Street) on August 12. W. J. Sharp (11317 – 63 Street) and S. Ash (11130 – 61 Street) also built garages at their homes, a kind of infill that would become more common as post-war prosperity and availability of cars made garages more attractive.

The community league voted on 7 October 1941 that the Highlands Forty Red Cross Club be accepted into the league as its War Services Club. At a later meeting it was decided to ask the Edmonton Public Library to send the library streetcar out to the Highlands. A new floor was placed in the skating shack

during the winter. A raffle was held to raise some of the funds for hockey team sweaters and stockings. Fred Adby, soon to become a major developer in Edmonton, advanced the money to the league for these uniforms.

In 1942 the housing shortage increased with the influx of wartime military and construction personnel. The east end of the Highlands also saw a bit more building. One unusual permit was issued to J. H. Guenette, of 11142 – 68 Street, for a dwelling and chicken house on half of Block X (11210 – 53 Street). Thomas Cooke of 11249 – 68 Street also obtained a permit for "accessory buildings" on Lots 1–2 Block X (5410 – 112 Avenue). Clearly the undeveloped east end of the Highlands was seeing more development in contravention of the original building restrictions placed on the neighbourhood than ever before. On July 2 J. A. Taylor received his permit to construct a house on Lot 10 Block 12 (11242 – 61 Street); on August 7 A. J. Brown of 11217 – 64

Street obtained a permit to build a dwelling on Lot 23 Block 23 (11150 – 64 Street); on September 25 Mrs. F. E. Gray, of 11305 – 61 Street, received a permit to build a house on Lot 26 Block 23 (11128 – 64 Street), and a garage on 23 November 1943; on November 12 J. W. Brown received a permit to build a house on Lot 12 Block 7 (11228 – 62 Street). The stucco bungalow built in 1942 at 11121 – 64 Street remains a relatively unaltered reminder of the type of houses built in the Highlands during the war.

A mammoth blizzard hit Edmonton in 1942, throwing the entire city into crisis. The schools were closed for two days, and Enid Hart and Jean Robbie remember that both their fathers had to walk downtown to work by following the streetcar tracks. The Edmonton Radial Railway itself was not operating. The United States Army were out with their equipment to help clear the snow, the perfect guests. Despite the turmoil, the horse-drawn milk delivery sleigh still made it into the Highlands.

Horses remained an important part of the Highlands scene at this time, with home deliveries of milk, bread, ice, wood, coal, and sometimes groceries. In the summer kids followed the ice wagon to pick up slivers off the streets. Sleighs were used in the winter, and children loved to ride on the runners whenever they could manage it. Enid Hart remembers a barn located behind her home where draft horses were kept. These horses were put out to pasture on 60 Street, and were a familiar sight in the neighbourhood. They would pull hayrides loaded down with Christmas carollers in the winter. Gradually trucks replaced horses, and one of the first delivery vans was the little green truck in which a Chinese-Canadian grocer delivered fresh vegetables to Highlands doors.

In 1943 substantial alterations were undertaken, some undoubtedly to accommodate more renters. W. Winklaur (11142 – 62 Street, now known as the Humphreys residence) had a thousand dollars of alterations done by H. Thompson in February. Other houses were built at quite low cost, such as that built in April by L. S. M. Bonk (11718 – 54 Street) on part of Block C (5307 – 118 Avenue). D. Mc-Nicoll (11436 – 67 Street) received a permit for a house nearby on Lot 11 Block 22 (11145 – 66 Street). Thomas Cooke (11249 – 68 Street) undertook renovations to the property at 11227 – 68 Street. B. Dancer built another chicken house near his home at 5540 Jasper (111) Avenue. Charles Curtis (11215 – 63 Street) on June 29 hired Charles M. Dean to build a house on Lot 13 Block 3 (11324 – 63 Street); this permit was increased in value in September to reflect a larger residence, while O. G. Kelly, now living at this address, built a garage in March 1945. On July 8 Nick Spachinsky received a permit to a house on Lot 11 Block 7 (11236 – 62 Street). John W. Brown obtained two permits on July 16 to cover all the construction of a house on Lot 2 Block 7 (11209 – 63 Street), with a permit for a significant addition let on December 13. A garage was added in April 1944. The contractor Charles M. Dean obtained a building permit for a dwelling on Lot 4 Block 3 (11323 – 64 Street) on August 10, and a permit for its garage in October. J. L. McIntyre, of 5618 Jasper (111) Avenue, built a substantial house at 5624 Jasper Avenue in August 1943, while L. H. Mase built another at 6325 Jasper Avenue, both constructed by the contractor D. B. McCready. On September 23 George Phillips got his permit for a house on Lot 5 Block 3 (11329 – 64 Street). Elsie Dean arranged to build a house on Lot 18 Block 25

BUILDING PERMITS

J. W. Brown
11228 – 62 Street

L. S. M. Bonk
5307 – 118 Avenue

D. McNicoll
11145 - 66 Street

Thomas Cooke
11227 - 68 Street
Renovation

Charles Curtis
11324 – 63 Street

Nick Spachinsky
11236 – 62 Street

John W. Brown
11209 - 63 Street

Charles M. Dean
11323 – 64 Street

J. L. McIntyre
5624 – 111 Avenue

L. H. Mase
6325 – 111 Avenue

George Phillips
11329 - 64 Street

Elsie Dean
11336 – 64 Street

(11336 – 64 Street) on October 16, and for a garage on October 29. A. Gravelle received his permit for a house on Lot 16 Block 24 (11248 – 64 Street), valued at only $2,000. (A further $1,650 in value was added by permit issued on 26 March 1945.)

The pressure for more housing continued throughout Edmonton during 1944. While housing values were sometimes pushed upward by wartime demands, the old Highlands restrictions had crumbled, and in the east end of the Highlands, E. R. Dunbar built a house valued at only $650 on part of Block Y at 5307 Jasper (111) Avenue in March. On May 6 J. S. Agnew, who lived at 6423 - 112 Avenue, was issued a building permit for a house at 6512 - 111 Avenue valued at $6,000. The war years would see a wide divergence in housing costs in the Highlands.

H. W. Marchment obtained a permit for a house and garage on Lot 19 Block 30 (5658 Ada Boulevard) on 13 May 1944. Also that May the War Services Council obtained a building permit for a dwelling on Lot 23 Block 24 (11204 – 64 Street), designed by Margaret Findlay, architect, and built by C. H. Whitham Ltd. On June 26 J. J. Slamko received his permit for a house on Lot 9 Block 7 (11246 – 62 Street), valued at $3,000. On September 20 H. E. Rowswell obtained a permit for a house on Lot 14 Block 7 (11214 – 62 Street), to be built by R. Vollan. Mrs. H. Coone received her permit to build a house on Block X (5406 – 112 Avenue) later that month, valued at $1,200. James Shea, of 11909 - 58 Street, was issued a permit on October 3 for a dwelling at 11329 – 63 Street, valued at $3,200. A. F. Potter then received a permit for a house on Lot 6 Block 6 (11335 – 63 Street) to be constructed by J. J. Cornwell, and valued at $4,500. A permit was

issued to S. A. Graham on October 27, for a house on Lot 13 Block 30 (5516 Ada Boulevard), valued at $4,500. During 1944 more low cost housing was permitted on the Highlands Survey, while at the same time costs of some housing continued its inflationary push. The Ericksen residence (11234 - 65 Street) was built in 1944. Andrew Ericksen, who lived there from 1944 to 1951, was the founder of Sunburst Motor Coaches.

Dr. H. C. Newlands outlined plans for post-war reconstruction put forward by the Edmonton Federation of Community Leagues at his last annual report to the Highlands and District Community League on 20 October 1944. At the same meeting a council was struck "for the express purpose of providing a sound platform to deal with Juvenile Delinquency and provide facilities for the Teen-Age Young people." The juvenile delinquency issue had become a widespread concern, developing during the war when many parents were absent, or working in war industry. That winter the league put on a moccasin dance at the rink, and planned for the coming season.

In 1945, 34 building permits were issued for projects in the Highlands. While several of these were merely for garages, a growing trend as the war neared its end, many more new houses began to be constructed this year. This trend was particularly evident during that spring. Even garages were growing in value by 1945. K. N. Alton, for example, took out a permit to build a $450 garage at the house at 11243 - 63 Street in March, at about the same time he received his permit to build a house at this address. E. Marsh, who now lived at 11350 - 67 Street, received a permit to build a house on Lot 7 Block 6 (11341 - 63 Street). Ada Boulevard was beginning to see more building activity as well, and William Hannish of 11240 – 65 Street obtained a permit to build a house on Lot 12 Block 30 (5308 Ada Boulevard), to be constructed by the contractor J. A. Boisvert. The contractor R. Eggert also began building a house on Lot 8 Block 18 (11126 – 60 Street) for E. B. Donald, who took out his permit on March 21. L. A. Grove took a permit to build a house on Lot 3 Block 30 or 5617 Jasper (111) Avenue, built by the contractor E. Bernard. R. H. Rae was hired to construct a house for M. Merryweather on Lot 9 Block 18 (11118 – 60 Street), to a permit issued on April 3. On April 18 Mrs. M. Eckert received her permit for a house on Lot 13 Block 18 or 6024 Jasper (111) Avenue. J. A. Price, then living at 11329 – 53 Street, obtained a permit on April 30 to build a house to be constructed by E. B. Killips on Lot 16 Block 17 (11202 – 60 Street).

In February 1945 the Highlands and District Community League organized a carnival event at the skating rink. The evening event included eight races: boys or girls under the age of 10 (one lap), boys or girls under the age of 12 (two laps), boys or girls under the age of 14 (three laps), and boys or girls under the age of 16 (three laps). This was followed by a girls' hockey game, the official opening and the crowning of the carnival queen. Finally there was a grand march of costumed skaters, door prizes, and general skating to Fred Dear's five-piece orchestra.

Victory in Europe Day (VE Day) on 8 May 1945 marked the formal end of hostilities in Europe. During that spring and summer, the growing realization that the world had been fundamentally changed swept through the global community. At the same time, a sense of exhilaration and hopefulness found expression among the returning veterans as they turned

their energy toward post-war reconstruction and civil re-establishment. This change was reflected in a more buoyant atmosphere in the Highlands.

May 1945 was a very busy month in the neighbourhood. L. H. Butler, an employee of Crane Ltd., received a permit to build his house on Lot 6 Block 3 (11335 – 64 Street) on May 2. H. E. Reid was issued a permit to build a house on Lot 1 Block 4 (11403 – 64 Street) on May 3. A. G. Naunton received his permit for a dwelling to be built by J. D. McDearmid on Lot 15 Block 17 (11210 – 60 Street) on May 15. Robert H. Rae Sr., of 6004 Ada Boulevard, received a permit to build a house on the adjacent Lot 11 Block 10 (6008 Ada Boulevard) on May 19. On May 28 William Tomyn was issued his permit for a house to be built by J. Semotiuk on Lot 8 Block 30 or 5517 Jasper (111) Avenue. Edna Bittorf then took out a permit for a dwelling to be constructed by R. Vollan on Lot 14 Block 30 (5524 Ada Boulevard).

L. G. Coutts received a permit to build a small house on Lot 2 Block 4 (11409 – 64 Street) on June 4. Edward Echert arranged to build a house on Lot 6 Block 18 (11132 – 60 Street) on June 21. On August 8 Robert N. Norn received a permit to build a dwelling on Lot 8 Block 1 (11150 – 63 Street). Two days later J. L Richards was issued a permit to build a house on Lot 23 Block 26 (11402 – 64 Street). On August 30 R. S. Gurr arranged to have a house built by M. Iverson on Lot 4 Block 4 (11423 – 64 Street). Victory over Japan Day (VJ Day), 15 August 1945, removed the final wartime concerns for many, and "post-war reconstruction" picked up even more.

Construction remained active in the Highlands as the fall of 1945 approached. On September 4 George A. Mix got his permit to

BUILDING PERMITS

E. B. Donald
11126 - 60 Street

L. A. Grove
5617 – 111 Avenue

M. Merryweather
11118 – 60 Street

Mrs. M. Eckert
6024 – 111 Avenue

J. A. Price
11202 – 60 Street

L. H. Butler
11335 – 64 Street

H. E. Reid
11403 – 64 Street

A. G. Naunton
11210 - 60 Street

Robert H. Rae Sr.
6008 Ada Boulevard

William Tomyn
5517 – 111 Avenue

Edna Bittorf
5524 Ada Boulevard

L. G. Coutts
11409 – 64 Street

Edward Echert
11132 - 60 Street

Robert N. Norn
11150 – 63 Street

J. L. Richards
11402 - 64 Street

R. S. Gurr
11423 - 64 Street

build a house on Lot 6 Block 8 (11145 – 63 Street). Robert Horn received his permit for a house on Lot 1 Block 2 (11205 – 64 Street) on September 12. H. N. Nelson got a permit for a house on September 14, to be built on Lot 17 Block 26 (11440 – 64 Street). On October 24 A. Tunstall, who lived at 6416 – 118 Avenue, obtained his permit for a dwelling to be built by M. Iverson on Lot 18 Block 26 (11436 – 64 Street). On November 15 George Brown Leach was granted a permit to have the contractor Myers build a house on Lot 6 Block 4 (11433 – 64 Street). Finally, Don Titus received a building permit on November 20 to build a house on Lot 16 Block 3 (11304 – 63 Street).

The venerable Edmonton Radial Railway line that had been such an integral part of life in the Highlands from its inception, and part of the negotiations which created it, ended its service at the end of the war. The last run took place on 21 July 1945. This event seemed to signal the end of one phase of Highlands development, and the beginning of another.

13
The Second Boom, 1946–1959

The Highlands began to be developed more energetically toward its north, west, and east margins at the end of the Second World War, and many of the semi-agricultural developments in the eastern part of the community began to disappear during the post-war boom. The Clyde Smith property, owned by an early Edmonton auctioneer, is one such example. His Arts and Crafts-influenced house at 11243 – 58 Street had a barn located behind it, as could be found on many properties in this district. His daughter Frances recalled that her father also had chicken coops, connected by plank sidewalks. Buttercup, the Smith's cow, has entered into neighbourhood lore. She lived in the barn until the area began to be built up. But things were about to change fairly rapidly.

About half the houses in the Highlands were built between 1946 and 1960, according to the 2001 federal census. After the war many homes were built "on spec," with contractors buying lots, often from the city to which they had reverted for tax delinquency. These contractors then would usually build a house and place it on the market. Harvey Gordon was one such custom builder in the Highlands at this time. Vera Rourke, who moved with her family into 11315 – 61 Street in 1946, remembers this as a time when most new buyers were ex-servicemen "with young families and no money." The little one-storey stucco bungalow at 11409 – 63 Street, built in 1950, is a fair example of the homes built at this time. This house remains virtually unchanged today.

In 1946, 38 building permits were issued in the Highlands for new houses or substantial improvements to existing houses. Men living in the neighourhood built many of the residences in the immediate post-war years. Ralph Vollan, for example, built houses for G. Rowswell at 11240 – 63 Street and F. W. Chalmers at 6121 Jasper (111) Avenue, as well as another at 5509 Jasper Avenue. These were the first of many.

Peter Sturko also began considerable construction in the Highlands at this time. In 1946 he built a house for D. B. Nisbet at 11422 – 63 Street and E. Ward at 11246 – 61 Street.

⚒ BUILDING PERMITS

G. Rowswell
11240 – 63 Street

F. W. Chalmers
6121 – 111 Avenue

D. B. Nesbitt
11422 – 63 Street

E. Ward
11246 – 61 Street

Peter William Sturko, born 13 July 1901, married Pearl Sarah Borchert, who died in 1945, and later married his second wife Ella. He had been a member of the Highlands Baptist Church at 55 Street and 112 Avenue. Sturko would die at his home at 11114 – 65 Street on 27 August 1971, having left a permanent legacy of houses in the Highlands.

Other notable Highlanders built new houses in 1946. Henry and F. S. Martell, 6205 Jasper (111) Avenue, were issued a permit to build a house on Lot 2 Block 10 (11227 – 61 Street) on April 24. The Martells also completed a garage there in November 1949. Frances Martell, Henry's wife, recalls how the house was built. Brothers Henry and Herbert built the house themselves. Frances drew up the plans on 42 X 30 graph paper, and this was the blueprint accepted by the city. Henry redrew the plans "neater" before construction began. The Martells were friends of Allan McBain, and they received a good rate on building materials. It cost $35 to hire a bulldozer to prepare the basement excavation. The basement at first had a dirt floor that was finished later. Construction commenced in April 1946. They borrowed $4,000 from Herman Martell to finish the house, and moved in on Halloween. Like many other post-war Highlanders, the Martells took in boarders at their new home.

The Highlands and District Community League also finally took out a permit for the long-delayed alterations to its hall on Lots 2–5 Block 13 (11327 – 62 Street) on May 17. Fred Adby was the contractor for this project. Long-time Highlander Stuart Pearce recalls that Adby was well known in the neighbourhood as a go-getter during the war, when he started a second-hand business with an old truck, later buying up gravel lots and selling it to the Americans during the wartime construction boom. Adby Construction would become much larger in the coming years.

The community league hall was a popular focus for the Highlands during the 1950s. The old hall had been taken down, and a new one with change rooms, a members' lounge, and caretaker's residence upstairs was completed between 1954 and 1957. Ted Reynolds, who was the hall rental agent after 1953, recalls the teen parties, which attracted hundreds to the Starlight Club events. Weddings were very common as well. Sometimes the party spilled out onto the community league grounds, with scuffles, drinking, and running through residential yards, which caused a bit of local consternation.

By the 1950s tennis and skating were no longer under the direct control of the community league. However, winter carnivals would take over in a big way, with their carnival queens, figure skating shows, and booths and games held in the hall. The carnival queen was selected simply on the basis of the most tickets of support sold as a fundraiser. On Friday nights, into the 1960s, local bands like Willy and the Walkers, The Nomads, and The Rebels would entertain teenage patrons from across the city.

Vera Rourke remembered in later years that the community hall was a sort of combination YMCA and YWCA with its well-trained leadership. Ninety children attended the Highlands Playschool just after the war, and before the advent of kindergarten in Edmonton. The Highlands Playschool seems to have been an inspiration for the kindergarten movement in Edmonton, a necessary response to the rising tide of the baby boom. Children of all ages shared dance programs, gymnastics, and arts and crafts. Eve Henderson, known for her radio and television presence, started a seniors' program similar to the Lions' Club. The Highlands playground also had a director to organize daily programs. Vera recalls Bette Anderson in particular, the director in the early 1950s, who started Children's Theatre in Edmonton under the Edmonton Junior League. The Highlands saw parades to open the playground, hot dog booths at the exhibition each year, bingos for a turkey at Christmas, and a ham at Easter. She feels that the hall was used daily by at least a hundred people in the 1950s.

The business district along 112 Avenue extended much further east into the Bellevue Addition during the early post-war years. Very shortly after the war 112 Avenue was finally paved, upgraded from the gravel, dirt, and cinders, with the ERR rails running down the centre, which had vexed Highlanders for decades.

Bob Bills and his son Gary later recalled that this western section had its own life, now disappeared since the completion of the Capilano Freeway bisected it in the late 1960s following a decision to cross the river at 66 Street rather than 50 Street. The Johnson brothers first opened a service station near Dan's Grocery in 1945, but they sold it to Bob Bills in 1947. Bills remembered that Dave Adams, a long-time Highlander, was his first customer and he remained faithful to the Esso station for years. Bob Bills described the business strip along 112 Avenue west of the Highlands when he started his business as including a barbershop and drugstore near his station, as well as Dan's Grocery. Other businesses he recalled were Quilley's Polar Bar, an ice cream and milkshake emporium, Quist's Meat Market, which later became Bellevue Grocery, and a

bank branch built shortly after the war. A Shell station also was located across 112 Avenue diagonally from Bills Service, and Highlands Motors, a Texaco station, at 70 Street. The Highlands, strictly speaking, did not get its own station until North Star opened one in 1959. He also recalled many small houses built in the Bellevue Addition by miners working in the east-end mines. This busy commercial section has now disappeared, and would have been where the bridge across the Capilano Freeway currently runs.

During the 1950s several businesses appeared further east along 112 Avenue west of 53 Street. Many of these were regularly patronized by Highlanders during the 1950s and 1960s. Barbara's Ready to Wear started at 5335 – 112 Avenue in 1953; this became Duke's Beauty and Barber (1955), Mount Royal Drug Store (1956–1959), Wally's Super Market (1960) and Mount Royal Grocery (1960–1962). Next door at 5335a – 112 Avenue the Mount Royal Milk Bar opened in 1952; this became Joe's Snack Bar (1953–1954), Lott's Snack Bar (1955), Mount Royal Snack Bar (1956–1958), Mount Royal Café (1959), Sammy's Lunch (1960), and Inga's Beauty Lounge (1962–1964). On the same block the Piggly Wiggly grocery opened at 5339 – 112 Avenue in 1952; this became Tetreau's Super Market (1953), Happy's Meat Market (1954), Mount Royal Super Market (1955–1956), Wally's Royal Super Market (1957–1959), Vic's Super Drugs and Post Office (1960–1961), Vic's Patent Medicine and Cosmetics (1962) and Mount Royal Grocery (1963–1964).

In 1947, 54 building permits were issued in the Highlands, mostly for new houses, with several additions to existing houses. A diverse group of builders now was working

BUILDING PERMITS

J. Eastwood
11308 – 62 Street

Jasper Construction
Company
11344 – 63 Street

R. H. Rae
6012 Ada Boulevard

Leo Herder
11328 - 62 Street

Clifford Jones
11430 – 62 Street

Stewart Graham
5516 Ada Boulevard

William Aiken
11346 - 64 Street

Harold Sumison
11303 – 65 Street

Jim and Mary Parris
11307 – 65 Street

Leo Herder
Lot 3, Block 25

W. F. Brown
6202 – 111 Avenue

M. Milne
6115 Jasper Avenue

J. McLeod
5502 Ada Boulevard

Fred Adby
6210 Jasper Avenue

J. J. Millan
11207 - 60 Street

Steve Hrudey
Construction
13 permits on 57/58 St.

Peter Sturko
9 permits on 60/61 St.

in the district. C. H. Whitham, one of the larger city contractors, would build a house for J. Eastwood at 11308 - 62 Street; Eastwood later would add a substantial improvement to the house using a permit issued 24 May 1955. The Jasper Construction Company also would build a house at 11344 - 63 Street at this time. R. H. Rae, who would become one of the major developers in the city and in the Highlands continued to build houses as well, including the house at 6012 Ada Boulevard. Residents like Leo Herder (11158 - 65 Street) continued to develop properties in the Highlands, such as the house at 11328 - 62 Street. Clifford Jones built a house at 11430 - 62 Street, with cedar shakes specified in the building permit. Modern International Style-influenced homes, such at the one built in 1947 at 11445 - 64 Street, were beginning to appear in the district as well as the Stewart Graham house at 5516 Ada Boulevard.

John Duke reports that Ralph Vollan Construction built a house for grandparents William T. Aiken and his wife Sarah at 11346 - 64 Street; William Aiken retired as chairman of the Highway Traffic Board in August 1947 and moved into his new house that same month. Peter Green bought the house and moved into it with his mother in August 1973, living there for many more years. John Duke also indicates that the three lots operated as a market garden on 65 Street were sold and built one during the 1940s. Harold Sumison built and occupied a house at 11303 - 65 Street in 1942. Jim and Mary Parris built on 11307 - 65 Street in 1946, and occupied that address for many years. Leo Herder, the neighbourhood developer who lived at 11158 - 65 Street then built a small, stuccoed residence on Lot 3 Block 25 to a permit issued on 23 September 1947. Norman

and Marion Arnold moved in during December 1947; he worked for Alberta Government Telephones. The house was sold to Harry and Olive Duke in 1957; they occupied this house until selling it to John and Betty-Jean Duke in 1959. The house was sold to Derek and Ethel Kirby in 1965, and to Daniel and Helen Demchuk in 1968.

Local developers continued to build in the neighbourhood, for example, W. F. Brown (11150 - 64 Street), who constructed a large house at 6202 Jasper (111) Avenue that spring, and Ralph Vollan who built a house for M. Milne at 6115 Jasper Avenue and J. McLeod at 5502 Ada Boulevard, valued at $13,000. Fred Adby (11742 - 66 Street) also built houses at 6210 Jasper Avenue, and another for J. J. Millan at 11207 - 60 Street. Despite efforts to keep the value of houses up in the Highlands, several less expensive houses were built in the eastern part of the district. For example, a permit for a house located at 11209 - 54 Street valued at $1,500 was issued on September 19. The east of the Highlands was becoming a district with a distinct mixture of housing styles and values.

Two developers were prominent in the Highlands during 1947. Steve Hrudey Construction (11018 - 76 Street) took out its first thirteen building permits for houses in the district on 13 June 1947. These were located north of 112 Avenue on 57 Street and 58 Street, as well as a house at 11206 - 57 Street. Peter Sturko, then living at 11202 - 68 Street, also constructed nine more houses north of 113 Avenue on 60 Street and 61 Street, most of them during that summer.

As the veterans returned during the decade between 1947 and 1957, Edmonton's population and average personal income doubled.

Between 1947 and 1960, seven annexations were added to Edmonton. As the city amalgamated new districts, services struggled to keep pace with the rapid development, including the north and east sections of the Highlands. Many streets and sidewalks remained unpaved for some time in the suburban sprawl moving rapidly outward from the city centre, echoing the experiences of suburban districts during the first building boom. The discovery of oil on 13 February 1947 ushered in Edmonton's long-awaited second boom. When Imperial Oil Leduc #1 blew in amidst much fanfare, it set in motion developments continuing to this day.

More Highlanders worked in the oil industry or its related businesses at this time. Bob Bills, who later opened his service station in Bellevue, was an Imperial Oil employee who had been transferred to Edmonton from Moose Jaw in 1945 to work as a geological cartographer with the team that brought in the Leduc well. Maxwell and Doris Peacock, who moved into 11108 – 64 Street, the house built by W. F. Brown in 1927 (E. T. Love's house during the 1930s), were transferred from Calgary to Edmonton in January 1948 to work for a law firm deeply involved with Imperial Oil in assembling the land for the first refinery in Strathcona County. Their neighbours the Coulthards also were a family whose breadwinner worked for Imperial Oil.

During 1948, 84 building permits were issued for dwellings and business premises, including the first apartment buildings in the district since construction of the Gibbard Block. Developers descended upon the Highlands even more energetically than during the first building boom, which had been prematurely cut short by the financial crunch of 1913. This

Lucien J. Belanger, who worked for Northwest Utilities, and his wife Irene, purchased the Peter Sturko-constructed house at 11227-56 Street about 1948.
City of Edmonton Archives Photo EA-64-54.

time, the new oil economy promised a longer run of prosperity. Businesses that would become household names began to show up on the scene. Nu-West Homes received a permit to build a house at 11414 – 62 Street. K & D Ltd. built a house at 11115 – 60 Street. W. F. Brown, still active in real estate development, received his permit to build a house at 6007 Jasper (111) Avenue. Ralph Vollan built other large houses at 5525 Jasper Avenue and 5660 Ada Boulevard. Leo Herder also took out a permit for a house at 11211 – 58 Street on May 31, for another at 11138 – 61 Street on September 3, and a third at 11408 – 62 Street on November 5. George Basiuk, of 6403 – 118 Avenue, received a permit on May 19 to build a small barbershop and dwelling on Lot 12 Block 27 (6411 – 118 Avenue).

But the real action rested with a few serious developers. Peter Sturko was issued a permit for a house at 11333 – 61 Street on April 6. Then on May 19 he took out eleven permits for houses north of 111 Avenue on 56 Street and 57 Street. On June 28 Steve Hrudey received seventeen permits for homes north of 112 Avenue and 113 Avenue on 57 Street and

⚒ BUILDING PERMITS
Nu-West Homes 11414 - 62 Street
K & D Ltd. 11115 - 60 Street
W. F. Brown 6007 – 111 Avenue
Ralph Vollan 5525 - 111 Avenue 5660 Ada Bouleard
Leo Herder 11211 - 58 Street 11138 – 61 Street 11408 – 62 Street
George Basiuk 6411 – 118 Avenue
Peter Sturko 11333 – 61 Street, plus 11 homes on 56/57 St.
Steve Hrudey 11303 – 58 Street 17 homes on 57/58 St.

BUILDING PERMITS

Larry I. Peers
10 homes on 60 Street
11306 – 60 Street

Municipal Construction
8 homes on 58 Street

Bruce McClean
11323 – 60 Street

P. Ripley
4 apartment buildings at
118 Avenue and 57 Street

58 Street. Hrudey also took out a permit for a house at 11303 – 58 Street on September 15. Larry I. Peers entered into development of the Highlands in 1948, taking out ten building permits for houses north of 113 Avenue on both sides of 60 Street on July 7, and another at 11306 – 60 Street on November 5. Municipal Construction was issued a further eight permits on 15 July 1948, for houses north of 113 Avenue along 58 Street.

Bruce McClean, a veteran discharged from the Royal Canadian Navy Volunteer Reserve in 1946, moved to the Highlands that June to visit his brother-in-law Ken Mackenzie. In 1948 Larry Peers built a house for the McCleans at 11323 – 60 Street, part of the substantial development stretching north along that street from 112 Avenue to 118 Avenue. Houses were being built at such a hectic rate that although Peers told McClean that he could move into the new house on December 1, construction was not yet completed by that date. Apparently the family moved in anyway and caught up later. McClean recalls that their friends kidded them about moving out to the country. The only house between 60 Street and Beverly he can remember was the Wheeler house on 58 Street.

Several innovative houses were built along 67 Street during 1948. Among those that remain substantially unchanged are the three attached flat-roofed buildings on 113 Avenue and 67 Street, the flat-roofed house at 11326 – 67 Street with its eclectic design features, and another flat-roofed house at 11328 – 67 Street.

Strathearn Heights and the Bel-Air Apartments defined a new lifestyle as people flocked to the city during the post-war years, raising their new families in moderately priced accommodation offered by apartment blocks. The Highlands at this time saw its first such

simple apartment blocks, as opposed to the more substantial apartments exemplified by the Gibbard Block. P. Ripley was issued four building permits to construct four 4-suite apartment blocks at 118 Avenue and 57 Street on 17 August 1948.

Several new businesses appeared along 112 Avenue after the war. Jamison's Coffee Bar opened in 1947 at 6417 – 112 Avenue. The Highland Hardware (6421 – 112 Avenue) opened in 1948, operating at this location until 1964. A taxi service also briefly moved in next to Stone's Meats (6507 – 112 Avenue) during 1948, where a series of grocery stores had operated since 1931.

"The Highlands, long a fine but lightly built up area, has developed fastest of any city district," the *Edmonton Bulletin* reported on 12 June 1948. "And its homes compare favourably with any in the city for variety, quality and design," the article continued, describing what was occurring in the Highlands as a boom. "A market garden was thrown open to Highlands housing last year, and this week the last two lots were up for sale for $1,000 each. Ten years ago the whole large garden site could have been bought for a like amount."

More veterans began to take up residence in the Highlands. For example, Stuart Pearce was a Highlander who returned to his old childhood neighbourhood after serving overseas during the war. He met his wife, Ethel Larkin, while she was working at the service canteen in Tholthorpe, Yorkshire. They were married, and Ethel came to Canada as a war bride on the *Aquitania* nine months after her husband had been returned on the same ship. By 1948 Stuart was hoping to return to the Highlands, where he had been raised. He describes all the land from 111 Avenue (named

Jasper Avenue until 1949) between 66 Street and 67 Street, as far as Ada Boulevard, as vacant in 1948. He bought a lot from the city for $400, minus 20 percent for returning veterans, and five percent for cash payment. Lots on Ada Boulevard at this time were only $500. He then built a house at 6611 – 111 Avenue, in which the family lived until 1953. His neighbour Robert Grierson bought an adjoining lot, and the two men built the two-bedroom bungalow together that summer, completing it in September. Many post-war houses were self-built, in keeping with a longstanding tradition in the development of Edmonton residential districts.

Acting City Engineer J. D. A. Macdonald reported to the board of city commissioners in February 1949 that several changes would soon be made to street names in the Highlands. "For some time there has been confusion regarding certain street names in the Highlands District," he reported, "and to clarify this we have recently circularized the owners affected and the results of a mail ballot show that there is overwhelming favor (sic) to changing street names...." On 17 April 1949 new street signs indicated that the roadway named Jasper Avenue between 53 Street and the lane west of 71 Street would be named 111 Avenue. Also, the roadway previously known as Jasper Avenue between 69 Street and 75 Street would be known as Ada Boulevard.

The year 1949 saw even more growth in the Highlands, with house prices beginning to escalate throughout the neighbourhood. Adby Construction completed a house valued at $9,000 at 11430 – 63 Street that November. D. Karvellas built another at 6250 Ada Boulevard valued at $10,000. Such projects were beginning to set the normal values in the district.

Steve Hrudey took out 23 building permits on 24 March 1949, for houses north of 112 Avenue along 56 Street and 57 Street, evaluated between $7,500 and $8,800. This block of residences was completed by November. One of these houses belonged to Frank and Jean Southam. Frank worked for Huron and Erie (later Canada Trust). Their daughter is Betty-Jean Duke, who married John Duke. They moved into the house in October 1949, until May 1959 when Frank Southam was transferred to Calgary. Stanley Uren, with Molstad and Company, then purchased it, living there until 1965. Ron Kryviak, a technician with Sherritt Gordon Mines, then occupied the house in 1967. On 4 October 1949 Hrudey received permits to build an additional thirteen houses north of 113 Avenue along the west side of 56 Street and the east side of 57 Street. On August 9 Peter Sturko was issued building permits for eleven houses north of 111 Avenue along the west side of 55 Street and the east side of 56 Street.

Several other interesting residences were built in the Highlands in 1949. The architect J. B. Turner designed a residence for C. D. MacGillivary at 6226 Ada Boulevard, constructed to a permit issued on March 31. J. Fekete, who would soon become a force in Edmonton residential development, built his first houses in the Highlands at 6220 – 111 Avenue, and at 11346 – 69 Street, for K. Schickle. L. I Peers (11223 – 61 Street) also built another dwelling at 11302 – 60 Street. H. Ward (11525 – 65 Street) built another house in the neighbourhood at 6111 – 111 Avenue, valued at $12,000. John Hyde built a house at 11441 – 63 Street. A. Traynor raised a new house at 5318 Ada Boulevard, and Ralph Vollan built another modest house at

BUILDING PERMITS

Stuart Pearce
6611 – 111 Avenue

Adby Construction
11430 – 63 Street

D. Karvellas
6250 Ada Boulevard

Steve Hrudey Construction
36 permits on 56/57 St.

Peter Starko
11 permits on 55/56 St.

C. D. MacGillivary
6226 Ada Bouleard

J. Fekete
6220 – 111 Avenue

K. Schickle
11346 – 69 Street

L. I. Peers
11302 – 60 Street

H. Ward
6111 - 111 Avenue

John Hyde
11441 – 63 Street

A. Traynor
5318 Ada Boulevard

Ralph Vollan
5532 Ada Boulevard

5532 Ada Boulevard, completed by November 1949.

Commercial development was growing along 112 Avenue and 118 Avenue, and the Karpetz Brothers undertook a large renovation to the radio store on 118 Avenue and 64 Street, while H. Saik (11135 – 62 Street) was issued a permit to build a store at 11336/11138 – 58 Street; the store seems to have opened by January 1950. C. H. Whitham also built a regulatory station for Northwestern Utilities at 5815 – 118 Avenue, completed by November 1949.

Construction had felt the drastic effects of the financial brakes being applied in the Highlands during the interwar years, as had been the case throughout Edmonton. In 1945 the City Charter was amended (Section 533) to deal with some of the housing left over from this slack period. Outstanding examples of such conditions include three homes that Felix X Frederickson, who lived at 11342 – 67 Street, began on that street during 1937. These flat-roofed bungalows still had not been completed by November 1950. The unfinished dwellings – 11322 – 67 Street, 11326 – 67 Street, and 11328 – 67 Street (Lots 22–24 Block 10 Bellevue Addition) – were becoming a matter of concern to neighbours, and W. R. Nicoll (11330 – 67 Street) took up a petition to the board of city commissioners and city council on November 27, noting that the houses were dilapidated and apt to depreciate the value of adjacent properties. Nicoll, constructing a house just to the north of 11328 – 67 Street, was denied a loan because the Frederickson properties supposedly posed a fire hazard, since the three were joined by a common arched façade, still covered in bare unstuccoed building paper and wood lath, as were the

interiors of two of the unoccupied houses. The only occupied dwelling was 11322 – 67 Street, where R. Poff, Frederickson's daughter, and son-in-law, lived.

Dr. Jerry Cotter, a second-generation Highlander, and his wife Laurie Parkhill recalled that some things had not changed a great deal in the Highlands just after the war. George and Florence Cotter took up residence on Ada Boulevard in July 1950, and Jerry recalled watching the harvest in the wheat fields across the river during the autumn.

The Highlands was, in 1950, the eastern edge of Edmonton. The transit ended at the 60th Street and 112 Avenue turnabout. At that time the milk delivery came by horse drawn enclosed wagons.... The horses wore blankets and ear protection in the cold weather and had feed bags provided at meal time. They had the best of care and loved their work!

With the advent of the Fifties, the boom continued unabated. In 1950, 70 building permits were issued for the Highlands. The development pattern remained the same, with neighbourhood builders continuing to provide some of the growth as they built a house here, a house there. Larger developers, intent on riding the regional wave of prosperity, continued to build contiguous tracts of houses. Many garages were built that year as residents began to turn away from the Edmonton Transit Service and drive their own cars.

In April 1950 Peter Sturko began the construction of three houses north of 111 Avenue on the west side of 55 Street, as well as at 5504 – 111 Avenue and 5512 – 111 Avenue in May, at 11429 – 65 Street in June, and at 11125 – 55 Street in November. Steve Hrudey began work in the same area in April, taking out permits for 21 houses filling the block north of 112 Avenue along the west side of 55 Street and the east side of 56 Street. In August Hrudey Construction received its permit to build a house on the corner lot at 11202 – 55 Street, finishing that block of residences. At the same time he built on the corner lot at 11203 – 56 Street, followed by a permit in December to build at 11218 – 56 Street, completing that block. R. H. Rae and Sons built three new houses west of 53 Street on the south side of 111 Avenue to permits issued on May 15. Tom Cooke was issued building permits for houses at 11142 – 56 Street and 11249 – 68 Street in May and June.

The east end of Highlands continued to fill up in 1950. J. H. Hutton was issued a permit to build a house at 5603 – 111 Avenue; M. Demchuk for a house at 11139 – 56 Street; P. Philip for a house at 5321 – 111 Avenue; R. Brunlees for a house at 5337 – 111 Avenue; E. J. New for a house at 5317 – 111 Avenue; and M. Peroz for a house at 5325 – 111 Avenue. F. Frederickson also was contracted to build a house for T. E. Pinch at 5334 Ada Boulevard in October 1950.

Several new residences appeared on Ada Boulevard as well. W. E. James decided to build on Lot 14 Block 10 (6110 Ada Boulevard) in May. G. and L. C. Cotter received a permit to build their house on Lot 15 Block 30 (5528 Ada Boulevard), to be constructed by A. Anderson. Valued at $17,000, this residence signalled the beginning of somewhat more imposing homes built along the eastern stretch of Ada Boulevard.

The second building boom in the Highlands was slowing a bit by 1951. Much of the northern, eastern, and western periphery of the original Old Highlands was filling up.

The packing plants along the northern boundary of The Highlands played an important role in its development. This aerial view from October 1932 shows the meatpacking complex. City of Edmonton Archives Photo EA-160-1313.

Many of the new residents worked for the expanding packing plants just to the north of the neighbourhood. Harold Jaqes, who moved to Edmonton as Swift's credit manager in 1951, bought a house in the Highlands, where many other company employees lived. He remembers that the Highlands was "well developed and there were no vacant lots." As an indication of the importance of the packing plants to the Highlands, Jaqes recalled nineteen neighbours who worked for Swift's. These included Charlie Bohannan, transportation; Elmer Burns; Archie Chorley, dairy and poultry; Don Cormack, provision department (pork); Peter Farr; Murray Greenfree, master mechanic; Bill Hodgkinson, assistant controller; Bob Jackson, buyer; Claire Malcolm, superintendent; Harvey Marples; John Peter, general manager; Gordon Price, controller; Mrs. Rydeham, superintendent; Vic Sands, purchasing agent; Les Spalding, controller; Alex Symington, killing floor foreman; Jack Thomas, personnel; Bob White; and Harry Young, purchasing agent.

The Highlands Golf Club became even more active during the prosperous 1950s. Harold Jaqes recalls that after moving into the Highlands in 1951 he began starting his day with a 5:30 round with a group of regulars. Jaques, Charlie Rietsma, Johnny Segati, and

⚒ BUILDING PERMITS

Steve Hrudey Construction
11203 – 56 Street
11218 – 56 Street

R. H. Rae and Sons
3 homes on 111 Avenue

Tom Cook
11142 - 56 Street
11249 – 68 Street

J. H. Hutton
5603 - 111 Avenue

M. Demchuk
11139 - 56 Street

P. Philip
5321 – 111 Avenue

R. Brnlees
5337 – 111 Avenue

E. J. New
5317 - 111 Abenue

M. Peroz
5325 - 111 Avenue

T. E. Pinch
5334 Ada Boulevard

W. E. James
6110 Ada Boulevard

G. and F. Cotter
5528 Ada Boulevard

K. Chernichan
11235 – 61 Street

E. Maloney
5304 Ada Boulevard

M. Dunsworth
11239 – 63 Street

D. J. Lavender
11408 – 68 Street

K. Maslowski
7417 - 111 Avenue

Peter Sturko
5516 – 111 Avenue

Demchuk store and
apartment
6419 - 112 Avenue

Dr. Dorsey
5322 – 111 Avenue

L. Buray & Sons Stores
5335/5339 – 112 Avenue

Peter Sturko
5358 – 111 Avenue
5352 – 111 Avenue

M. Hewko
11307 – 56 Street

W. Kent
11302 – 55 Street

F. Steperyk
6002 – 111 Avenue

P. Ashton
11203 - 56 Street

Leo Herder
11306/11322 – 55 Street

Highlands Baptist Church
5351 – 112 Street

C. Rolf
5322 Ada Boulevard

Val Berg formed a group that would golf and share breakfast each day. Other such groups bonded neighbours together in special ways.

In 1951, 21 building permits were issued for the Highlands. During February 1951 K. Chernichan was issued a permit to build a house at 11235 - 61 Street, and E. Maloney for a house at 5304 Ada Boulevard. In April M. Dunsworth was issued a permit for a house at 11239 - 63 Street, D. J. Lavender for a house at 11408 - 68 Street, K. Maslowski for a dwelling at 7417 - 111 Avenue, and Peter Sturko for a house at 5516 - 111 Avenue. During May the Demchuks, who lived at 11305 - 61 Street, received a permit for a store and apartment at 6419 - 112 Avenue, designed and built by G. Flak. The Highlands Barber Shop opened here in 1953, the Highlands Studios in 1954, Airview Photos in 1954–1955, the Highlands Beauty Salon in 1955, and Paula's Beauty Salon and Highlands Barber Shop from 1955 until 1964. Victoria's Studio and Camera seems to have shared this address in 1957, while Meyer's Studio appears in city directories between 1958 and 1961.

In May 1951 Dr. Dorsey (6703 - 111 Avenue) was issued a permit for a residence located at 5322 - 111 Avenue. During the same month L. Buray & Sons took out a permit to build stores located at 5335/5339 - 112 Avenue, designed by Dewar, Stevenson, and Stanley. Peter Sturko built two houses at 5358 - 111 Avenue and 5352 - 111 Avenue in June and July. M. Hewko of 11212 - 62 Street also took out a permit for a house at 11307 - 56 Street in July. W. Kent received his permit for a house at 11302 - 55 Street in August. During September F. Steperyk (11245 - 66 Street) got his permit to build a dwelling at 6002 - 111 Avenue, and P. Ashton (11310 - 58 Street) for a house

at 11203 - 56 Street. Leo Herder decided to build two new houses in October, at 11306 - 55 Street and 11322 - 55 Street.

The Highlands Baptist Church was issued a building permit to build a new church hall on Lot 26 Block 36 (5351 - 112 Street) on 2 October 1951. Peter Sturko was the contractor selected to build the new hall.

There were 26 building permits issued in the Highlands during 1952. During March, C. Rolf was issued a permit for a house at 5322 Ada Boulevard, and W. W. Butchart for a house at 5316 Ada Boulevard. Houses were also built during April at 11315 - 56 Street, and at 11311 - 56 Street. During April G. Sherwin (11329 - 63 Street) also was issued a permit for a house at 5333 - 111 Avenue. In May Peter Sturko (5512 - 111 Avenue) received a permit to build a house at 5343 - 112 Avenue, and another at 11107 - 55 Street; A. Hneidan (5308 - 111 Avenue) for a house at 5328 - 111 Avenue; S. P. Reynolds (11318 - 67 Street) for a house at 11332 - 62 Street; V. Belland for a house at 11319 - 56 Street; and A. Rebus for a house at 11219 - 58 Street. During June, P. Stuparyk took out a permit for a dwelling at 11314 - 55 Street, and Peter Sturko for a house at 11107 - 55 Street. During August, J. R. Peach took out a permit to build "upstairs rooms" for his residence at 11322 - 56 Street, while W. Kent indicated the need for a $5,000 adjustment to the dwelling at 11302 - 55 Street, and W. Bank (5307 - 118 Avenue) received a permit for a new house at 11328 - 53 Street. Three houses appear to have been started in September, with permits issued to Peter Sturko for a house at 5339 - 112 Avenue, to J. Bonk (11718 - 54 Street) for a house at 11324 - 53 Street, and to William Krank (11212 - 70 Street) for a house at 11326 - 55

Street. Finally, G. Jamison (living at 6417 – 112 Avenue, the address of Jamison's Coffee Bar) was issued a permit for a house located at 11103 – 54 Street in October 1952.

Another twenty building permits were issued in the Highlands during 1953. Steve Hrudey Construction built two 2-suite apartment buildings on Block 26A during that summer, at 5607 – 118 Avenue, and 5615 – 118 Avenue. In March, J. Kulmatyski (11942 – 62 Street) received a permit to build a house at 11223 – 53 Street, and N. Suprovich for a house at 5311 – 112 Avenue. During May J. Fleese (11311 – 56 Street) was issued a permit for a dwelling located at 11329 – 61 Street; P. Koroluk (7555 – 112 Avenue) for a dwelling and garage at 11133 – 60 Street; and Peter Sturko for a house at 11247 – 58 Street. In June, E. Tingstad was issued a permit for a residence at 11112 – 62 Street; Dr. D. Russell for a dwelling and garage at 5521 – 111 Avenue; and R. H. Mundy (11203 – 61 Street) for a house at 11128 – 53 Street. Permits were let out for four houses in July: to V. McDonald for 6023 – 111 Avenue and to Peter Sturko for 5336 – 111 Avenue, 5340 – 111 Avenue, and 5344 – 111 Avenue. J. Fleese also received a permit for a house and garage at 11325 – 61 Street that August.

Eastglen High School (11430 – 68 Street) opened in 1953, as a direct response to the flood of baby boomers that were arriving at high school age in the east end of the city. Eastglen, designed by Rule Wynn and Rule, was one of the largest city high schools when it opened, and would be attended by many Highland students after this date.

The Thistle Curling Club opened its rink at 6920 – 114 Street in 1953. The Thistle Curling Club was established in 1920, but curling had been promoted and played in the Highlands

BUILDING PERMITS

W. W. Butchart 5316 Ada Boulevard	G. Jamison 11103 – 54 Street
G. Sherwin 5333 – 111 Avenue.	Steve Hrudey Construction 2 two-suite apartment buildings at 5607 and 5615 – 118 Avenue
Peter Sturko 5343 – 112 Avenue 11107 – 55 Street	J. Kulmatyski 11223 – 53 Street
A. Hneidan 5328 – 111 Avenue	N. Suprovich 5311 – 112 Avenue
S. P. Reynolds 11332 – 62 Street	J. Fleese 11329 – 61 Street
V. Belland 11319 – 56 Street	P. Koroluk 11133 – 60 Street
A. Rebus 11219 – 58 Street	Peter Sturko 11247 – 58 Street
P. Stuparyk 11314 – 55 Street	E. Tingstad 11112 – 62 Street
Peter Sturko 11107 – 55 Street.	Dr. D. Russell 5521 – 111 Avenue
J. R. Peach 11322 – 56 Street Addition	R. H. Mundy 11128 – 53 Street
W. Kent 11302 – 55 Street Addition	V. McDonald 6023 – 111 Avenue
W. Bank 11328 – 53 Street	Peter Sturko 5336 – 111 Avenue 5340 – 111 Avenue 5344 – 111 Avenue
Peter Sturko 5339 – 112 Avenue	J. Fleese 11325 – 61 Street
J. Bonk 11324 – 53 Street	
William Krank 11326 – 55 Street	

BUILDING PERMITS

W. Allan	A. Markowich
5530 Ada Boulevard	5327 – 112 Avenue
B. Mailo	5331 – 112 Avenue
11345 – 64 Street	G. McClary
P. J. Achtemichuk	5640 Ada Boulevard
11312 – 55 Street	A. Marchmount
Edmonton Public School Board,	5658 Ada Boulevard Addition
addition to Highlands School	K. C. Jamieson
11509 – 62 Street	11226 – 55 Street Addition
City of Edmonton Parks and Recreation	A. G. Waddel
Department	11124 – 53 Street
Playground shelter,	S. Chorney
62 Street & 112 Ave	11411 – 65 Street.
M. Mix	J. Eshow
11110 – 61 Street	11327 – 53 Street
A. Gordon	N. Humen
11413 – 63 Street	11108 – 56 Street
G. L. Monson	Garfield Hardie
5309 – 111 Avenue	11356 – 56 Street
Highlands and District Community	P. Koroluk
League	6211 – 111 Avenue
Wading pool	
Lots 1–8, Block 12	
Fred Steparyk	
11355 – 55 Street	

from its inception through the efforts of W. J. Magrath, a curling enthusiast. Betty Jameson began curling at the club in 1953, and in 1980 was the skip for the team that won Provincial and Canadian Curling Championships. In 2007 the club hosted the World Curling Federation Men's and Women's Senior World Curling Championship.

The Beverly Bridge opened for motor traffic in 1953, diverting drivers from 112 Avenue to 118 Avenue. While this restored some of the previous peace and quiet valued by Highlanders, it also hit at the little commercial strip along 112 Avenue. When the Safeway left the Highlands in 1990, another magnet for commercial visitors disappeared. Despite a renewal of interest in the 112 Avenue corridor through the Highlands, this shift of commercial activity to the north has proven to be permanent, although somewhat mitigated by the creative energies of those re-establishing businesses in the past several decades.

Only five building permits were issued in the Highlands during 1954. In May, W. Allan (6220 – 111 Avenue) received permission to build a house at 5530 Ada Boulevard, to be built by Fekete Construction. In June, E. Mailo (11214 – 55 Street) received his permit for a house and garage located at 11345 – 64 Street, and in August, P. J. Achtemichuk (11327 – 58 Street) received his permit to build a house at 11312 – 55 Street.

On 30 September 1954 the Edmonton Public School Board was issued a building permit for an addition to Highlands School (11509 – 62 Street). This was a significant addition, to be built by R. H. Rae and Sons, and valued at $209,200.

On 25 October 1954 the City of Edmonton Parks and Recreation Department took out a permit to build a playground shelter on Block 12, on 62 Street north of 112 Avenue.

Five more permits were issued for the Highlands during 1955. M. Mix was issued a permit for a house and garage at 11110 – 61 Street in April, as was A. Gordon (11237 – 66 Street) for a dwelling at 11413 – 63 Street. In October, G. L. Monson was issued a permit for a house and garage at 5309 – 111 Avenue.

On 23 August 1955 the Highlands and District Community League was issued a building permit for a wading pool on Lots 1–8 Block 12. City of Edmonton Building Maintenance constructed this pool as part of a program that built such pools for community leagues in Glenora, Ritchie, King Edward Park, Grovenor, Queen Mary, and Queen Alexandra.

Six building permits were issued for the Highlands during 1956. In March Fred Steparyk (11245 – 66 Street) received a permit to build a house at 11355 – 55 Street; A. Markowich (11834 – 64 Street) for dwellings at 5327 – 112 Avenue and 5331 – 112 Avenue; G. McClary for a house at 5640 Ada Boulevard; A. Marchmount for an addition to his residence at 5658 Ada Boulevard; and K. C. Jamieson for an addition to his residence at 11226 – 55 Street, to be completed by Highlands Construction.

Only one new house was begun in 1957, when A. G. Waddel received a permit that April to build at 11124 – 53 Street. Adrian L. Magrath received a permit to build a garage at his property located at 11136 – 62 Street. The Highlands and District Community League also hired Ralph Vollan at the end of September, to undertake alterations to the sports centre on Lots 1–3 Block 13.

Five building permits were issued in the Highlands during 1958. Among these, during

April, S. Chorney was issued a permit to build a house at 11411 – 65 Street. In May, J. Eshow (11329 – 53 Street) got his permit to build a house next door, at 11327 – 53 Street, while N. Humen was permitted to build a dwelling and garage at 11108 – 56 Street, to be constructed by R. Holzer. Garfield Hardie, an agent with Bluebird Real Estate Ltd., received a permit to build a house at 11356 – 56 Street in December.

Jamison's Coffee Bar in 1958. Photograph courtesy of Jamison family.

A closer view of the signage on Jamison's Coffee Bar, after renovation in 1958. Photograph courtesy of Jamison family.

Two new houses were built in the Highlands during 1959. P. Koroluk (11237 – 51 Street) was issued a permit for a house at 6211 – 111 Avenue in May, while Cindy Pawlenchuk received her permit for a house at 5507 – 118 Avenue in June. The contractor F. Negraiff built the Pawlenchuk house. North Star Oil Ltd received a building permit for the first service station in the heart of Old Highlands on 10 April 1959, to be built at 5905 – 118 Avenue. A. Lakusta also took out a permit in May 1959 to build offices and stores at 5809/5819 – 118 Avenue, designed by the architect Nick Flak.

By 1956 Edmonton and Calgary shared the distinction of being the fastest growing cities in Canada. Edmontonians loved their cars, and by 1956 Waterloo Motors led all the North American dealers in sales. The city sought a new, modern look expressed in International architecture, ranch houses, and arborite. Innovative builders such as Clifford E. Lee and Merrill Muttart pioneered prefabricated homes and drywall construction. Edmonton suburbs began to expand even more rapidly than before the First World War. The Highlands would be transformed by this construction boom as well.

Afterword
Hope and Renewal, 1960-2011

Like many other mature neighborhoods, the Highlands suffered some decline during the 1960s. The commercial strip along 112 Avenue assumed a somewhat seedy look in the minds of many. During the 1970s, however, more families moved into the neighborhood, seeking out the special charms offered by a mature community environment with historical character homes. When La Boheme opened in the old Gibbard Block, and Ernst and Carol Eder invested in its careful restoration after becoming tenants in 1979, it became a model for other business initiatives, and for the entire city. In 1992 the province designated the Gibbard Block as a Registered Historical Resource.

Realizing that the future of the Highlands in many ways resided in its past, and the preservation and respect of that past, the community developed plans for the systematic preservation of the built heritage in 1983. Plans were put forward for municipal "direct control" of future development in the Highlands, but this was defeated by city council.

In 1988 the Highlands Historical Foundation was created by residents who realized the importance of preserving both the stories as well as the architecture of the Highlands. A walking tour guide was one of their first projects, and this guide was reissued in 2012. In 2006 the HHF (later renamed the Highlands Historical Society) was influential in leading the effort to have an inventory of historic houses completed in the Highlands. In March 2007 Heritage Collaborative Inc. completed the Highlands Neighborhood Survey and Inventory Project, which identified three promising enclaves of significant structures as suitable for designation as heritage districts. In addition, 40 of the community's buildings were added to the city's inventory of historic buildings. Of those, five were officially designated and placed on the *Register of Historic Resources in Edmonton*.

The demolition of buildings in the community does not occur without a great deal of controversy. In spite of differing opinions the old community league hall was torn down in

March 2007 after serving six decades as the centre of social and recreational life in the Highlands. The remaining hall was in such dire need of renovation that the community decided to build a new, more consolidated community hall. This project is still ongoing.

The Highlands neighborhood has broad appeal. Eighteen-year-old Christine Hirschi recently moved to the community with her family. "I love the idea of walking my dog and being able to see the most beautiful, unique homes in Edmonton. With the river valley being so close and the historic homes to look at, it's easy to see why someone of any age would want to live in such a special neighborhood."

Longtime residents who move away from the neighborhood often do so with heavy hearts. In a recent issue of the *Highlands/Bellevue Highlights*, Lynn Spyker said goodbye to "friends from the (community) garden, music club, the library, the coffee shop, ladies' shinny hockey, kid's soccer, school, the community league, fellow walkers, dinner club, community theatre, Friday night fire pit, her neighbors, men's hockey and pub night."

Like all communities, the Highlands continues to evolve. Homes are renovated, others are restored and some are new. Residents come and go but each, like Lynn Spyker, takes a piece of this community with them. After all, their "Heart's in the Highlands."

Johanne Yakula
Chair, Book Committee
Highlands Historical Society

Notes

Those Confusing Magrath Companies

William John Magrath and Bidwell Arthur Holgate were partners in a number of firms during their heyday before the First World War. Sometimes it is difficult to keep these many corporate identities clear. This overview of the more important examples taken from the Alberta Corporate Registry may be helpful.

Magrath Holgate Company, Limited

W.J. Magrath and B.A. Holgate took over complete control of this firm the day after **Magrath Holgate Company, Limited**, capitalized at $200,000, filed its articles of association with the Registrar of Joint Stock Companies on 1 February 1911. The four subscribers were William John Magrath, Edmonton broker, Bidwell Arthur Holgate, broker, Rev. Arthur W. Coone, accountant and company secretary, and Bertram H. Tayler, another Edmonton broker. In 1916-1918 Tayler served overseas with the 49th Battalion, Canadian Expeditionary Force, while remaining a subscriber of the company. By 1916 the company office was registered as being located in the Orpheum Arcade on Jasper Avenue. Mabel S. Holgate became a member of the board in 1917, assuming ownership of most of the Holgate shares, with Bidwell retaining only one share.

The company memorandum and articles of association, drawn up by Boyle, Parlee and Company, and filed the same day, indicated that the company object was primarily "to carry on the business of a land company, with the right to buy, own, develop, improve, clear, settle, cultivate, let, secure, exchange and sell real property and lands cultivated or not, and any interests therein...." Also, "to construct, erect, build and maintain in and on the said lands streets, ways, sidewalks, bridges and other means of communication, houses and manufactures, and other buildings and works necessary or suitable for the occupation or the improvement of any of the said lands, and to put into operation and make any work or improvement thereon." Finally, "to build dwelling-houses and other buildings on the said property or any part thereof."

Another 26 articles covered an array of objects involving the right to sell its property, make loans to purchasers, provide mortgages, work the land with mines, work as contractors, and a full range of activities supportive of the main aim to develop areas like the Highlands.

When William John Magrath died in 1920, his widow Ada T. Magrath took over his role in the company, but in November 1921 and November 1922 the Registrar of Companies sent her two letters demanding annual company returns be filed, and threatening to strike the company from the register. A combination of Tayler's absence, the death of Magrath and other circumstances seems to have led to a general decline in the company activities commensurate with the general economic malaise in Edmonton at that time. By 1923 Tayler was living in Vancouver and working there as a broker, and Rev. A.W. Coone was a clergyman in Nanton, Alberta. Ada Magrath and Mabel Holgate seem to have been the most active directors at this time. The company became very inactive, and was struck from the Register on 31 January 1927. The company was in tax arrears under the Corporations Taxation Act when this occurred.

Magrath Holgate, Limited

A new company, **Magrath Holgate, Limited,** capitalized at $100,000, was formed at a meeting of the Magrath Holgate Company, Limited on 15 January 1912. Rev. A.W. Coone, the secretary-treasurer, reported that a resolution was passed: "That a new company

be formed and that said new company be at liberty, and permission is hereby given to the same, to use as the name of said new company the name of 'Magrath Holgate, Limited'."

Magrath Holgate, Limited filed its memorandum of association on 18 January 1912, with William John Magrath, Bidwell Arthur Holgate, Bertram Harold Tayler and Frederick John Whitcroft, all Edmonton brokers, as its subscribers. The objects of this company were very similar to those of the Magrath Holgate Company, Limited, established the previous year by the same principals. By 1915 Fred Whitcroft was on active service, joining Bert Tayler, and leaving active control to Magrath and Holgate. By 1920, the year of Magrath's death, Whitcroft was living in Vancouver, where he had been since 1918, although he remained a director with Ada Magrath, Bidwell Holgate and Bert Tayler. In 1922 Mabel Holgate joined the board, but there are no further records for this company following 1922.

Magrath and Holgate, Limited

A second company was formed in 1912, with the very similar name **Magrath and Holgate, Limited**. This company had the same directors as Magrath Holgate, Limited: William J. Magrath, Bidwell A. Holgate, Bertram H. Tayler and Frederick J. Whitcroft. Its articles of association were filed on 18 September 1912. Its memorandum and articles of association indicate a similar object to those of the other Magrath and Holgate companies established at this time, "to develop and turn to account any land [it] acquired...."

Bidwell Holgate left as a director in 1913, and D.L. Robinson became a provisional director. In 1914 the only directors were Tayler, Whitcroft and T.C. Johnston, the company accountant, with the Scott Fruit Company Ltd. Both Tayler and Whitcroft would join the Canadian army in 1915, leaving Johnston to run the show alone. Returns were not filed from 1919 until 1921, and, like the other Magrath and Holgate companies, it was threatened with removal from the Register. This company seems to have been carried on as a shell company by the William Magrath estate, B.H. Tayler, A.W. Tayler and Fred Whitcroft. Finally, on 31 December 1925, the provincial Registrar sent a letter inquiring whether Magrath and Holgate, Limited "was carrying on business or in operation, but to date no reply has been received." No further records survive for this company.

Magrath, Hart & Co. and Magrath Hartt, Limited

For some time William John Magrath and Bidwell Arthur Holgate worked as general commission real estate agents and as brokerage, insurance and financial agents under the name **Magrath, Hart & Co.,** with offices at 44 Jasper Avenue East. W.J. Magrath and B.A. Holgate took over control of this firm the day after Magrath Holgate Company, Limited was formed in 1911.

This name was used again when the articles of association were filed for Magrath Hartt, Limited on 10 July 1915. The directors were W.J. Magrath, Ada T. Magrath, Bidwell A. Holgate, and Mabel S. Holgate. The principal aim of Magrath Hartt, Limited was to purchase Magrath Hart & Co. This company's assets at the time included the Highlands office block, a Jasper Avenue lease, an oil lease at Ponoka, Western Canada Securities Limited and several other items.

Documentation in the Alberta Corporate Registry also includes a considerable list of accounts receivable, mortgages receivable, rents receivable, "sundry debtors" and properties such as the Anderson Garage, Hunt House, Ash House and Wells House. It also included equity in "syndicates" such as the Gibbard Apartments, a horse and scales at the Bush Mine, "fixtures" at the Orpheum Theatre, as well as stocks and shares in several companies. This 1915 inventory also identified ten houses and lots in Highlands, Brown Estate and Bellevue Addition and the Hudson's Bay Reserve; 263 lots in the Highlands, with an additional 238 lots still for sale in Plan No. 4393 A.Y.; 26 unsold lots in Bellevue; and 88 unsold lots in the Bellevue Addition.

Perhaps this confusing plethora of Magrath companies can be explained by an interesting case that took place in 1932. Magrath Hartt, Limited, with Magrath Ltd., about which the author could find no information, would be struck off the Register of Companies on 30 June 1930, but in 1932 was briefly restored for the purposes of facilitating a legal case. Abbott and McLaughlin, solicitors for Northern Trusts Company, requested this action be applied to both companies, in order to allow foreclosure of a mortgage for Lot 16 Block 8 on the Highlands Survey. Magrath Ltd. held this property, having received it from Magrath Hartt Ltd. on 2 July 1924. The movement of properties among various companies was one purpose of so many overlapping directorships and company organizations, and may have provided some benefit through their coinciding interests.

Highlands Boundaries

The Highlands has had several surveys and changes to the neighbourhood boundaries over the years. The author based his research into the Highlands story on a survey of all the properties for which building permits were granted on the Highlands Survey as recorded by the City of Edmonton between 1912 and 1960. It was not until 1960 that the boundaries of the Highlands finally were filled up with residential and commercial construction, fulfilling the long-delayed dream of the developers who began to systematically open the district in 1910.

Some of the narrative touches on neighouring districts as well, especially Bellevue and the Bellevue Addition, which have always seemed an organic extension of the Highlands. Today the completion of the Capilano Bridge and freeway defines the west boundary of the neighbourhood in reality. The Saskatchewan River is the obvious southern border of the Highlands, and 118 Avenue is the northern limit. The early businesses and residences along 112 Avenue since replaced by the freeway development have also received some attention.

Key to Historic Edmonton Street Names

Following is a list of historic street names that are used in this book, along with their current names. Most of the street names were changed in 1914 when Edmonton and Strathcona amalgamated.

Ada Street: Ada Boulevard

Agnes Avenue: 115 Avenue

Agnes Street: 128 Avenue

Alberta Avenue: 118 Avenue (still used as an alternative name)

Campbell Street: 61 Street

Elm Avenue: 113 Avenue

Elm Street: 81 Street

Fraser Avenue: 98 Street

Gibbard Street: 57 Street

Government Street: 92 Street

Grace Street: 62 Street

Griesbach Street: 105A Avenue

Houston Street: 64 Street

Irwin Street: 63 Street (north of 112 Avenue)

Johnston Street: 63 Street (south of 112 Avenue)

Knox Avenue: 112 Avenue

Kinistino Avenue: 96 Street

Kinnaird Street: 82 Street

Kirkness Street: 95 Street

Lake Street: 60 Street

Magrath Avenue: 113 Avenue

Namayo Avenue: 97 Street

Pine Avenue: 112 Avenue (before it became Knox)

Queen's Avenue: 99 Street

Spruce Avenue: 114 Avenue

Stewart Street: 101A Avenue

Sutherland Street: 106 Avenue

Wadleigh Street: 67 Street

Willow Avenue: 115 Avenue

Wilton Street: 65 Street

Thank You

The Highlands Historical Society gratefully acknowledges the following people for their contributions to the centennial book project:

Author Ken Tingley, who worked long and hard and generously shared his expertise and experience with us.

Halkier & Dutton Strategic Design: for their consultation and expertise with the creation of our new visual identity and tagline.

The Highlands Golf Course: for their generosity in providing their beautiful facilities for our events.

Ted Smith: for his ongoing support of the HHS and donation of a piece of stained glass.

Anita Jenkins: for her impressive book editing skills.

Linda Blanchett of Diva Communications: for her advice about book production.

Sid and Nellie Braaksma: for their unfailing support of the HHS and for making their historic home available for our fund raising event.

Arlene Blood: for sharing her lovely home with the HHS in order to raise funds.

Margaret Husband: for providing many exceptionally interesting photographs.

Lu Ziola: for her patience and creativity in providing the layout.

Bob Snyder: for his experience, advice and contacts in the book publishing industry.

Nancy Power: for her contacts and enthusiasm for this project.

The HHS Book Committee:
Johanne Yakula, Denise Harmon, Helen Gillespie and Carol Snyder.

Highlands Historical Society

Highlands Historical Society board members: Upper row (l to r): Vicki Wheeler, Helen Gillespie, Gail Rydman, Johanne Yakula, Mark Milne, Cathy Chalmers, Mike Harmon. Bottom row (l to r): Laurie Parkhill, Halina Lesko, Francine Gregory, Shelli Carder Drozd, Laurel Erickson, Carol Snyder, Denise Harmon, Stuart Drozd.

About the Author

Ken Tingley has lived in Edmonton since 1956, and has worked as a historical resource consultant there since 1973. He was named the first Historian Laureate for the City of Edmonton in 2010. Most of Ken's research and work has focused on his home city. His many projects include a history of the Cloverdale community and *Ride of the Century – The Story of the Edmonton Transit System*. Ken believes that one of the fundamental themes of Edmonton history is a nexus of community-based interests developing in complementary and competitive ways.

Index

A

Abbott, Percy W. 26
Achtemichuk, P.J. 124
Ada Boulevard 2, 12, 47, 60, 86, 133
Adams, Dave 115
Adams, H.M.B. 61
Ada Street 133
Adby Construction 114, 119
Adby, Fred 108, 114, 116
Ad Club 66
Adrian Avenue 50, 51
Agnes Avenue 133
Agnes Street 133
Agnew Drugs 33
Agnew, J.S. 110
Aiken, Sarah 116
Aiken, William T. 116
Aird, Dorothy 51, 52, 74, 76, 86, 87
Airview Photos 122
Alberta Avenue 21, 25, 47, 51, 61, 133
Alberta Board of Health 67
Alberta Government Telephones 116
Alberta Lumber Co. Ltd. 58
Alberta Marble and Granite Company 57
Alberta Moral Reform League 64
Alexander, W.H. 79
Algonquin Apartments 32, 46
Allan, W. 124
Allardice Grocery 61
Allardice, James 61
Allen, William A. 106
All-numerical System 55
Alton, K.N. 110
Anderson, A. 121
Anderson, Bette 115
Anderson, C.A. 76
Anderson, Jack 67
Anderson, J. Lyle 62
Anderson, Mrs. C.A. 74, 87
Anderson, Mrs. J.L. 91

Anderson, Pete 24
Aquitania 118
Arlington 32
Armistice Day 68
Arnold, Marion 116
Arnold, Norman 116
Ash Brothers Diamond Hall 60
Ash, J.R. 108
Ash, Mrs. 77
Ash, S. 108
Ashton, P. 122
Ash, William Thomas 50, 60
Assessor and Collection Department 65
Assiniboine 5
Atkinson, Dr. W.A. 51, 56, 59, 64, 68
Atkinson, Mrs. W.A. 87, 92
Atkinson Residence 57
Ault, M. 74
Avenue Theatre 71

B

Baker, A.G. 58
Baker, C. Harvey 73, 81, 86
Baker, Herbert 29, 81, 82, 94
Baker, Howard G. 61
Baker, Mrs. Herbert 29, 68, 91
Bancroft, W.J. 82
Bank, W. 122
Barbara's Ready to Wear 115
Basiuk, George 117
Beacon Heights 29, 47
Beacon Heights Annex 47
Beecroft, Mrs. H.J. (Mamie) 62, 67
Beecroft, William J. 51, 62, 79, 92
Bel-Air Apartments 118
Belland, V. 122
Bellevue 21, 23
Bellevue Addition 23, 36, 46, 73
Bellevue Community League 105
Bellevue Grocery 115

Bell Residence 27
Belvedere 23
Bennett, C.B. 64
Berg, Val 122
Bernard, E. 111
Beverly 11
Beverly Annex 35
Beverly Board of Health 68
Beverly Bridge 124
Beverly Coal and Gravel Co, Ltd. 60
Beverly Heights 25, 29, 35, 47
Beverly Heights Annex 48
Beverly Mine 35
Beverly School District 14, 40
Bidwell Holgate 49, 60
Big House 69
Bills, Bob 115, 117
Bills, Gary 115
Bills Service 115
Bishop, George 65
Bittorf, Edna 111
Blackfoot 5
Black, Mrs. J.H. 88
Blakey, W.G. 82
Blaynay, J.D. 28, 51
Blayney, Mrs. J.D. 29
Bluebird Real Estate Ltd. 125
Blue, John 44
Bohannan, Charlie 121
Boisvert, J.A. 111
Bond, Edward H. 64
Bond, Edward J. 27, 30, 31, 64, 79
Bond, John L. 63, 78
Bond, Mrs. E.J. 84, 91
Bond, Rev. Stephen 29
Bonk, John 107, 122
Bonk, L.S.M. 109
Borchert, Pearl Sarah 114
Borden Park 23, 55, 71
Bouillon, A.V. 13
Boulevard Heights 25, 26
Bowker, E.C. 15
Boyle, John R. 26
Boyle Parlee & Co. 26
Brown, A.J. 108
Brown, Ernest 27
Brown, Frank G. 66, 81
Brown, George 62
Brown, John W. 109
Brown, Mabel Edna 83
Brown, William F. 26, 31, 32, 50, 51, 54, 65, 74, 79, 80, 82, 83, 116, 117
Brunlees, R. 121
Buchanan, Rev. T.C. 77

Bullman, J.A. 54
Bullock, R.A. 81, 82
Burns, Elmer 121
Burt, A.L. 80
Bury, A.U.G. 2, 72, 76, 79, 86, 106
Bury Residence 62
Bush Mine 35, 71
Butchart, J.J. 108
Butchart, W.W. 122
Butler, L.H. 111
Buttercup Farm house 59
Byron-May 15

C
Caledonia Temperance Hall 70
Campbell Street 61, 133
Canada Candy Company 77
Canada Safeway 91
Canadian Consolidated Rubber Company 63
Canadian Expeditionary Force 66
Canadian Ladies Golf Union 107
Canadian National Railway 88
Canadian Northern Railway 65
Canadian Pacific Railway 11
Capilano Bridge 3
Capital EX 20
Capitol Hill 12
Card, Charles F. 94
Carder Drozd, Shelli vii
Carey Street 18
Carswell, James E. 65
Cashman, Tony 7
Central Women's Christian Temperance Union 88
Chalmers, Cathy vii
Chalmers, F.W. 113
Chalmers, J. 55
Chambers, Mrs. 87
Chernichan, K. 122
Children's Theatre 115
Chorley, Archie 121
Chorney, S. 125
Chown Hardware 63
Chown, R.C. 54
Chown, Russell C. 63
C.H. Whitham Ltd. 110
City Beautiful 12, 41
City Capital 13
City of Edmonton Ladies Amateur Championship 107
City of Edmonton Parks and Recreation Department 124
City Park Annex Addition 23
City Park Grocery 61

City Park Meat Market 61
City Stores and Works Department 63
CJCA 71
CKUA 71
Clark, C.I. 35
Clarke, George C. 27, 51, 65
Clarke, Joseph A. 12, 42
Clark, George C. 42, 54
Classified Historic Site 40
Clover Bar 12
Clover Bar Heights Land Co. Ltd. 47
Coal Setters Ltd 59
Cobbledick, Marjorie 73
Cobbledick, Rev. G.H. 30, 67
Cockburn, Robert 65
Coles, H.P. 73
Coles, Miss B. 73
Collegiate Gothic King Edward Park 50
Colter, G. 121
Colter. L.C. 121
Communist Party 91
Concordia College 70
Cooke, Thomas 108, 109
Cooke, William 76
Cook, Tom 121
Coone, Mrs. H. 29, 110
Coone, Rev. Arthur W. 21, 29, 54, 61, 68
Co-operative Commonwealth Federation 91
Coote, Charles T. 64
Cormack, Don 121
Corner Drugstore 33
Cornwell, J.J. 110
Cottage Construction Company 63
Cotter, Dr. Jerry 120
Cotter, Florence 120
Cotter, George 120
Coutts, L.G. 111
Cox, Harry 105
C.P.R. Station 14
Cresswell and Atherton Grocery 62
Cresswell, Frederick 62
Crispy, William 67
Crow, John 66
Crown Paving Co. Ltd. 94
Cryderman, Bill 67
Cryderman, Helen 67
Cryderman, Lil 67
Cryderman, Manley R. 51, 64, 81, 87
Cryderman, Ruth 67
Cunningham, Mrs. O.W. 68
Cunningham, William C. 50
curling rink 33
Curtis, Charles 109
C.W. Carry Ltd. 53

D

Dalziel, J. 87
Damsell, Mrs. 2
Dancer, B. 109
Dando, Thomas L. 48
Dando, T.R. 81
Dan's Grocery 115
Davidson, Adam J. 34, 57, 59, 69, 81, 82, 83, 86, 87, 92, 93, 106
Davidson Avenue 35
Davidson, Cora 34
Davidson, Mrs. Del 35
Davidson Residence 34, 92, 94
Davidson Street 35
Davies, Rev. T.R. 105
Davis, G.H. 76
Dean, Charles M. 109
Deane, G. 53
Dean, Elsie 109
Dear, Fred 111
Delton 23
Demchuk, Daniel 116
Demchuk, Helen 116
Demchuk, M. 121
Dempsey, Alex C. 51
Demschuk Store and Apartment 122
Dewar, Stevenson, and Stanley 122
Dirty Thirties 89
Dixon, John S. 66
Dobson, H.E. 68
Dominion Meteorological Office 84
Dominion of Canada 7
Donald, E.B. 111
Dorsey, Dr. 122
Dreamland Theatre 71
Drozd, Stuart vii
Duggan, D.M. 72
Duke, Betty-Jean 116, 119
Duke, Harry 116
Duke, John 116, 119
Duke, Olive 116
Duke's Beauty and Barber 115
Dunbar, E.R. 110
Dunkraker, Henry 65
Dunsmore, Robert G. 26, 27, 51, 64
Dunsmore Residence 64
Dunsworth, M. 122
Durham, C 27

E

East Edmonton District 29
East Edmonton Municipal Association 54
East End Park 12, 23, 55
Eastglen High School 123
Eastham, Mrs. 88
Eastwood, J. 116
Eastwood School 93
Eaton, Cyrus 44
Echert, Edward 111
Eckert, M. 111
Edina Coal Mine 92
Edmonscona System 55
Edmonton Ad Club 58
Edmonton Agricultural Society 19
Edmonton Bulletin 3, 4, 9, 14, 15, 40, 42, 43, 44, 45, 118
Edmonton Capital 12, 13, 14, 15, 16, 22, 24, 25, 35, 37, 47, 48, 49, 56
Edmonton Commercial Grads 71
Edmonton Daily Capital 15
Edmonton Federation of Community Leagues 70
Edmonton House 5
Edmonton Industrial Association 46, 58
Edmonton Journal 88, 90, 91, 94
Edmonton Junior League 115
Edmonton Police Department 105
Edmonton Public Library 76, 108
Edmonton Public School Board 50, 80
Edmonton Radial Railway 12, 14, 29, 34, 44, 55, 61, 86, 105, 112, 115
Edmonton Real Estate Association 72
Edmonton Real Estate Exchange 72
Edmonton Saturday Mirror 34
Edmonton Saturday News 29
Edmonton Settlement 3, 9, 11
Edmonton Transit Service 120
Edwards, Thomas W. 65
Edwards, William H. 62
Eggert, R. 111
Elm Avenue 133
Elm Street 133
Emmerson, Mrs. 87
Emmott, Mrs. Stanley 92
Ericksen, Andrew 110
Erickson, Laurel vii
Esdale Press 65
Eshow, J. 125
Esson, Alex S.P. 65
Ewing, A.F. 43

F

Faculty Row 71
Farr, Pete 121
Faulkner, Ambrose C. 27, 64
Federated Leagues Cup 87
Fekete Construction 124
Fekete, J. 119
Ferguson, William A. 61
Ferguson, Zola M. 93
Field, Dr. T.H. 69
Field, Ethel 61
Field, James Williamson 61, 69
Field's Cash Store 61
Findlay, Margaret 110
First Street 22
First World War 12, 15, 33, 59, 72
Flak, G. 122
Fleese, J. 123
Fort Augustus 5
Fort Edmonton 5, 6, 7
Fort McMurray 53
Fort Pitt 9
Fort Saskatchewan 5, 7
Fourth Street 22
Fraser Avenue 133
Fraser, Colin 8
Fraser, John 8
Frederickson, Felix X 87, 120, 121
Freeman, Churchill L. 26, 94
Fulton, James H. 65
Fyfe, C.S. 61

G

Gallagher's Flat 24
Gallinger, Claude 40
Gem Theatre 71
Gibbard Block 32, 61, 117, 118
Gibbard Street 33, 133
Gibbard, Thomas 32
Gibbard, William T. 32
Gibson, George E. 27, 51
Gibson, William 32, 51, 64
Gilken, R.H.M 94
Gillespie, Helen vii
Gilmour, M.H. 93
Gimby, Charles Wellington 66
Gimby, Miss 56
Gimby, Mrs. P.W. 87
Glenora 13
Gold Bar 4
Good, James 61
Gordon, A. 125
Gordon, Harvey 113

Gourlay, William S. 65
Government Street 12, 133
Grace English Lutheran Sunday School 70
Grace Street 133
Graham, S.A. 107, 110
Graham, Stewart 116
Grand Trunk Pacific Railway 58
Grant, Major A.C. 91
Grant, Wilbur G. 64
Gravelle, A. 110
Gray, F.E. 109
Gray, Sidney 61
Great Depression 12
Greater Edmonton 4
Great Lone Land 7
Great War 12, 46, 55
Great War Veterans' Association 70
Greenfree, Murray 121
Green, George 51
Greenough and Blair 69
Green, Peter 116
Gregory, Francine vii
Grierson, Allie 30, 91
Grierson, Edmnd 30
Grierson, Mrs. Robert W. (Allie) 91
Grierson Presbyterian Church 65
Grierson, Robert 119
Grierson, Robert W. 81
Grierson, Robert Walter 2, 30
Griesbach 23
Griesbach Street 133
Griesbach, William 18, 80
Griffith, Frederick and Helen (Ella) 31
Griffith, Gladys 31, 51, 74, 80
Griffith, May 31, 32, 79, 80
Groat Estate 23
Groat, Malcolm 8
Grove, L.A. 111
Guenette, J.H. 108
Gullion, George 8, 9
Gullion, James 8
Gullion, James Ingram 9
Gurr, R.S. 111
Gyro Playgrounds 76

H
Haggish, Rev. W.J. 30, 91
Haggith, Mrs. W.H. 87, 91
Hall, Marion P. 84
Halmon, Denise vii
Hambley Confectionery Store 75
Hamilton, Robert 43
Hamilton, William 46, 62

Hammond, Marjorie 83
Hamon, Mike vii
Hannish, William 111
Happy's Meat Market 115
Hardie, Garfield 125
Harrison, A.G. 12
Harris, Wilson 80
Hart, Enid 52, 67, 71, 76, 78, 81, 86, 105, 109
Haugen, O.J. 31
Hayman, Pearl 67
Hecla Block 82
Heintzman and Company 64
Henday, Anthony 5
Henderson, Eve 115
Henderson's directory 27, 34, 50, 61, 64
Henry, William T. 46
Herder, Leo 116, 117, 122
Hewko, M. 122
Highland Drugstore 33
Highland Golfer 106
Highland Hardware 118
Highlands and District Community League 2, 34, 70, 72, 78, 86, 88, 89, 92, 105, 110, 111, 114, 125
Highlands Baptist Church 114, 122
Highlands Barber Shop 94, 122
Highlands Beauty Parlor 94
Highlands Beauty Salon 122
Highlands boat yard 51
Highlands Bowling Club 79
Highlands Cash Grocery 61
Highlands Community League Memorial Centre 105
Highlands Construction 125
Highlands Curling Club 61
Highlands Forty Red Cross Club 108
Highlands Golf Club 106, 121
Highlands Grocery Store 61, 64
Highlands Hardware Store 61
Highlands Historical Foundation 1
Highlands Historical Society vii, 87
Highlands Junior High School 93
Highlands Lawn Bowling Club 34, 105
Highlands Meat Market 61
Highlands Methodist Church 21, 50, 61, 65, 68, 77, 82
Highlands Motors 115
Highlands Normal School 70
Highlands Orchestra 67, 73
Highlands Parent-Teachers' Association 72
Highlands Playschool 114
Highlands Presbyterian Ladies Aid Society 67
Highlands Public School District 72
Highlands School 21, 36, 50, 62, 78, 124

Highlands School Annex 62
Highlands Shoe Repair 94
Highlands Studios 122
Highlands United Church 21, 58, 67, 77, 82, 91
Highlands Women's Missionary Society 68
Highway Traffic Board 116
Hillaby, Violet 88
Hillaby, W.H. 88
Historian Laureate viii
Hneidan, A. 122
Hodgkinson, Bob 121
Hoff, Henry J. 30
Holden, Albert 66
Holgate 55
Holgate, B.A. 28, 50
Holgate, Bidwell A. 21, 27, 54, 69
Holgate, Mabel 30
Holgate-Magrath 46
Holgate, Mrs. B.A. 76, 91
Holgate Residence 28, 60, 67
Hollands, Andrew 80
Hollands, Andy 79
Holmes, G.B. 76
Holzer, R. 125
Hooson Company 31
Hooson-Racey insurance company 31
Hooson Residence 30
Hooson, William Knight 31
Hopkins, Marshall W. 65
Horn, Mrs. D. 80
Horn, Robert 112
Horticultural and Vacant Lots Association 79
Hotchkiss, Charles S. 11
Houston, Robert J. 51
Houston Street 50, 51, 56, 64, 133
Hrudey Construction 121
Hrudey, Steve 108, 117, 119, 120
Hudson's Bay Company 5, 6, 7
Hudson's Bay Reserve 26
Hudson, William 61
Humberstone Coal Company 59, 75
Humen, H. 125
Humphreys, Erica 62
Humphreys, J. Leonard 62, 73, 76, 79, 80, 86
Humphreys residence 109
Hunter, Mrs. 91
Husband, Dorothy May 32
Husband, Margaret xiii, 29, 30, 31, 32, 37, 49, 57, 66, 73, 74, 82, 86, 91, 95, 104, 135
Husband, Maude 88
Husband, Walter 32
Husband, William 106
Huston, Robert J. 65
Hutton, J.H. 121

Hyde, E.E. 93
Hyde, John 119

I

Illustrated London News 48
Imperial Agencies Ltd. 49
Imperial Bank Building 49
Imperial Canadian Trust Company 65
Imperial Life Assurance Company 64
Imperial Order of the Daughters of the Empire 94
Industrial Pavilion 23
Inga's Beauty Lounge 115
Irwin Street 51, 56, 133
Iverson, M. 111, 112

J

Jackson, Arthur 88
Jackson, Bob 121
Jackson Brothers jewelers 65
Jameson, Betty 124
James Ramsay Company 57
James Warmington Grocery 75
James, W.E. 121
Jamison, G. 123
Jamison, K.C. 125
Jamison's Coffee Bar 118
Jaqes, Harold 121
Jasper Avenue 12
Jasper Construction Company 116
Jasper Place 11
Jeffery, George F. 80, 88
Jennings, R. 93
J. J. Montgomery and Company 65
Joe's Snack Bar 115
Johnston Street 133
Jones, Clifford 116
Jones, David 57
Jones, Jonathan H. 65
Junior Girls Club 107

K

Karpetz Brothers 120
Karrer, Dr. Powell 65
Karvellas, D. 119
K & D Ltd 117
Kean, E. 27
Kelly, O.G. 109
Kelly, Wilmer J. 65, 74, 79, 80, 81, 82, 84, 86, 87, 93
Kent, W. 122
Killips, E.B. 111
Kinistino Avenue 56, 133
Kinnaird Street 12, 133

Kirby, Derek 116
Kirby, Ethel 116
Kirby, Rev. 29
Kirkness, James 8
Kirkness Lake 35
Kirkness Street 18, 133
Klondike Days 20
Knox Avenue 48, 50, 51, 60, 133
Koroluk, P. 123, 126
Kozak, Muzz 107
Krank, William 122
Kreig, E.M. 49
Kryviak, Ron 119
Kulmatyski, J. 123

L

LaFleche Brothers 65
Lake Street 133
Lakusta, A. 126
Larkin, Ethel (Pearce) 118
Laurier, Sir Wilfrid 11
Lavender, D.J. 122
lawn bowling 33
L. Buray & Sons 122
Leach, George Brown 112
Lee, Cliford E. 126
Lee, E.J. 40
Leeman, Mrs. F. 74
Lee, Robert 13
LeMarchand Mansion 32
Lesko, Halina vii
Logie, Dr. N. Burton 80
Lott's Snack Bar 115
Loughlin, S. 15
Love, E.T. 117
Lower Edmonton Settlement 6, 7
Low Level Bridge 55

M

Macdonald, J.D.A. 119
MacDonald, J.M. 43
Macdonald, Kenneth 8
MacGillivary, C.D. 119
MacGregor, John 67
MacKay, A.G. 68
MacKay, A.J. 88
MacKenzie, D.S. 15
Mackenzie, Kenneth W. 30, 69, 118
MacKenzie, Mary 15
Mackenzie residence 69
MacLean, Harry A. 51
Macleod, Bruce 1
Macleod, Loretta 67, 87
Macleod, Loretta Conley 1
MacLeod. M. 86

Macleod, Malcolm 1, 67, 87, 89
Macleod, Marjorie 1
MacLeod, Mrs. Malcolm 91
Macleod, Norman (Bill) 1
Macleod, Violet 1, 26, 67, 87, 89
Madison, Harold "Harry" B.C. 53
Madison, Jean 53
Magrath 55
Magrath, Ada 34, 46, 74, 75, 105
Magrath, Adrian L. 46, 62, 125
Magrath and Holgate 32
Magrath Avenue 133
Magrath coach house 105
Magrath, Hartt & Company 13, 14, 57, 60
Magrath Holgate 2, 14, 21, 23, 25, 48, 57
Magrath, Holgate & Company 13, 14, 16, 18,
    21, 50
Magrath Holgate Limited 27
Magrath-Holgate Limited 35
Magrath-Holgate Ltd. 40
Magrath Mansion 31, 60, 68, 74, 105
Magrath, Mrs. W.J. 87
Magrath residence 37
Magrath, W.J. 21, 22, 27, 40, 49, 50, 62, 66, 72,
    74, 124
Mailo, E. 124
Malcolm, Claire 121
Maloney, E. 122
Marchment, H.W. 110
Marchmount, A. 125
Margaret Marshall Residence 63, 94
Markowich, A. 125
Marples, Harvey 121
Marshall, Daisy-May 94
Marshall, Duncan 11
Marshall, J. 94
Marshall, Margaret 94
Marshall Residence 82, 94
Marshall, Robert Colin 94
Marsh, E. 110
Martaugh, John 61
Martell, Frances 2, 77, 82, 105
Martell, F.S. 114
Martell, Henry 105, 114
Martell, Herbert 114
Martell, Herman 114
Martland, John 108
Mase, L.H. 109
Maslowski, K. 122
Massey Manufacturing Company 82
Matheson, Annie 53
Matheson, Bruce 80
Matheson, Captain John 52
Matheson, Gordon 80

Matthews, Herbert C. 65
May, Carmie H. 57
Mayor Armstrong 42
McBain, Allan 114
McClary, G. 125
McClean, Bruce 118
McCormack, Sam G. 78, 84, 86, 87, 93
McCready, D.B. 109
McCutcheon Bros. 25
McDearmid, J.D. 111
McDonald, V. 123
McDonald, W. Harland 53
McDonald, William S. 32
McDougall Heights 14
McDougall, John A. 8, 14, 18, 27
McGillivray, Mrs. C 74
McGillivray, Rev. Russell 88
McGrath, Mrs. W.J. 88
McIntyre, J.L. 109
McKay, A.G. 92
McKenzie, Ethel 73
McKinney, Charles 61
McLean, Harry A. 64
McLeod, Donald 8
McLeod, J. 116
McLuhan, Herbert E. 51, 65
McLuhan house 31, 32
McLuhan, Marshall 51
McLuhan Sullivan and McDonald Ltd. 65
McManus, G. 72
McManus, Mrs. G. 73
McNally, Fred 79
McNicoll, D. 109
McPhee, M. Clifford 51
McQueen, Edward 40
McSweyn, Margaret 67
McSweyn, W. 76, 82
McSweyn, William F. 64
McTavish, Rev. R. Lorne 79
Meiklejohn, Garnett M. 27, 51, 84
Merrick, J.H. 106
Merryweather, M. 111
Methodist parsonage 31
Meyer, A.C. 56
Meyer, A.E. 61
Meyer's Studio 122
Millan, J.J. 116
Miller, Sydney M. 61
Milne, M. 116
Milne, Mark vii
Mix, George A. 111
Mix, M. 125
Moffatt, Mr. 77
Monaghan, C.W. 56

Monson, G.L. 125
Montgomery, A. 56
Montgomery, Dr. R.G. 49, 51
Montgomery, John J. 65
Montgomery, R.O. 50
Mooney Biscuit and Candy Company 62
Moorehouse, E.W. 54
Morehouse, Ernest 36, 64
Morehouse, Ernest W. 28, 30, 32
Morehouse, E.W. 29, 31, 34, 40, 49, 63, 69, 73, 74, 75, 105
Morell and Nicholas 41
Morell, A.U. 41
Morrison, Donald A. 65, 81
Morrison, Mrs. 74
Morrison Residence 51
Morrison, Wesley R. 51
Mould, Mrs. E.M. 107
Mount Royal 25, 73
Mount Royal Café 115
Mount Royal Drug Store 115
Mount Royal Grocery 115
Mount Royal Milk Bar 115
Mount Royal Park 73
Mount Royal Snack Bar 115
Mount Royal Super Market 115
Municipal Construction 118
Mustard, William J.A. 26
Muttart and Wright 79, 84
Muttart, Merrill 126
Myles, Andrew 61

N

Namayo Avenue 23, 133
Naunton, A.G. 111
Negraiff, F. 126
Nelson, H.N. 112
Nesbitt and Morehouse 28
Nesbitt, ARthur 28
New, E.J. 121
New France 7
Newland, Frank G. 49, 62
Newlands, Dr. H.C. 110
Newnham, Helen Carswell 68
Nicoll, W.R. 120
Nisbet, D.B. 113
Norn, Robert N. 111
Northcote 7
North Edmonton 11
Northern Alberta Railway (NAR) 53
Northern Boat Building Company 52
Northlands Park 20
North Saskatchewan River 3, 5, 7, 11

North Star Oil Ltd 126
North Star station 115
Northwest 7, 9
Northwest Company 5
North-Western Territory 6
Northwestern Utilities Ltd. 80
North-West Mounted Police 7
Norwood 23
Norwood Boulevard 12, 22
Norwood School 68
Nowyny 56
Nu-West Homes 117
Nye, Mrs. 74

O

Oakes, Joseph W. 56
O'Connor, George 45
Oliver, Frank 8
Oliver, jesse 74
Oliver, Jesse 61
Olynyk, Alex 107
One Big Union 70
Order of the British Empire 94
Orser, Bruce R. 29, 65
Owen, Eda 84
Owen, Evelyn 106
Owen, Herbert W. 64
Owen, Quint 106
Owen Residence 84

P

Palmer, L.A. 51
Parkdale 23
Park Grocery 75
Parkhill, Laurie vii, 120
Parkview Red and White Store 75
Parlee, Bill 26
Parlee, Harold H. 26, 54, 80, 81, 86
Parlee, Steven 26
Parris, Mary 116
Patrick, G. 57
Paula's Beauty Salon 122
Pawlenchuk, Cindy 126
Peach, J.R. 122
Peacock, Doris 117
Peacock, Maxwell 117
Pearce house 89
Pearce, Stuart 52, 114, 118
Pearson, Fred 66
Peers, Larry I. 118
Peers, L.I. 119
Pepper and Sons 50
Peroz, M. 121

Peter, John 121
Peterson, Jack 74
Pettis, H. 81
Phelps, Miss 74
Philip, P. 121
Phillips, George 109
Piggly Wiggly grocery 115
Pinch, T.E. 121
Pine Avenue 12, 48, 133
Plum, A.W. 75
Poff, Fern 53
Poff, Howard G. 53
Poff, R. 120
Potter, A.F. 110
Powell, Rev. Thomas 29
Premier Mine 71, 72
Presbyterian Ladies Aid Society 68
Price, Gordon 121
Price, J. 80, 84
Price, J.A. 111
Provincial Historical Resource 30
Pugh, Frank 51

Q

Queen's Avenue 133
Quilley's Polar Bar 115
Quist's Meat Market 115

R

Rae, R.H. 93, 108, 111, 116
Rae, Robert H. Sr. 111
Ralph Vollan Construction 116
Rat Creek 7
Raymond family 53
Raymond, Jack 1
Rebus, A. 122
Red Deer News 70
Reeves, Miss 79
Registered Historical Resource 63, 127
Reid, H.E. 111
Revillon Bros. Wholesale 62
Rex Fruit Store 65
Reynolds, Dorothy 53
Reynolds, S.P. 122
Reynolds, Ted 114
R. H. Rae and Sons 121, 124
Richards, J.L. 111
Richards, Mrs. R.A. 88
Rietsma, Charlie 121
Ripley, P. 118
Ritchie, Harry W. 60
Robbie, Jean 52, 67, 71, 76, 78, 81, 86, 105, 109
Robertson-Davidson 48

Robertson-Davidson Limited 47
Robertson-Davidson Real Estate Company 35
Robertson, G.D. 47
Robertson, George 34
Robinson, R.J. 21, 29
Robinson, Robert J. 51, 64
Rolf, C. 122
Rose, W.J. 84
Ross, Alex 66
Rossdale Flats 19
Ross, Donald 8
Ross Flat 6
Ross Flats 7
Ross, James A. 93
Rourke, Vera 113, 114
Rowland, James 8
Rowland, William 8
Rowswell, G. 113
Rowswell, H.E. 110
Roxburgh, Rev. Frank D. 65
Roxford, Marge 67
Roy, Mr. 80
Rupert's Land 7
Russell, Dr. D. 123
R. W. Grierson and Co. 30
Rydeham, Mrs. 121
Rydman, Gail vii
Rymer, J.E. 61

S

Sage-Appleton Company 25
Sageon, W.J. 50
Saigeon, Gladys V. 64
Saik, H. 120
Sammy's Lunch 115
Sands, Vic 121
Saturday News & Alberta Homesteader 15
Saunders, F.A. 21
Schickle, K. 119
Schroffel, F. 94
Schwermann Hall 70
Scott, Creighton A. 65
Scott, Thomas M. 51
Scriver, Arthur W.G. 63
Second World War 81
Seeman, T.R. 74
Segati, Johnny 121
Seller, Mrs. 86
Semotiuk, J. 111
Sharp, W.J. 108
Shaw, Henry 107
Shea, James 110
Sheldon, Carleton G. 58, 73, 75, 80, 92, 93

Sheldon Coal Company 59
Sheldon, G. 80
Sheldon, Mrs. Carleton G. 93
Sheppard, W.A. 107
Sherritt Gordon Mines 119
Sherwin, G. 122
Shook, Morton 66
Shortridge, Harold 80
Short, William 23, 40
Siddell, George L. 50, 60
Sifton, Clifford 11
Simpson, James B. 65
Sinclair, John 8
Singer, Matilda 60
Singer, Philip 60
Sisson, Cephas 30, 32, 51, 65
Sissons Drug Store 77
Slamko, J.J. 110
Slate, Frank 84
Slate, Herbert 73, 75, 76, 77
Slater, Andrew 79
Smith, Bill 61
Smith, Clarence 27, 64, 76, 77, 79, 80
Smith, Clyde 2, 59, 113
Smith, Frances 59
Smith, George P. 70
Smith, Minnie 59
Smith, R. 87
Smith, Rev. J.W. 29, 30, 58
Smith, Rev. W.A. 30
Smith, W. McKay 56
Snew, Alfred 62
Snyder, Carol vii
Social Credit movement 91
Somers, Milton S. 66
Southam, Frank 119
Southam, Jean 119
Spachinsky, Nick 109
Spalding, Les 121
Spanish influenza 2, 67
Spruce Avenue 133
Standard Mine 71
Starke & Franklin 18
Starlight Club 114
Steparyk, Fred 125
Steperyk, F. 122
Steve Hrudey Construction 116, 123
Stevens, H. Bewlay 15
Stewart Street 133
St. Mary's Roman Catholic Church 58
Stoker, Robert 91
Stone's Meats 118
Strange, General 9
Strathcona 11, 55

Strathcona Hospital 42
Strathearn Heights 118
Stuparyk, P. 122
Sturko, Peter 113, 116, 119, 120, 122, 123
Sumison, Harold 116
Sunburst Motor Coaches 110
Sunshine Club 94
Suprovich, N. 123
Sutherland 23
Sutherland, F.G. 68
Sutherland Street 133
Swift Canadian Company 64
Swift's 121
Symington, Alex 121

T

Tanner, Eldon 62
Tappenden, Mrs. 87
Tappenden, Mrs. Fredrick 87
Tardrew, Katherine 63
Tardrew, Mary 63
Taylor, Alfred S. 64
Taylor, Bertram A. 27
Taylor, B.H. 36
Taylor, C.E. 12
Taylor, H.C. 15
Taylor, J.A. 108
Tetreau's Super Market 115
The Best Edmonton Stories 7
The Nomads 114
The Rebels 114
Thistle Curling Club 33, 123
Thom, J. MacGregor Residence 88
Thomas, A.W. 92
Thomas, Jack 121
Thompson, H. 109
Thompson, J.J. 42
Thompson, Mrs. C.J. 74
Thomson, William 65
Till, Mrs. 88
Tingley, Ken viii
Tingstad, E. 123
Titus, Don 112
Toby, L.F. 50
Tomyn, William 111
Topping, Alice 67
Topping, Eileen 68
Topping, Frank 68
Topping, Miss 73
Towns, Roy 2
Traynor, A. 119
Tretheway, George 44
Triple Realty Company 83

Truesdale, John 94
Truman, Mr. 26
Tunstall, A. 112
Turnbull, D.M. 15
Turner, G.E. 36, 50
Turner, J.B. 119
Tuxedo Park 23
Twin Cities 11

U

Union Sunday School 21, 29
Upper Edmonton Settlement 7
Upper Fraser Avenue 23
Uren, Stanley 119
Urquhart, F. 79

V

Vail, Albert M. 62
Vail, A.M. 79
Van Allen, George H. 83
Vancouver Symphony 67
Vanderburg, Roland G. 28, 62
Van Der Voort, Dr. Percy 64
Vanderwell, Richard 60
Vic's Patent Medicine and Cosmetics 115
Vic's Super Drugs and Post Office 115
Victoria Place 42
Victoria Pool Room and Barber Shop 61
Victoria's Studio and Camera 122
Vollan, R. 111
Vollan, Ralph 113, 116, 117, 119, 125
Voluntary Aid Detachment 56

W

Wachowich, Allan H. 57
Waddel, A.G. 125
Wadleigh Street 133
Wakeman, Mrs. E. 79
Wally's Royal Super Market 115
Wally's Super Market 115
Walter, John 8
Ward, Edward (Harry) 57, 113
Ward, E.T. 74
Ward, H. 119
Ward, Mrs. E.H. 74
Ward, Muriel 57
Ward Residence 30, 57
War Services Club 108
War Services Council 110
Waterloo Motors 126
Waterways 53
Watson, George 36
Watson, Mrs. J. 107

Webb, F.H. 26, 27, 31
Webb, L.H. 62
Webb, M. Francis 50
Wellman-Gibbs Company 25
Wellman, Norman B. 27, 51
Wells, Cyrus 65
Wells, Ethel 65
Wells, Harry L. 62
Wells, Miss 73
Wells, Muriel 67
Western Canadian Foundry and Machine 46
Western Foundry 48
Western Foundry and Machine 35, 59, 60
Western Veteran Publishing Company 75
Westgate, Mrs. 67
West Houston Street 26
Westminster Apartments 32
Wheeler, Vicki vii
Whitcroft, Fred J. 27
White, Bob 121
Whitecroft, Fred 36
White, Mrs. Bertha 50
Whitham, C.H. 116, 120
Wight, Rev. Louis S. 65
Wight, Rev. L.S. 29
William Brown Residence 83
William Mitchell Residence 51
Williams, Edward B. 65
Williams, J.W.H. 73, 75, 80
Williams, Mrs. Fred 91
Williams, Mrs. J.W.H. 91
Williams, William Pring 63
Willing, Mrs. 67, 88
Willow Avenue 133
Willy and the Walkers 114
Wilton Street 133
Winklaur, W. 109
Winnipeg General Strike 70
Women's Missionary Society 29
Woodroofe, W.T. 55
Wright, J.E. 56
Wright, Mrs. J.L. 79

Y

Yakula, Johanne vii
Yellowhead Pass 9
YMCA 114
Yorath, Christopher J. 80
York Factory 6
Young, G.F. 75
Young, Harry 121
Young, Thomas 21, 49, 64
YWCA 114

Addresses

The street index acknowledges the high interest in the built heritage of the Highlands. Every building permit for the Highlands Survey between 1912 and 1960 was recorded during research for the book. While this approach provided a systematic methodology, a small number of the buildings that were granted permits may not in fact have been built. Also, at one time part of 111 Avenue was designated as the end of Jasper Avenue, and addresses were given in the text as originally recorded on the building permits when granted. Present addresses may sometimes vary from the original, but in many cases lot and block numbers are given, which should allow interested readers to cross reference for location.

27 Jackson Block 28
44 Jasper Avenue East 27
112 Avenue 60
155 Jasper Avenue East 26
451 – 5 Street 26
624 – 15 Street 26
785 – 5 Street 52
1146 – 65 Street 66
1650 West Houston Street 27
1725 Campbell Street 28
1745 Irwin Street 27
1755 Irwin Street 27
1765 Irwin Street 27
1778 Irwin Street 27
1804 Houston Street 26
1892 Wadleigh Street 52
3246 Jasper East 26
5202 – 118 Avenue 61
5304 Ada Boulevard 122
5307 - 111 Avenue 110
5307 – 118 Avenue 109, 122
5308 – 111 Avenue 122
5308 Ada Boulevard 111
5311 – 112 Avenue 123
5316 Ada Boulevard 122
5317 – 111 Avenue 121
5318 Ada Boulevard 119
5321 – 111 Avenue 121
5322 – 111 Avenue 122
5322 Ada Boulevard 122
5325 – 111 Avenue 121
5327 – 112 Avenue 125
5328 – 111 Avenue 122
5331 – 112 Avenue 125
5333 – 111 Avenue 122
5334 Ada Boulevard 121
5335 – 112 Avenue 115

5335/5339 – 112 Avenue 122
5336 – 111 Avenue 123
5337 – 111 Avenue 121
5339 – 112 Avenue 115, 122
5340 – 111 Avenue 123
5343 – 112 Avenue 122
5344 – 111 Avenue 123
5351 – 112 Street 122
5352 – 111 Avenue 122
5358 – 111 Avenue 122
5406 – 112 Avenue 110
5410 – 112 Avenue 108
5502 Ada Boulevard 116
5504 – 111 Avenue 120
5507 – 118 Avenue 126
5512 – 111 Avenue 120, 122
5516 – 111 Avenue 122
5516 Ada Boulevard 110, 116
5517 – 111 Avenue 111
5521 – 111 Avenue 123
5524 Ada Boulevard 111
5525 Jasper Avenue 117
5528 Ada Boulevard 121
5530 Ada Boulevard 124
5532 Ada Boulevard 120
5540 – 111 Avenue 109
5603 – 111 Avenue 121
5606 – 118 Avenue 61
5607 – 118 Avenue 123
5610 – 111 Avenue 61
5615 – 118 Avenue 123
5617 – 111 Avenue 111
5618 – 111 Avenue 109
5640 Ada Boulevard 125
5650 Ada Boulevard 34, 35, 106
5658 Ada Boulevard 110, 125
5660 Ada Boulevard 117
5702 – 118 Avenue 61
5704 – 118 Avenue 61
5706 – 118 Avenue 61
5802 – 118 Avenue 61
5806 – 118 Avenue 61
5808 – 118 Avenue 61
5809/5819 – 118 Avenue 126
5812 – 118 Avenue 61
5815 – 118 Avenue 120
5905 – 118 Avenue 126
6002 – 111 Avenue 122
6004 Ada Boulevard 111
6008 Ada Boulevard 111
6010 - 111 Avenue 69
6010 – 111 Avenue 60
6012 Ada Boulevard 116
6013 Jasper Avenue 94

6018 Jasper Avenue 59
6023 – 111 Avenue 123
6024 – 111 Avenue 111
6110 Ada Boulevard 121
6111 – 111 Avenue 119
6115 Jasper Avenue 116
6121 – 111 Avenue 113
6124 Jasper (111) Avenue 30
6202 – 111 Avenue 116
6205 – 111 Avenue 94, 114
6210 Ada Boulevard 28, 60
6210 Jasper Avenue 116
6211 – 111 Avenue 126
6212 – 118 Avenue 61
6220 – 111 Avenue 119, 124
6226 Ada Boulevard 119
6229 – 111 Avenue 105
6240/6250 Ada Boulevard 49
6240 Ada Boulevard 37, 107
6250 Ada Boulevard 119
6270 Ada Boulevard 79
6274 Ada Boulevard 82
6306 – 111 Avenue 26
6318 – 111 Avenue 94
6318 –111 Avenue 68
6319 – 111 Avenue 107
6322 – 113 Avenue 77
6327 – 118 Avenue 61
6335 Jasper Avenue 94
6401 – 118 Avenue 61
6401 Alberta Avenue 56
6403 – 118 Avenue 61, 117
6403 Ada Boulevard 58
6406 – 118 Avenue 61
6411 – 118 Avenue 117
6416 – 118 Avenue 61, 112
6417 – 112 Avenue 118
6420 Ada Boulevard 88
6421 – 112 Avenue 118
6423 – 112 Avenue 60
6424 – 118 Avenue 61
6427 – 112 Avenue 32, 33, 61
6507 – 112 Avenue 118
6510 – 112 Avenue 94
6512 – 111 Avenue 110
6512 – 118 Avenue 61
6703 – 111 Avenue 122
6920 – 114 Street 123
7417 – 111 Avenue 122
7543 – 112 Avenue 70
7555 – 112 Avenue 123
7599 – 112 Avenue 75
10071 Jasper Avenue 51
10530 – 103 Street 53

11023 – 64 Street 84
11103 – 54 Street 123
11107 – 55 Street 122
11107 – 63 Street 63, 106
11108 – 56 Street 125
11110 – 61 Street 125
11112 – 62 Street 123
11115 – 60 Street 117
11115 – 65 Street 65
11116 – 64 Street 65
11118 – 60 Street 111
11119 – 60 Street 30
11119 – 61 Street 61
11119 – 62 Street 63, 94
11119 – 65 Street 65
11120 – 65 Street 66
11121 – 63 Street 108
11121 – 64 Street 109
11122 – 62 Street 62, 106
11122 – 64 Street 56, 65
11123 – 61 Street 62
11123 – 65 Street 65
11124 – 53 Street 125
11125 – 60 Street 30, 57
11125 – 65 Street 65
11126 – 60 Street 111
11127 – 63 Street 31, 64, 78
11127 – 64 Street 32, 64
11128 – 53 Street 123
11128 – 62 Street 49, 62, 75
11128 – 63 Street 93
11128 – 64 Street 109
11129 – 61 Street 49, 62
11130 – 61 Street 108
11130 – 65 Street 66
11131 – 65 Street 65
11132 – 60 Street 111
11133 – 60 Street 123
11133 – 64 Street 32, 64
11134 – 64 Street 108
11135 – 63 Street 64
11136 – 62 Street 62
11136 – 62 Street 62, 125
11137 – 65 Street 65
11138 – 61 Street 117
11139 – 56 Street 121
11141 – 62 Street 63
11141 – 63 Street 32, 64
11141 – 64 Street 32, 64
11141 – 65 Street 65
11142 – 56 Street 121
11142 – 62 Street 62, 109
11142 – 63 Street 108
11142 – 64 Street 27, 58, 65

11142 – 65 Street 66
11142 – 68 Street 108
11145 – 63 Street 112
11145 – 65 Street 65
11145 – 66 Street 109
11149 – 64 Street 27
11149 – 65 Street 65
11150 – 63 Street 111
11150 – 64 Street 26, 83, 109, 116
11153 – 64 Street 30, 64
11154 – 66 Street 106
11156 – 64 Street 65
11158 – 64 Street 50
11158 – 65 Street 116
11202 – 55 Street 121
11202 – 60 Street 111
11202 – 68 Street 116
11203 – 56 Street 121, 122
11203 – 61 Street 123
11204 – 61 Street 76
11204 – 64 Street 110
11205 – 64 Street 112
11206 – 57 Street 116
11207 – 60 Street 116
11209 – 54 Street 116
11209 – 63 Street 109
11209 – 127 Street 64
11210 – 53 Street 108
11210 – 60 Street 111
11210 – 63 Street 64
11211 – 58 Street 117
11212 – 61 Street 88
11212 – 62 Street 62, 122
11212 – 64 Street 79, 84
11212 – 70 Street 122
11213 – 65 Street 65
11214 – 55 Street 124
11214 – 62 Street 110
11215 – 61 Street 28, 62, 92
11215 – 63 Street 64, 109
11215 – 65 Street 65
11216 – 61 Street 88
11216 – 65 Street 66
11217 – 64 Street 32, 80, 108
11218 – 56 Street 121
11218 – 63 Street 64
11218 – 65 Street 66
11219 – 58 Street 122
11220 – 61 Street 88
11220 – 62 Street 88
11220 – 64 Street 92
11222 – 65 Street 66
11223 – 53 Street 123
11223 – 61 Street 119

11223 – 63 Street 32, 64
11223 – 64 Street 64, 84
11224 – 63 Street 50, 64
11224 – 64 Street 56, 65
11226 – 55 Street 125
11227 – 61 Street 114
11227 – 63 Street 27, 64, 84
11227 – 68 Street 109
11228 – 62 Street 109
11228 – 64 Street 75
11232 – 70 Street 108
11233 – 63 Street 27, 64
11233 – 64 Street 93
11234 – 61 Street 75
11234 – 63 Street 64
11234 – 65 Street 110
11235 – 61 Street 122
11236 – 62 Street 109
11237 – 51 Street 126
11237 – 66 Street 125
11239 – 63 Street 27, 64, 122
11239 – 64 Street 81
11239 – 65 Street 65
11240 – 63 Street 113
11240 – 65 Street 111
11242 – 61 Street 108
11242 – 62 Street 79
11242 – 64 Street 56, 79
11243 – 58 Street 59, 113
11243 – 63 Street 110
11245 – 64 Street 81
11245 – 66 Street 122, 125
11246 – 61 Street 113
11246 – 62 Street 110
11247 – 58 Street 123
11248 – 63 Street 64
11248 – 64 Street 110
11248 – 65 Street 66
11249 – 68 Street 108, 121
11302 – 55 Street 122
11303 – 65 Street 116
11304 – 63 Street 112
11304 – 64 Street 65
11305/17 – 64 Street 31, 33
11305 – 61 Street 109, 122
11305 – 66 Street 52
11306 – 55 Street 122
11306 – 60 Street 118
11306 – 61 Street 67
11307 – 56 Street 122
11307 – 65 Street 116
11308 – 62 Street 116
11308 – 67 Street 61
11310 – 58 Street 122

11311 – 56 Street 122, 123
11312 – 55 Street 124
11312 – 64 Street 30, 65
11314 – 55 Street 122
11315 – 56 Street 122
11316 – 91 Street 75
11317 – 63 Street 64, 108
11317 – 64 Street 65
11318 – 67 Street 122
11319 – 56 Street 122
11319 – 65 Street 65
11320 – 65 Street 92
11321 – 68 Street 52
11322 – 55 Street 122
11322 – 56 Street 122
11322 – 62 Street 62, 80, 88
11322 – 67 Street 120
11323 – 60 Street 118
11323 – 64 Street 109
11324 – 53 Street, 122
11324 – 63 Street 109
11324 – 64 Street 65, 68
11325 – 61 Street 123
11326 – 55 Street 122
11326 – 67 Street 118, 120
11327 – 53 Street 125
11327 – 58 Street 124
11327 – 62 Street 114
11328 – 53 Street 122
11328 – 62 Street 116
11328 – 67 Street 118, 120
11329 – 53 Street 125
11329 – 61 Street 123
11329 – 63 Street 110, 122
11329 – 64 Street 109
11330 – 63 Street 49, 64
11330 – 64 Street 50, 65
11330 – 67 Street 120
11331 – 65 Street 65
11332 – 62 Street 122
11333 – 61 Street 117
11335 – 64 Street 111
11336 – 64 Street 110
11336/11138 – 58 Street 120
11340 – 62 Street 78
11341 – 63 Street 110
11341 – 64 Street 30, 65
11342 – 64 Street 31, 32, 65
11342 – 67 Street 120
11344 – 63 Street 27, 116
11345 – 64 Street 124
11346 – 64 Street 116
11346 – 67 Street 52, 53
11346 – 69 Street 119

11350 – 67 Street 53
11350 – 67 Street 53
11355 – 55 Street 125
11356 – 56 Street 125
11402 – 64 Street 111
11403 – 64 Street 111
11408 – 62 Street 117
11408 – 68 Street 122
11409 – 64 Street 111
11411 – 65 Street 125
11413 – 63 Street 125
11414 – 62 Street 117
11422 – 63 Street 113
11423 – 64 Street 111
11424 – 64 Street 30, 65
11425 – 63 Street 36
11425 – 65 Street 65
11429 – 64 Street 65
11429 – 65 Street 65
11430 – 62 Street 116
11430 – 68 Street 123

11431 – 65 Street 65
11433 – 64 Street 112
11436 – 64 Street 112
11436 – 67 Street 109
11440 – 64 Street 112
11440 – 65 Street 66
11441 – 63 Street 119
11442 – 65 Street 66
11445 – 64 Street 116
11448 – 67 Street 89
11451 – 64 Street 65
11466 – 64 Street 65
11509 – 62 Street 124
11525 – 65 Street 119
11718 – 54 Street 107, 109, 122
11742 – 66 Street 116
11825 – 61 Street 62
11831 – 61 Street 62
11834 – 64 Street 125
11942 – 62 Street 123
12005 – 66 Street 62